Romantic Literature and Postcolonial Studies

T0386738

Postcolonial Literary Studies

Series Editors: David Johnson, The Open University and Ania Loomba, University of Pennsylvania

Visit the Postcolonial Literary Studies website at
www.euppublishing.com/series/epls

Romantic Literature and Postcolonial Studies

Elizabeth A. Bohls

EDINBURGH
University Press

Edinburgh University Press Ltd
22 George Square, Edinburgh EH8 9LF

www.euppublishing.com

Typeset in 10.5/13 Sabon
by Servis Filmsetting Ltd, Stockport, Cheshire, and
printed and bound in Great Britain by
CPI Antony Rowe, Chippenham and Eastbourne

A CIP record for this book is available from the British Library

ISBN 978 0 7486 4199 4 (hardback)
ISBN 978 0 7486 4198 7 (paperback)
ISBN 978 0 7486 7874 7 (webready PDF)
ISBN 978 0 7486 7875 4 (epub)
ISBN 978 0 7486 7876 1 (Amazon ebook)

Contents

Illustrations

Series Editors' Preface

Postcolonial Literary Studies foregrounds the colonial and neo-colonial contexts of literary and cultural texts, and demonstrates how these texts help to understand past and present histories of empires. The books in the series relate key literary and cultural texts both to their historical and geographical moments, and to contemporary issues of neo-colonialism and global inequality. In addition to introducing the diverse body of postcolonial criticism, theory and scholarship in literary studies, the series engages with relevant debates on postcolonialism in other disciplines – history, geography, critical theory, political studies, economics and philosophy. The books in the series exemplify how post-colonial studies can re-configure the major periods and areas of literary studies. Each book provides a comprehensive survey of the existing field of scholarship and debate with a timeline, a literature survey, discussion of key critical, theoretical, historical and political debates, case studies providing exemplary critical readings of key literary texts and guides to further reading. At the same time, each book is also an original critical intervention in its own right. In much the same way that feminism has re-defined how all literary texts are analysed, our ultimate aim is that this series will contribute to all texts in literary studies being read with an awareness of their colonial and neo-colonial resonances.

DJ and AL

Acknowledgements

David Johnson and Ania Loomba have been ideal interlocutors as this book came into being. I am grateful for the opportunity to spend time thinking about these topics and to join a series that already includes such distinguished contributors.

Ian Duncan and Courtney Thorsson read individual chapters and offered valuable feedback. My colleagues Karen Ford, Mark Quigley and Sangita Gopal kindly answered questions and gave suggestions. Louise Bishop, Kathleen Karlyn and Joanne Kent lent their ears as I talked through knotty sections on our morning walks, dispensing pep talks as needed.

My thanks go to Jenny Daly, Jackie Jones and the staff of Edinburgh University Press for their professionalism and expert support, and to the staff of the University of Oregon's Knight Library (especially Interlibrary Loans) for filling my copious book orders. Dan Rosenberg has my eternal gratitude for organising the purchase of the Gale Group's Eighteenth-Century Collections Online database (ECCO). And I thank the English Department, in particular Harry Wonham and Paul Peppis, for an indispensable research term.

This book is dedicated to Marilyn Butler, whose pioneering work has shaped studies of Romanticism and colonialism. She gave me my first break by recruiting my book for Cambridge Studies in Romanticism in the 1990s and is an enduring intellectual inspiration.

Timeline

Date	Historical Events	Literary and Other Publications
1707	Union of England and Scotland	
1745–6	Jacobite uprising in Scotland fails	
1760	Slave rebellion in Jamaica	James Macpherson, *Fragments of Ancient Poetry* (the Ossian poems)
1763		Hugh Blair, *Critical Dissertation on the Poems of Ossian*
1768–71	Captain James Cook's first voyage	
1771		William Jones, *Poems Consisting Chiefly of Translations from the Asiatic Languages*
1772	Mansfield Decision	
1772–6	Cook's second voyage	
1773		John Hawkesworth, *Account of the Voyages* [of James Cook]
1775	American Revolutionary War begins	
1776		Adam Smith, *Wealth of Nations*
1776–9	Cook's third voyage; killed in Hawaii	

1783	Treaty of Versailles ends American war	
1784	Asiatic Society of Bengal founded Pitt's India Act extends parliamentary control of East India Company	
1785		William Cowper, *The Task*
1786		Robert Burns, *Poems, Chiefly in the Scottish Dialect* William Beckford, *Vathek*
1787	Society for Effecting the Abolition of the Slave Trade (SEAST) founded Warren Hastings impeached	
1788	Australia colonised by British Joseph Banks founds African Association	William Cowper, 'The Negro's Complaint'
1789	Fall of Bastille begins French Revolution	William Blake, *Songs of Innocence* Olaudah Equiano, *Interesting Narrative*
1790		Edmund Burke, *Reflections on the Revolution in France* James Bruce, *Travels . . . to Discover the Source of the Nile*
1791	Slave revolt on Saint-Domingue (Haiti)	Thomas Paine, *Rights of Man* William Fox, *Address . . . on the Propriety of Abstaining from West India Sugar and Rum*
1792	September Massacres in Paris Abolition Bill passes Commons, dies in House of Lords	Mary Wollstonecraft, *Vindication of the Rights of Woman*

1793	France and Britain at war	Robert Burns, 'Tam o' Shanter'
		Bryan Edwards, *History of the West Indies*
1794	Habeas Corpus suspended Horne Tooke, Holcroft and Thelwall treason trials	William Blake, *Songs of Experience*
		Ann Radcliffe, *Mysteries of Udolpho*
1795	Treason and Sedition Acts New Zealand colonised Mungo Park goes to Africa Warren Hastings acquitted	Samuel Taylor Coleridge lectures on slave trade Samuel Hearne, *Journey . . . to the Northern Ocean*
1796		John Gabriel Stedman, *Narrative of . . . Surinam*
1797	Sailors mutiny at Spithead and Nore	Robert Southey, *Poems*
1798	United Irishmen rebellion French in Egypt	William Wordsworth and Samuel Taylor Coleridge, *Lyrical Ballads*
1799	Napoleon Bonaparte is elected First Consul of France	Mungo Park, *Travels in . . . Africa*
1800	Act of Union with Ireland	Maria Edgeworth, *Castle Rackrent*
		William Earle, *Obi*
1801		Robert Southey, *Thalaba*
1802	Peace of Amiens	
1803	War with France renewed	Walter Scott, *Minstrelsy of the Scottish Border*
1805	Battle of Trafalgar	Walter Scott, *Lay of the Last Minstrel*
1806	Vellore Mutiny in India	Sydney Owenson, *The Wild Irish Girl*
1807	Slave trade abolition passed	
1808	Peninsular War begins	
1809		*Quarterly Review* founded
1810		Roberty Southey, *The Curse of Kehama* *Travels of Mirza Abu Taleb*

1811	Prince of Wales is Regent	Jane Austen, *Sense and Sensibility*
		Sydney Owenson, *The Missionary*
1812	Anglo-American War	Lord Byron, *Childe Harold* (Cantos 1 and 2)
1813		Jane Austen, *Pride and Prejudice*
		Lord Byron, *The Bride of Abydos*, *The Giaour*
1814	Napoleon abdicates; Treaty of Paris between Allies and France	Jane Austen, *Mansfield Park*
		Walter Scott, *Waverley*
1815	Battle of Waterloo ends war	
1816		Percy Shelley, *Alastor*
		Samuel Taylor Coleridge, *Kubla Khan*, *Christabel*
1817	Suspension of Habeas Corpus	James Mill, *History of British India*
		Blackwood's Magazine founded
		Thomas Moore, *Lalla Rookh*
1818	Arctic expedition launched	Mary Shelley, *Frankenstein*
		John Keats, *Endymion*
		Walter Scott, *Heart of Midlothian*
1819	Peterloo Massacre	Lord Byron, *Don Juan*
	Sir Stamford Raffles takes Singapore	
1819–25	Revolutions against Spanish Empire in South America	
1820	Accession of George IV	Percy Shelley, *Prometheus Unbound*
1821		Thomas De Quincey, *Confessions of an English Opium Eater*
1823	Slave rebellion in Demerara (British Guiana)	

1824		James Hogg, *Confessions of a Justified Sinner*
1827		Walter Scott, *Chronicles of the Canongate*
1829	Catholic Emancipation Act	
1830	Accession of William IV	
1831	Slave rebellion in Jamaica	Mary Prince, *The History of Mary Prince*
1832	First Reform Act enfranchises more of middle classes	
1833	Parliament emancipates slaves	
1834		Thomas Pringle, *Poems Illustrative of South Africa*
1835		Thomas Babington Macaulay, *Minute on Education*
1837	Accession of Queen Victoria	

Romantic Literature from the Margins

In three decades, the study of Romantic literature has changed dramatically. When I entered graduate school in 1982, a narrow canon still dominated the field, with the six well-known poets at the forefront and Jane Austen and Sir Walter Scott inhabiting a kind of parallel universe. Deconstructionists were busily deconstructing Romantic lyrics; a still nascent feminist criticism was rediscovering a few Romantic women writers, such as Dorothy Wordsworth and Mary Shelley. In 1983, Jerome McGann published *The Romantic Ideology*, with the influential thesis that scholarship on the period was dominated by an 'uncritical absorption in Romanticism's own self-representations' (McGann 1983: 1). The surge of self-critical reflection that followed led many scholars towards historically situated research with a theoretical grounding and a political edge – in short, New Historicism. This trajectory is well known. Like scholars in other areas of literary study, many Romanticists were persuaded that works of literature could not be properly understood in isolation from the historical moment and cultural matrix in which they were produced. But although the late 1980s and early 1990s produced much important historicist work, not until the very end of the twentieth century did a critical mass of scholars of Romantic literature come to see colonialism and empire as crucial parts of that matrix. In 1998, Tim Fulford and Peter Kitson, editors of a landmark collection of essays on *Romanticism and Colonialism,* could still write that the relationship between the two had been 'relatively little studied', with a few notable exceptions (Fulford and Kitson 1998: 1). Writing in 2012, I am able to draw on postcolonial criticism in all areas of Romantic literature. Much more work remains to be done, but there is now a general consensus that the fact of empire and its effects are fundamental to the study of Romantic culture.

With this methodological shift has come a gradual broadening of that narrow canon (and a realisation that it is itself a historical arte-fact).[1] We now read more of the poets people were reading during the Romantic period, including numerous women, from Anna Barbauld and Charlotte Smith to Anna Seward and Felicia Hemans. Scholars have finally acknowledged that in the 1780s and 1790s, when 'critical attention shifts to the supposedly lyrical advent of Romanticism', it was actually the novel that 'took off' to become the dominant literary genre.[2] Other prose genres, such as travel writing – so influential during the Romantic era – have garnered increasing attention and respect. Romanticism must now be understood through all of the genres that fall under its purview. But this happened after my own graduate training was finished. In graduate school, obsessed with 1790s novels and travel writing, I did not seriously consider calling myself a Romanticist. Given the state of the field in the 1980s, that would have involved spending too much time and energy studying and teaching those six canonical poets, whom I admired, but could not love. I have thus been employed as an eighteenth-century specialist while continuing to study the Romantic decades, from the 1780s to the 1820s. So I come to this book as some-what of an outsider – which I consider to be, in an important sense, an advantage.[3]

Postcolonial criticism troubles the distinction between inside and outside. In addition to elevating lyric poetry by a few canonical men, a mid-twentieth-century construction of Romantic literature also 'fet-ishized' what Clara Tuite labels England's 'green core' (Tuite 2000: 109). Much attention was paid to poets' and novelists' representations of the English countryside, its natural beauty and rural society, but little to England's connection with the wider world. The British Empire, if mentioned, was thought of as being 'out there', safely separate from the 'little England' so beautifully evoked by Romantic literature. Postcolonial critics call into question this 'enduring fiction of moral and geographical separateness' between metropole and colony, home and abroad, maintained with so much work over so many years (Wilson 2004: 16). They challenge us to ask what is happening at the margins of empire – in the 'contact zones' where imperial eyes, boots and guns enter unfamiliar territory – and demand that we take into account the experi-ences of subalterns, those who bear the brunt of colonial power.[4] But they also help us to discern within the 'green core' the traces of imperial exploitation and the scars of colonial warfare. Postcolonial critics argue that the experience of colonialism and empire was central to the forma-tion of Western nations, implicating everyone, even those who took no overt part in imperial activity. This book will survey the impact of postcolonial criticism on the study of British Romantic literature. Because postcolonial criticism is deeply historical in character, we must begin by revisiting the eventful history of Britain in the Romantic era.

Worldwide War and Imperial Expansion

Romantic literature has often been characterised as a literature of revolution. It is true that the events in France, launched when a crowd tore down the Bastille prison in 1789, unleashed idealism and optimism across the Channel. At that moment, for young intellectuals like the poet Helen Maria Williams, everyone, everywhere, was French: 'It was a triumph of human kind; it was man asserting the noblest privileges of his nature; and it required but the common feelings of humanity to become in that moment a citizen of the world'.[5] Mary Wollstonecraft, William Godwin, Thomas Paine, William Wordsworth, Samuel Taylor Coleridge, Robert Southey – a generation of young writers shared the enthusiasm. Their liberal politics encompassed other issues as well, such as domestic political reform and slavery. Many were abolitionists: colonial slavery epitomised 'a system of arbitrary government that, at home and abroad, enriched a few at the expense of others' freedom' (Fulford 2008: 182). Ideals of liberty and hatred of tyranny made these young Britons into so-called Jacobins[6] and anti-imperialists. The Scottish poet Robert Burns almost lost his government job on suspicion of Jacobinism. William Blake's hatred of empire, like his sympathy for the French Revolution, was long-lived and uncompromising, expressed in works such as *America: A Prophecy* (1793). But many of his more moderate compatriots (though by no means all) shared the early sympathy with the French, whom they saw as oppressed by an authoritarian regime and lacking the liberty that free-born Britons enjoyed.

For all but the most hard-core, this sympathy did not last. The prison massacres of 1792, the king's execution the same year, and the increasing radicalism of revolutionary leaders such as the Jacobins made a pro-revolution stance increasingly hard to sustain. When France declared war on England in 1793, aligning Britain with Austria, Prussia and eventually most of Europe against the revolutionary armies, supporting the revolution began to look like aiding the enemy. As the war dragged on – it would last a full two decades – the lines hardened and the British government cracked down on anything smelling of treason. In 1794 three home-grown radicals, Thomas Hardy, John Thelwall and John Horne Tooke, were tried for treason (a jury acquitted them). The following year the Pitt government passed the first of the famous

'Gagging Acts', suspending habeas corpus and outlawing treasonable practices such as mass meetings. The year 1796 saw the first invasion scare when a French force of 14,000 actually sailed to Ireland, but failed to land. The fear of invasion galvanised British patriotism and support for the war, especially after a further major scare in 1803. By this time, the political climate had decisively changed. Conservative reaction and wartime patriotism prevailed and would continue throughout the war years. While of course this does not mean no one opposed government policies, even radical leftists were rethinking their position.[7] Indeed, most of the Romantic era was a time of profound conservatism, a fact not adequately reflected by many literary histories of the period.

What the French were doing in Ireland in 1796 (and again in 1798) was helping the colonised Irish to resist the British Empire at a time when its armies were busy elsewhere. The war against revolutionary France was an imperial war, fought on various fronts worldwide. France was an empire too, with colonies in the Caribbean and ambitions in India. The two nations were long-time enemies that had faced off repeatedly during the eighteenth century, most recently when France helped Britain's North American colonies to become the United States of America. Aiding anti-imperial rebellion in the British Isles was not a new idea for the French, either. Long before sailing to Ireland at the invitation of the anti-colonial United Irishmen, they had helped Scottish Jacobites,[8] hosting the Pretender's court in exile and giving the Jacobite rebels of 1745 hope of French reinforcements (which never arrived). Though the chance to strip the French Empire of its colonies was not Britain's prime motive for going to war in 1793, it was considered a welcome benefit (Duffy 1998: 186). The two empires fought in the Caribbean, trading colonies back and forth over the war years. Britain, as the winner, ended up keeping all but one of France's Caribbean possessions.[9] Its prime target was Saint-Domingue (present-day Haiti), the richest single colony of all the European empires, but a massive slave revolt starting in 1791 foiled that plan. Though some British slave holders initially rooted for the slaves against the hated French, the threat of a slave rebellion spreading through the region changed their minds.

Imperial warfare took place in India as well, with British garrisons overrunning French bases at Pondicherry, Surat and elsewhere early in the war. French influence on Tipu Sultan, the ruler of Mysore, gave the East India Company an excuse to storm his capital at Seringapatam, a key victory in the wartime expansion of Company rule on the subcontinent. When Napoleon invaded Egypt in 1798, the British feared he was heading for India (he was not) and sent more troops there, as well as establishing additional bases on islands in the Mediterranean (Duffy 1998: 187, 196–8). Napoleon's final defeat at Waterloo in 1815 left the British Empire the world's paramount military and naval power. From twenty-six colonies in 1792, it had grown to forty-three. Though many of these were small strategic islands, others included Ceylon (present-day Sri Lanka), and the Cape Colony (present-day South Africa), as well as substantial territorial gains in India (controlled by the East India Company). In this process of expansion, the Company transformed itself from a trading concern into the equivalent of a colonial state, and was subjected to increased Parliamentary control.

During these twenty years of war which dramatically expanded the empire, Britain added more territory than it had done since creating the colonies of settlement in Ireland and America in the seventeenth century. By 1820, Britain ruled more than a quarter of the world's population (Bayly 1989: 100, 3). From a diverse collection of colonies, acquired at various times, in various ways, Britain had become the first modern empire. Up to 1783 the British Empire had been mainly Atlantic-based, consisting of colonies of settlement linked by trade in a maritime, mercantile system: North America and the Caribbean, along with the four nations of the British Isles. The loss of America and the expansion of British India shifted the empire's centre of gravity to the east. Its armed forces ballooned as well. Forced to respond to the French *levée en masse*, or military draft, it enlarged its army. At the start of the wars British land forces numbered some 40,000 men; by 1814 they had grown to a quarter million at home and abroad. The Royal Navy grew from 16,000 to 140,000 between 1789 and 1812 (Colley 1992: 287). The navy became a global agent of 'ecological imperialism', busily turning timber into ships from Canada to India, Australia to the Caribbean.[10] The need to finance all this was part of what drove the rapid expansion of the empire: more lands meant more revenue.[11] In 1799, England also got its first consolidated income tax, made permanent during the war.

With increased size came significant changes in the character of the British state and society. To tax its subjects properly, the government needed to know more about them. Collecting statistics and surveying land increasingly became part of the business of government. In England, Scotland and Ireland – and in India, Canada and South Africa – soldiers and civil servants collected facts on population and production. They surveyed land: only by measuring, settling and making it pay could the empire maintain the military forces to defend its possessions.[12] (An outstanding example of data collection in a colonial context was carried out by the hated French: Napoleon's *Description de l'Egypte* (1809–29), the encyclopaedic multivolume study produced by the team of scientists and scholars who accompanied the general between 1798 and 1801.) The patriotic rationale for collecting data in this way was that it laid the basis for agrarian improvement. At home, this was seen as the way to assimilate the Gaelic-speaking population of the Scottish Highlands into the British mainstream. On the other side of the globe, agrarian reform also drove Lord Cornwallis's settlement of the Bengal land revenues in 1793. The goal was to stabilise a local landed aristocracy, apply capital to land, and bring waste land under the plough, though this proved to be wishful thinking rather than sound policy (Bayly 1989: 123–4, 156). Information collection, increased revenue, bigger government and a bigger military: the imperial state was acquiring a more sophisticated apparatus of control.

In some ways, however, the state seemed to be turning towards the past. Faced with revolution and regicide across the Channel, Britain took on more of the character of an *ancien régime*, enhancing the rituals of royalty as a symbolic focus for a nation at war. The British monarchy might have been competing with the French revolutionary government, which held elaborate patriotic festivals such as the 1790 Festival of the Federation, stage-managed by the painter Jacques-Louis David and others. In 1797, for example, George III staged a state procession through London before a crowd of 200,000 to give thanks at St Paul's Cathedral for recent British victories (Colley 1992: 216). Napoleonic-era military uniforms were another symptom of this renewed national pomp and display. 'Never before or since', Linda Colley comments, 'have British military uniforms been so impractically gorgeous, so brilliant in colour, so richly ornamented or so closely and cunningly tailored.' In tight breeches, high boots and extravagant headgear, officers were literally 'dressed to kill' (Colley 1992: 186). The aristocracy and gentry played a newly expanded role in the army and colonial service of the imperial state at war (Bayly 1989: 135). Popular patriotism flourished too, if not universally. Britons volunteered for local militias, motivated by the recurrent threat of a French invasion, though recurrent labouring-class unrest made state authorities somewhat wary of arming the populace (Colley 1992: 305, 310).

It is important to remember that the pressures that strengthened and modernised the imperial state included revolt from within as well as war on the Continent. The recent successful uprising by the Creole colonists of North America had made clear the empire's vulnerability to its own unhappy citizens. The protracted slave revolt in French Saint-Domingue – the Haitian Revolution – targeted Britain's enemy, but terrified British slave holders. Popular uprisings such as naval mutinies by ill-treated sailors at Spithead and the Nore in 1797 and food riots protesting recurrent wartime shortages kept the government aware of the need for repressive force. In 1798 came the bloody United Irishmen rebellion (with belated, ineffective help from the French). It was suppressed, but left over 10,000 dead. In Vellore, India, in 1806, native Hindu and Muslim East India Company troops (sepoys) staged a violent mutiny against changes in the military dress code that both groups perceived as disrespectful to their respective religions. (Such disrespect was also the perceived cause of the much bigger and bloodier Indian Mutiny of 1857.) The repressive apparatus of the modernising state had to be ready when less overt methods of social control failed, as they repeatedly did.

Important among these tactics were religion and morality. Both moral reform of the lower classes at home and religious assimilation in the overseas empire served the purpose of social control. The conservative mood of the war years had a religious cast. Although Dissenters, Unitarians and deists aired liberal opinions in the early 1790s, such voices grew rare as the war dragged on. The French threat helped to forge a stronger link in Britain among evangelical Protestantism, nationalism and empire. Evangelicals were already active in the movement to abolish slavery (though converting slaves to Christianity remained controversial). The 'spirit of the revived empire of the Napoleonic Wars was thoroughly infused with a kind of Anglican providentialism which acted more or less subtly on policy' (Bayly 1989: 137). Though the East India Company did not officially permit missionary activity in the areas it controlled until 1813, the new moral seriousness of the times affected the Company's employees. For example, Fort William College in Calcutta (Kolkata), a distinguished centre for language study, founded in 1800 by Governor-General Wellesley to teach Company employees the languages of India, segregated its students from the 'habitual dissipation and corruption of the people of India' while they completed their training. In general, in Bayly's words, a 'new moral racism came to confirm the vision of disciplined Christian people' that wartime fears had helped to mould (Bayly 1989: 115). Ideologies of racial separation and domination would later evolve different rationales, but they would continue to mark British imperialism for the duration of the empire and beyond.[13]

Forged in the crucible of war and imperial expansion, the British Empire at the end of two decades of victorious conflict differed in significant ways from that of 1789. That conflict took place around the globe: on bloody battlefields, but also in the day-to-day struggle and negotiation between colonisers and colonised, 'a long process of political dialogue, of challenge and response, and of accommodation' (Bayly 1989: 75). The imperial centre did not just impose change on its peripheries. They changed one another: both took part in a turbulent process of mutual constitution, from which the cultural discourse of Romanticism emerged (Makdisi 1998: 175). Romantic literature was written in a time of transition – a time experienced by those living through it as extraordinary, even apocalyptic. What would the future bring? Anna Letitia Barbauld's poetic prophecy *Eighteen Hundred and Eleven* floated a bizarre possibility: the downfall of Britain and the rise of America as an imperial power. Hearing the news of Napoleon's improbable escape from Elba in 1815, the journalist Leigh Hunt remarked, 'We want nothing now, to finish the romantic history of the present times, but a visit from the Man in the Moon' (quoted in Roe 2005: 3). He is using the word 'romantic' in the sense, common at the time, of 'fantastic, extravagant'. The history of these decades does read like a romance – a tale of exciting, unusual, improbable events, not like real life. The romantic history of war and empire generated a romantic literature, telling stories rooted in real-life events that seemed at times like a fantastic dream.[14]

Literature, Empire and Postcolonial Criticism

War and imperial expansion touched all areas of life in the British Empire. What about reading? With armed forces deployed around the globe and growing colonies in new areas, a flood of information flowed back to the imperial metropolis:

> Military men on reconnaissance, naval men on patrol, scientific explorers, industrial exporters, travelling gentlemen, and Christian missionaries penetrated to ever more remote, previously unvisited lands, bringing home shiploads of art and antiquities, plant and animal specimens, and diaries which told of their adventures and their discoveries. (St Clair 2004: 232–3)

Book production grew rapidly in travel and exploration writing, including what we would call anthropology, as well as in military history and politics. There was scarcely a spot on the globe that had not had a book written about it by the 1820s. Though travel books were often expensive, and print runs were small, literary journals carried notices and excerpts. Britain's reading elite, women as well as men, had increasing access to a whole world of geography and history, and they eagerly took it into their consciousness.[15] Of course, this also included creative writers. Romantic literature, especially poetry, was often set in places other than England. Poets and readers found Scotland, Ireland and

Wales appealing; even more so were Greece, Albania, Turkey, Persia, India, North and South America, even Australia or the North Pole. Though few poets (except for Byron) had travelled abroad, they had all read travel books, and they cited them in the long, well-researched footnotes of which Romantic authors were increasingly fond. For example, readers of a poem such as *Childe Harold's Pilgrimage,* which romanticised Lord Byron's travels, could also gain an intellectual perspective on modern Greece from his prose footnotes (St Clair 2004: 214–15).

What people read during the Romantic period differs in important ways from the literature later canonised as Romanticism. The poets most valued by twentieth-century literary criticism were by no means those most read or esteemed by their contemporaries, though there is some overlap. St Clair (2004) lists a canon of the eight literary authors most highly respected in the period and until the mid-nineteenth century. Of these, Walter Scott, a poet as well as a novelist, sold far and away the most books. Second came Lord Byron, followed by authors less familiar to modern students: Thomas Moore, Thomas Campbell, Samuel Rogers. Bringing up the rear were the Lake Poets, with Robert Southey outselling William Wordsworth and Samuel Taylor Coleridge, who trail at the end of the pack. John Keats and Percy Bysshe Shelley had tiny sales; William Blake, who insisted on hand-crafting his books, sold hardly any during his lifetime. More broadly, we need to remember that the idea that poetry is dense, relatively inaccessible, and requires special training to read was a product of later times. For the educated men and women of the Romantic era, verse – including stories told in verse – was normal, everyday reading. Novels, though they sold well, were barely considered respectable, except those of Scott, the only ones reading societies were willing to buy (St Clair 2004: 214–19, 254). Travel writing, on the other hand, was as highly respected as history or philosophy.

Postcolonial critics need to know what Romantic readers read, and did not read, because the type of criticism we practice is deeply historical. We believe literary texts cannot be properly understood apart from the historical moment in which they were written and initially read. This does not mean that works ignored by Romantic audiences – Blake's, for example – have nothing of interest to tell us. These works, too, open a revealing window onto Romantic culture as experienced and analysed by extraordinary contemporary observers.[16] Of all the texts in the historical archive, the imaginative writing that we now call 'literature' is of special interest precisely because literary forms gave scope to the imagination. What was it possible to imagine in this particular place and time, amid the unfolding events of war and empire? How could the literary imagination help to make sense of the increasingly wider world that Britain was exploring, mapping, trading with and colonising?

It is important to remember that we do not read literature as a historical document, a trove of information about the past. We are literary critics: as such, we are concerned with form as well as meaning, and we realise that meaning cannot be properly grasped apart from form, or genre. Literary forms themselves, and their histories, carry unique insights into the nature of past experience and consciousness. The quest romance, for example – a poetic form popular in the early nineteenth century, as we will see in Chapter 4 – appealed to Romantic poets as a means of imaginatively charting the far-flung spaces brought to Britons' attention by their country's extensive overseas ventures. A journey or quest has long served creative writers as a metaphor for a process of learning and growth, whether successful or failed. Southey's *Curse of Kehama*, Shelley's *Alastor*, and Coleridge's *Rime of the Ancient Mariner* are examples of Romantic poems about fantastic, fateful journeys to places that real travellers also visited on the more prosaic errands of empire. These poets' imagined journeys at the intersection of poetic form and imperial reality help us understand the intangible impact – and the real cost – of empire.

Postcolonial criticism, as practised by the numerous critics of Romantic literature on whose work this book draws, is eclectic and pragmatic. It invokes a wide range of theories, from deconstruction and psychoanalysis to Bakhtinian dialogism and the methods of Edward Said, influenced by Michel Foucault. With the historian of empire Kathleen Wilson, I assume that 'there is no universal colonial condition or imperial experience, but discrete practices of power and ways of imagining it in specific historical periods' and specific places (Wilson 2004: 11). Any generalisations we attempt to make must be tempered with caution and qualified with rigor. Postcolonial critics of Romantic literature do not 'apply' theories, a word suggesting that texts and histories are only of interest insofar as they illustrate the ideas of a few 'name-brand critics' (Loomba 2005: 4). Rather, we theorise those 'discrete practices of power and ways of imagining it' from the ground up, with the help of others' insights when they prove to be of use. We read texts historically, insisting on a history that is not Europe-centred, but international and global: a vision of 'interconnected and interdependent sites of historical importance, territorial and imaginative, that can disrupt oppositions between metropole and colony' (Wilson 2004: 3). Postcolonial critics of British Romantic literature study the entangled pasts and peoples of England, Scotland, Ireland, North America, the Caribbean, Africa and India through their literatures.

Plan of the Book

My choice of literary texts for inclusion in this book is designed to decentre the empire by exploring the intimate interpenetration between metropole and colonies, the British Isles and the rest of the world. The book presents the impact of postcolonial studies on British Romantic literature through carefully selected, linked case studies, rather than attempting a comprehensive survey. Chapter 1, 'Romantic Geographies', begins with exploration writing: the push to extend what was already a global empire into places as distant as the frozen Arctic and the African interior. For two travellers from British India, however, Britain itself was a contact zone. Abu Taleb and Dean Mahomed view the centre of empire with an outsider's eye. I then consider two canonical Romantic works in which the imperial 'outside' comes home to England: in *The Rime of the Ancient Mariner,* Coleridge's traumatised sailor will not shut up; the country estate in Austen's *Mansfield Park* is built on the proceeds of slavery. Chapter 2 takes up one geographical margin, the colonial Caribbean, which was both economically central and culturally contentious for the empire. Postcolonial criticism's concern with imaginary geography – the cultural construction of space in an imperial context – informs this chapter on 'Slavery and the Romantic Imagination' as I discuss abolitionist poetry by Cowper, Southey and Blake and a Romantic novel, *Obi*, about enslavement, escape and revolt. I finish with the slave autobiographies of Robert Wedderburn and Mary Prince. To what extent, postcolonial critics ask, could these subalterns speak?[17]

Chapter 3, 'Scottish Literature and Postcolonial Studies', treats a margin closer to home. Scotland, for many centuries an independent kingdom, became in 1707 officially part of Great Britain; Ireland followed in 1801. Once four nations (England, Wales, Scotland, Ireland), today the 'British empire in Europe' is a 'United Kingdom'. Scottish Romantic writers confronted the history and legacy of internal colonialism in diverse ways. Postcolonial critics have analysed the voices of this trilingual, multicultural nation in the poetry of Robert Burns and the novels of Sir Walter Scott and James Hogg. But the Scots were colonisers as well as colonised subjects, fanning out across the globe. The chapter ends by discussing the South African poetry of the Scottish poet Thomas Pringle. Chapter 4, 'Romantic Orientalisms', takes its title, of course, from Edward Said's *Orientalism*, a founding work of postcolonial studies. The discourse Said analyses took off during the Romantic period, with the British colonisation of India as an important motivation. The colonisers needed to know Persian, Sanskrit and Arabic in order to run the country; studying these languages, colonial administrators like Sir William Jones became fascinated with Eastern culture and religion. This convergence of scholarly knowledge and colonial power marked literary treatments of the East. Writers annotated poems and novels with extensive footnotes, drawing on the work of Jones and others for a more absorbing, encompassing presentation of the 'Oriental' stories and settings that Romantic readers loved. Sydney Owenson, Percy Shelley, and Lord Byron all spun tales of the East, rooted in imperial politics and culture in ways postcolonial critics have fruitfully explored.

My 'Coda' revisits some of the book's themes through a reading of a Romantic novel, Mary Shelley's *Frankenstein*, whose interpretation has been decisively changed by postcolonial studies. Like her educated contemporaries, Shelley read widely in the literature of travel, exploration and colonialism. The creature that Victor Frankenstein creates, using corpses and outdated theories, becomes the quintessential outsider when rejection and cruelty twist his innocence into rage. Postcolonial critics read *Frankenstein* in the context of racial discourse, slave revolt and Arctic exploration. I will then introduce a Romantic writer from the colonial margin: Henry Louis Vivian Derozio, a Eurasian from cosmopolitan Calcutta, was an educator and activist who protested against the practice of *sati*, or widow-burning. He features this controversial custom in his verse romance, *The Fakeer of Jungheera*, whose cultural hybridity reveals the emergence of a distinctively Indian, postcolonial modernity.

Rather than a comprehensive survey, *Romantic Literature and Postcolonial Studies* provides a selective introduction to a rich and varied field. The texts I have chosen to discuss in detail range from short lyrics to sprawling verse tales, exploration narratives and novels. I hope that the ideas and methods found in these analyses will help readers to make broader sense of the literature and culture of this eventful half-century. British Romantic writers included men and women, aristocrats and slaves, travellers and homebodies, radicals and reactionaries. They shared a public sphere filled with information about their nation's activities in various corners of the globe. Britain's rapidly expanding empire sparked writers' imaginations and often troubled their consciences; it changed and complicated the ways individual Britons could imagine the wider world and their place in it.

Notes

1. Butler (1990) traces its genesis to Cold War American academia.
2. Siskin 1998: 155; and see Garside et al. 2000, Heydt-Stevenson and Sussman 2008: 13.
3. Many scholars now designate the 'long eighteenth century', beginning anywhere from 1660 to 1740 and continuing to around 1830, as an appropriate period to study. Thomas Keymer and Jon Mee (2004) make a case for this periodisation, which 'enables an understanding of longer processes now increasingly seen as central to the formation of Romantic culture' and 'avoids marginalization of the many "Romantic period" writers who for one reason or another resist explanation in terms of the idioms or ideology of "high" Romanticism' (Keymer and Mee 2004: xi).
4. 'Contact zone' is Mary Louise Pratt's term, often borrowed by postcolonial critics, defined as 'the space of colonial encounters, the space in which peoples geographically and historically separated come into contact with each other and establish ongoing relations, usually involving conditions of coercion, radial inequality and intractable conflict' (Pratt 1992: 6). 'Subaltern' was a military term for officers under the rank of captain. This origin is inconsistent with its use in postcolonial studies to mean any oppressed person (Loomba 2005: 48–9). The Subaltern Studies group of historians, founded by Ranajit Guha in the 1980s, undertook to write a new history of India from the point of view of the subaltern or oppressed classes, rather than the colonial elite. Postcolonial studies – like feminist studies and working-class history – undertakes to recover the voices of the oppressed, but this is not a straightforward undertaking and has provoked a sustained debate among theorists, well summarised by Loomba (2005: 192–204).
5. Williams 2001: 69, quoted in Roe 2005: 1. Williams was responding to the Festival of the Federation (in July 1790), a mass celebration of the revolution, which she experienced at first hand (she lived in France and Switzerland for the rest of her life).
6. The Jacobins were the most famous political club of the French Revolution; moderate at first, they turned radical and implemented the so-called Reign of Terror in 1793–4. The term came to be used pejoratively for leftists and suspected French Revolution sympathisers during Britain's conservative reaction.
7. Mary Wollstonecraft, for example – who lived in Paris during Robespierre's Reign of Terror – wrote a history of the revolution troubled by, and at pains to justify, its violence: 'the retaliation of slaves is always terrible' (Wollstonecraft 1989: 234).
8. Jacobites were supporters of King James II of England and VII of Scotland, deposed in 1688, and of his son and grandson. They staged unsuccessful rebellions in Scotland in 1715 and 1745. See Chapter 3.
9. Britain gave back Martinique and Guadeloupe to lend respectability to the restored Bourbons after Napoleon's defeat (Duffy 1998: 206).
10. Bayly 1989: 126, 130. The phrase 'ecological imperialism' is Crosby's (Crosby 2004). On the environmental dimension of Romantic imperialism, see also Grove 1996.
11. Bayly 1998: 35. Napoleon used methods of fiscal extraction to finance French imperial expansion.
12. Bayly 1998: 39. See Edney 1997 on the ideological implications of mapping British India.
13. On the protean character of racial ideologies and the difficulty of pinning down

determinate chronologies, starting as far back as the medieval period, see the Introduction to Loomba and Burton 2007.

14. Nobody alive at the time thought of their age as one of 'Romanticism', nor did their contemporaries group the living poets of the day together as 'Romantic'. This classification did not emerge until considerably later in the nineteenth century.

15. St Clair 2004: 233. It is important to realise, however, that differential book prices meant far fewer readers had access to new, copyrighted books such as those of travel and romantic poetry. Those with more modest means read the out-of-copyright material that St Clair calls the 'old canon' (St Clair 2004), including poets from Geoffrey Chaucer to William Cowper, conduct literature, etc. Circulating libraries (which carried mostly novels, borrowed by women) and reading societies (which stocked non-fiction prose and had mostly men as members) widened the reading material available to elite readers, but did not significantly deepen access down the social ladder, with Scotland a partial exception. See St Clair 2004: 122–39, 234, 235–67; see also Suarez and Turner 2011.

16. See Makdisi 2003.

17. Spivak's famous article (1988) asks this questions and concludes they could not; other postcolonial critics have disagreed. See Loomba 2005: 192–204 and Parry 2004: 18–23.

Chapter 1

Romantic Geographies

European fiction from the age of empire rests on a crucial spatial or geographical foundation, a 'theoretical mapping and charting of territory', argues Edward Said in *Culture and Imperialism* (1993). Careful reading lets us recognise in these works 'the hierarchy of spaces by which the metropolitan centre and, gradually, the metropolitan economy are seen as dependent upon an overseas system of territorial control, economic exploitation, and a socio-cultural vision'. Without all these things – in short, without the empire – 'stability and prosperity at home . . . would not be possible' (Said 1993: 58–9). Scholars have taken up Said's challenge to think about the mental maps undergirding Romantic literary forms and to confront Romantic literature's engagement with Britain's global and imperial activities. British culture in the late eighteenth and early nineteenth centuries reveals an expanding 'planetary consciousness'.[1] We see this in the London popular culture that the poet William Wordsworth sampled in his youth and incorporated in his autobiographical poem, *The Prelude*. Book VII, 'Residence in London', contrasts the modern metropolis's inauthentic, international 'raree-show' with the 'simplicity and power' of rural English nature in the poet's Lake District home (*Prelude* VII, ll. 190, 720).[2] In the city crowd he spots diverse 'specimens of man' from around the world, including 'from remote/ America, the Hunter-Indian; Moors/ Malays, Lascars, the Tartar and Chinese' (ll. 236, 239–42). This casual list of nationalities encountered on the London streets reflects the reach of Britain's commercial and imperial interests by the late eighteenth century. London was very much a global city, hub of a worldwide network of trade and colonialism.

Wordsworth mentions American Indians again as part of the 'Parliament of Monsters' that helps generate the 'anarchy and din' of Bartholomew Fair: 'Albinos, painted Indians, Dwarfs,/ The Horse of knowledge, and the learned Pig' (ll. 691, 659, 680–1). Native people were exhibited, alongside other freaks and wonders, in the centre of empire, and had been since the sixteenth century (Altick 1978: 45–8). Curious Londoners could pay to see not just North American Indians, but a family of Laplanders, a Brazilian woman dubbed the 'Venus of South America', and, most notoriously, a South African woman, Sarah Baartman, known as the 'Hottentot Venus', shown in both London and Paris between her arrival in 1810 and her death in 1814 (Altick 1978: 268–75). Dissected by the French anatomist Georges Cuvier, Baartman involuntarily donated her preserved vagina to the Paris Musée de l'Homme, where it could be viewed well into the nineteenth century.[3] The emerging racial science of the time used Baartman's anatomy as evidence that there was more than one species of human being, a belief known as polygenesis.

The same curiosity that drew Londoners to such exhibitions fuelled the enduring popularity of travel writing in the Romantic print market. Travel writing had been important in England since at least the sixteenth century, informing readers about the wider world in which English commercial and territorial interests were steadily expanding. Travel accounts functioned as propaganda promoting overseas trade and settle-ment. The information travellers brought home informed the thinking of philosophers, natural historians and political economists, as well as poets and dramatists. Modern knowledge could not have been produced without it. Philosophical and political debates drew on travellers' obser-vations and opinions. Travel writing made the 'world of the intellectual and the reader . . . systematically international'. Popular and respected well into the nineteenth century, travel writing later lost its cachet; by the mid-twentieth century it was no longer taken seriously as literature.

This chapter considers travel writing as a way for readers to expe-rience Britain's global presence and as a literary form engaged with inter-cultural contact. I first consider travel writing as a genre and the challenges it presented to writers. I then discuss two popular 1790s exploration narratives: Samuel Hearne's *Journey from Prince of Wales's Fort in Hudson's Bay to the Northern Ocean* (1795) and Mungo Park's *Travels in the Interior Districts of Africa* (1799). These men are best understood as neither heroic adventurers nor ethnocentric imperialists. Rather, they were visitors to societies that tolerated their presence to dif-fering degrees and whose aid was vital to their missions. Seeing travellers as visitors lets us notice their uneasy negotiations with their hosts and the vulnerability that drives them (Lee 2001: xxii). Romantic travel was not a one-way affair. I will introduce two travellers to the British Isles from India: Abu Taleb, a Persian who worked for the English in India before travelling to the British Isles in 1799–1802, and Dean Mahomed, who joined the East India Company's army at the age of eleven and later emigrated to the British Isles. The chapter will finish with two canonical works whose interpretation has been transformed by postcolonial studies: Samuel Taylor Coleridge's *Rime of the Ancient Mariner* (1798) and Jane Austen's *Mansfield Park* (1814).

Romantic Travel Writing

Though Britons actively pursued travel and exploration throughout the seventeenth and eighteenth centuries, the 1770s brought a significant change. The three state-sponsored voyages of exploration led by Captain James Cook (1768–71, 1772–6, and 1776–9) ushered in a new era, forging crucial links among exploration and colonialism, the nation-state, science, visual art and the literary imagination. Cook's first expedition – promoted by Britain's national scientific organisation, the Royal Society, and funded by King George III to the tune of £4,000 – had a scientific pretext: to observe a rare celestial event, the transit of Venus, from the southern hemisphere. But Cook's secret instructions from the Admiralty made clear that he was to gather information bearing on future colonisation. They were told:

> carefully to observe the Nature of the Soil, and the Products thereof; the Beasts and Fowls that inhabit or frequent it, the fishes that are to be found in the Rivers or upon the Coast and in what Plenty; and in case you find any Mines, Minerals or valuable stones, you are to bring home Specimens of each, as also such Specimens of the Seeds of Trees, Fruits and Grains as you may be able to collect, and Transmit them to our Secretary, that We may cause proper Examination and Experiments to be made of them.
>
> You are likewise to observe the Genius, Temper, Disposition and Number of the Natives. (quoted in Smith 1985: 16)

Cook took along a party of scientists and artists under the leadership of Joseph Banks, a wealthy aristocrat and accomplished botanist. Banks would later become President of the Royal Society and the 'shadowy impresario of Britain's colonial expansion', dispatching explorers to remote areas and assembling specimens from around the world (Fulford and Lee 2002: 118). Banks's party included two more naturalists (one a student of the great Swedish taxonomist Linnaeus) and two artists, Alexander Buchan and Sydney Parkinson.[4]

John Hawkesworth's *An Account of the Voyages Undertaken by the*

Order of His Present Majesty for Making Discoveries in the Southern Hemisphere (1773), compiled from the journals of Banks, Cook and others, was the most popular travel book of the eighteenth century. Its images resonated for Romantic writers such as Dorothy Wordsworth, whose journal of her trip to Scotland compares Highland huts to the Patagonian dwellings in Hawkesworth's book (Wordsworth 1941: 1.224). The Scottish geographer John Pinkerton, editor of a collection of travel writing (Pinkerton 1808–14), lauds the voyages of 'our immortal Cook' as 'forming an illustrious epoch' in travel writing. Pinkerton's final volume provides a 'Retrospect of the Origin and Progress of Discovery, by Sea and Land, in Ancient, Modern, and the Most Recent Times'. Travel accounts before Cook 'are rather to be regarded as curious, than useful'.[5] Cook's accomplishments were unprecedented: the information he brought back about Tahiti, Australia, New Zealand and the North American coast, and the myths he disproved, including '*Terra Australis Incognita*', the southern continent, 'a grand imaginary feature' of earlier maps. Since Cook, the 'style, manner, and topics of books of voyages and travels' were 'greatly improved' (Pinkerton 1808–14: 17.xxix, xxxi). Modern travel writing incorporated science, geology, mineralogy, political economy.

   Romantic travel writing differed in several ways from that of the mid-eighteenth century. European exploration shifted from sea routes and coastlines to continental interiors, notably Africa and South America. Explorers like Mungo Park and Alexander von Humboldt confronted threats from inhospitable terrain to tropical disease, not to mention indigenous societies leery of intruders.[6] During two decades of war, many who travelled did so in uniform. Napoleon's invasion of Egypt generated the multivolume *Description de l'Egypte* (1809–29). This state-supported project embodied the 'encyclopedic ambition of Romantic "planetary consciousness"' and inspired Humboldt's even more massive account of his travels in the Americas (1807–32) (Leask 2002: 116–17). Lone explorers, such as Mungo Park in West Africa and his predecessor James Bruce in North Africa and Ethiopia, wore local dress and learned languages; subsequent expeditions to Africa (including Park's in 1805, from which he did not return) took larger parties and military power for protection. After the Napoleonic Wars, British travellers' situation changed as well. As Britain's colonies in Asia and Africa grew more Westernised, 'travel writers celebrated their emancipation from the necessity of cultural disguise alongside an increased separation from indigenous peoples' (Leask 2002: 3).

   Some important formal features distinguish travel writing as a genre.

At its core is the narrative of the journey, often presented in the form of a journal or log. Also popular were epistolary travelogues addressed to a real or fictional correspondent. An example is Mary Wollstonecraft's *Letters Written . . . in Sweden* (1796), which combines a report from a seldom-visited region of Europe with allusions to the writer's depression and romantic disappointment. This book (Wollstonecraft's most popular) exemplifies another key feature of travel writing: its element of fictionality, despite its factual content. 'The actual experience of a journey is reconstructed, and therefore fictionalised, in the moment of being told' (Korte 2000: 11). Wollstonecraft drew on the actual letters she wrote during her journey, but revised them for book publication. Other Romantic travellers, like Samuel Hearne and John Gabriel Stedman, kept records of their experiences and later wrote for publication (both men travelled in the 1770s, but did not publish until the 1790s). Additions and revisions reveal the difference between the young man, risking his life in the colonial contact zone, and his older self, back in civilisation, reworking the raw material of the journey for metropolitan readers.

This brings up another important feature of travel writing: its autobiographical element, which further troubles the border between fact and fiction. Readers naturally equate the narrator of a travel account with its author, but analysis reveals a distinctive persona – a character the writer creates according to the demands of the literary work. John Gabriel Stedman, for example, as he reworked his Suriname journal into his *Narrative of a Five Years Expedition Against the Revolted Negroes of Surinam* (1796), produced a 'retrospective and somewhat idealised vision of his youth'. He romanticised his relationship with his slave concubine, Joanna, presenting himself as a romantic hero rather than a soldier purchasing sexual services. This change 'had significant repercussions for his treatment of interracial sexual relationships in the *Narrative*' (Price and Price 1988: xxxii). A persona can be stoic and resourceful, like Hearne's, or melancholy and reflective, like Wollstonecraft's, but must always be distinguished from the historical individual who penned the account.

Historically, it is no doubt true that the late eighteenth century was more tolerant of autobiographical content. Earlier reviewers condemned travelogues with too much personal detail as egotistical. Scholars notice a turn from objective to subjective in Romantic-era travel writing.[7] For Nigel Leask, however, such a view 'elevate[s] . . . one, self-consciously literary, strain of travel writing at the expense of other discourses of travel . . . of equal importance'. To call all Romantic travel writing 'subjective' is 'to ignore not only the majority of travelogues produced during the period but also the testimony of contemporary commentators'. Scientific and literary travel writing eventually did diverge, but Leask is right that this happened after 1820, rather than before. The decades between 1790 and 1820 saw a fruitful struggle to integrate subjective experience with objective or scientific observation (Leask 2002: 6, 8, 7).

As a genre, travel writing is eclectic. Barbara Korte calls it an *omnium-gatherum:* a medley capable of including a broad range of elements, from scientific data to personal anecdote or philosophical reflection. This heterogeneous content generates a stylistic variety ranging from the self-consciously literary to plain, functional prose (Korte 2000: 5, 15). Alongside the narration of the journey, the other constant component of the travel book is description of places, things, and people. Many Romantic travel writers, like their predecessors, segregate narration from description. Mungo Park, for example, interpolates sections describing the manners and customs of the various African tribes he encounters along the way to the River Niger. Mary Pratt calls this convention 'textual apartheid' (Pratt 1992: 61). The ethnographic present tense in which generalisations about native peoples were made, she argues, functioned to fix them in a timeless present by interpreting anything they did as a normal habit rather than, for example, a reaction to the travellers' presence. Along with the 'global project of natural history', this mode of describing non-Europeans functions to 'dismantle the socioecological web that preceded them and install a Eurocolonial discursive order' (Pratt 1992: 64).

Explorers or Visitors?

Exploration narratives 'linked individual experience to corporate significance', Bruce Greenfield points out. The 'widely shared understanding that Europeans and Euro-Americans were fundamentally concerned with, even defined by, their global expansion . . . enabled the traveller . . . to gain a public hearing when he returned'. Going where few Europeans had ventured gave explorers' reports authority for readers (Greenfield 1992: 11). I will discuss two examples from very different latitudes. The first is Samuel Hearne's trek across northern Canada in search of elusive mineral wealth and a non-existent Northwest Passage. His *Journey from Prince of Wales's Fort in Hudson's Bay to the Northern Ocean* (1795) is 'the first recognised classic of northern exploration literature' (McGoogan 2004: 129). Hearne, like Cook, was a navy man who went to sea as a boy and worked his way up the ranks. After the Seven Years' War he joined the Hudson's Bay Company in Canada. Chartered by the Crown in 1670, the Company still exists today. Like the East India Company in South Asia, it functioned as a de facto government of parts of North America before formal colonisation. Its trappers and fur traders formed working relationships with Native Americans, and its network of trading posts facilitated the later extension of state authority. When Britain's victory over France won it much of Canada, the Company was positioned to extend its reach further into the interior.

This is where Hearne's mission comes in. The Company commissioned him to travel west with a twofold goal: to investigate Chipewyan (Dene) Indian reports – from as early as 1719 – that remarkably pure copper was available somewhere out there, and to find a shipping route to the Pacific. Transporting the copper by land could take over a year, but not with a water passage. Moses Norton, Governor of Prince of Wales's Fort, hired Hearne and recruited his Indian guides. The first guide deserted Hearne and two other hapless Britons 200 miles from the Fort (Glover 1958: xvii). Hearne made two more attempts before his third, successful expedition. This time he took more control of assembling the party, finally finding a competent guide, Matonabbee, a powerful Chipewyan whom Hearne calls 'the most sociable, kind and sensible Indian I had ever met' (Hearne 1958: 35–6). The expedition's success resulted, in a seeming paradox, from Hearne's relinquishing leadership and letting Matonabbee take charge. As a follower rather than a leader, Hearne could benefit from Indian survival techniques and return from the expedition alive (Fulford 2006: 65).

Matonabbee, writes Tim Fulford in *Romantic Indians:*

> appears in Hearne's text not as a 'savage' but as a great leader . . . Hearne is full of admiration and respect rather than the paternalism or condescension often found in white men's portraits of Native Americans. Hearne's deference toward the man who led him to the Arctic and back allows Matonabbee to appear as a complex human being rather than a stereotype of savagery (noble or ignoble). (Fulford 2006: 73–4)

This was a man whose life was shaped by British colonialism. Born of a match made by the governor of the fort between a Dene man and a slave woman bought from Southern Indians, Matonabbee was adopted by the governor, but later left the fort to join his father's relations. Hearne praises his resourcefulness and integrity, 'benevolence and universal humanity' (Hearne 1958: 224). He did have one flaw, however, namely jealousy. A polygamist, he was so possessive he once stabbed a man whose wife he had taken through the Chipewyan custom of wrestling for women, which Hearne describes (1958: 67). Hearne's portrait of Matonabbee so impressed the poet Robert Southey that he drew on it for his American epic, *Madoc* (1805). The great man's death seems shockingly out of character. When the French captured Prince of Wales's Fort in 1782, taking Hearne and the rest of the garrison to Europe as prisoners, but leaving their Indian employees behind, Matonabbee hanged himself. This seemingly self-sufficient leader had been from the outset:

> utterly dependent, for livelihood, status, and self-respect, on the British whom he served . . . Matonabbee, after the withdrawal of the British, had become foreign to himself, in his native land . . . [He] owes his power, his identity itself, to empire but he is also, ultimately, its victim. (Fulford 2006: 74–5)

The part of Hearne's narrative most often anthologised in collections of Canadian literature and analysed by critics concerns his guides' massacre of a group of Inuit at a site Hearne christens 'Bloody Falls'.[8] The explorer realises part way through the journey that this 'inhuman design' is his guides' main motive for travelling to the Coppermine River. When he tries to dissuade them, they call him a coward (Hearne 1958: 74). The isolated European's vulnerability becomes obvious:

> As I knew my personal safety depended in a great measure on the favourable opinion they entertained of me in this respect, I was obliged to change my tone, and replied, that I did not care if they rendered the name and race of the Esquimaux extinct.

He says he will kill as many Inuit as necessary 'for the protection of any one of my company', though they are no enemies of his (Hearne 1958: 74–5). Hearne's situation is ironic: 'He finally has a group of Indians doing what is necessary to get him to the mouth of the Coppermine, but upon learning of their reasons . . . he would like to stop them' (Greenfield 1992: 37).

Hearne's graphic narration of the massacre calls attention to another challenge inherent in producing exploration narratives. Explorers, though qualified for their work, tended not to be highly educated and often needed help preparing books for publication. One modern editor maintains that though someone corrected the manuscript, 'Hearne wrote it' (Glover 1958: xxx). But Fulford assumes extensive revision by someone else. A quarter of a century after his journey, Hearne's notes formed the basis for 'a dramatic narrative carefully shaped to fit the public taste for the picturesque, the romantic, and the sensational . . . a composite literary artifact, crafted with an eye to the market for travellers' tales of "savage" peoples and dangerous adventures' (Fulford 2006: 66). In any case, the revision took place following Hearne's return to England. Once again immersed in the tastes and sensibilities of metropolitan Britons, the explorer may well have changed his perspective on his experience.

The passage describing the Bloody Falls massacre was added to Hearne's original journal. As the Dene slaughter the Inuit, someone kills a young girl so close to Hearne 'that when the first spear was stuck into her side she fell down at my feet, and twisted round my legs, so that it was with difficulty that I could disengage myself from her dying grasps'. He begs for her life as his guides pitilessly stab her. They begin 'to ridicule me, by asking if I wanted an Esquimaux wife; and paid not the smallest regard to the shrieks and agony of the poor wretch, who was twining round their spears like an eel!' (Hearne 1958: 99–100). This striking simile carries 'more power because the rest of Hearne's description seems so bare and direct'. Likening the agonised girl to an animal 'reinforces the image of the indigene as nature'. At this point, however, Hearne's spare prose gives way to 'civilised circumlocution' (Goldie 1989: 45):

> I was at length obliged to desire that they would be more expeditious in dispatching their victim out of her misery, otherwise I should be obliged, out of pity, to assist in the friendly office of putting an end to the existence of a fellow-creature who was so cruelly wounded. (Hearne 1958: 100)

In contrast to his earlier direct language, these euphemisms, in the passive voice, strive for 'civilised' distance from the grisly scene. Hearne's summary of the incident is explicitly retrospective, alluding to the distance of time between the event and his tortured recollection:

> My situation and the terror of my mind at beholding this butchery, cannot easily be conceived, much less described; though I summed [sic] up all the fortitude I was master of on the occasion, it was with difficulty that I could refrain from tears; and I am confident that my features must have feelingly expressed how sincerely I was affected at the barbarous scene I then witnessed; even at this hour I cannot reflect on the transactions of that day without shedding tears. (Hearne 1958: 100)

These tears, not noted in his journal, were a retrospective addition by Hearne or an editor. They differentiate Hearne from his Dene companions: 'the white man feels guilt and pity when the Indians do not. If Hearne was complicit with murder, he purges his guilt by compassion of which tears are the bodily proof.' Hearne did not, that is, 'go native' – become a savage – like Joseph Conrad's fictional Kurtz (Fulford 2006: 68–9).

Hearne's *Journey* fascinated Romantic readers such as Wordsworth and Coleridge, who both wrote poems inspired by its portrayal of indigenous Americans. American Indians had been featured in the British press throughout the eighteenth century, with coverage intensifying during and after the Seven Years' War (1756–63), a conflict that put more Britons in proximity to Indians than ever before. Newspapers and magazines ran accounts of battles, redacted Indian leaders' orations, and excerpted travel accounts. Everyone in this imperially minded society had an opinion about the Indians' role in the struggle for control of North America. After mid-century, Indians were no longer featured as sentimentalised noble savages, but primarily as pitiless warriors. Other aspects of Native American culture drew metropolitan readers' interest (though the appeal of violence clearly persisted). Accounts of Indian spirituality and shamanism fit in with Romanticism's challenge to the Enlightenment insistence on empirically demonstrable knowledge. These are described, if sceptically, in Hearne's *Journey*. Coleridge's use of the supernatural in his *Rime of the Ancient Mariner* draws on these features.[9] Before and after the revolt of Britain's North American colonies, the continuing exploration of the continent and interactions with its native inhabitants loomed large in the imaginative geography of British culture.

Meanwhile, further south, another continental interior drew increasing interest from London's architects of empire. Of course, Britain and the rest of Europe had an established trade relationship with Africa, organised around the human commodity of slaves. British ships took their first human cargoes from Africa to the Caribbean as early as 1562, selling them to the Spanish. After Britain colonised several Caribbean islands and North America, British merchants could sell slaves to British planters. The slave trade peaked in the 1770s: Britain led the world in the volume of African captives transported and sold.[10] Captive Africans populated Britain's sugar islands (see Chapter 2). Earlier travel writing about Africa came largely from slave traders. In the 1780s, when the abolitionist movement got organised and became a major political force, both abolitionists and advocates of slavery drew on travel reports in support of their political views. Africa – in particular its vast interior – needed to be re-imagined as the anti-slavery movement gained popular support (Pratt 1992: 71).

Interior exploration opened a new chapter in metropolitan readers' acquaintance with Africa, starting with James Bruce's controversial *Travels . . . to Discover the Source of the Nile* (1790). The eccentric Scot cut a colourful swathe through the continent. Six feet four, wearing

Arab dress and speaking fluent Arabic, he set off in 1768 to discover the Ethiopian source of the Nile (not admitting that Europeans had already been there). Bruce arrived in London in 1774 – the same time as Omai, the Tahitian who came back with the Cook expedition – and became a celebrity. Horace Walpole wrote to a friend:

> Africa is, indeed, coming into fashion. There is just returned a Mr. Bruce, who has lived three years in the court of Abyssinia, and breakfasted every morning with the maids of honour on live oxen. Otaheite and Mr. Banks are quite forgotten. (Leask 2002: 55)

The live oxen story broke in the September 1774 issue of *London Magazine*: Ethiopians 'cut collops from live animals, which they tear to pieces with their teeth while warm, and palpitating with a vital motion' (quoted in Leask 2002: 55, 56). Bruce's *Travels* describe a 'Polyphemus banquet' where participants ate meat from a living cow and afterward had sex on the floor: 'there are no rooms but one, in which they sacrifice to both Bacchus and Venus' (quoted in Leask 2002: 92).

The reception of Bruce's book was mixed. Leask has analysed the widespread scepticism of metropolitan readers (Leask 2002: 54–101). This limited the stylistic options of subsequent travel writers if they wanted readers to believe them. Where Bruce's flamboyant tale tested readers' credulity, Mungo Park's *Travels in the Interior Districts of Africa* (1799) turned to simplicity and understatement. The credibility of Park's book mattered to more than just its author. His expedition was sponsored by the Association for Promoting the Discovery of the Interior Parts of Africa, known as the African Association, an influential group of aristocrats, businessmen and scientists formed in 1788 by Sir Joseph Banks (the natural historian who sailed with Cook). The expedition's aims included establishing trade, other than the slave trade, with the continent and discovering the source of the River Niger. By 1794, when Park left for Africa, the Association had sent three previous explorers into the interior. None had returned; surviving papers of the third indicated that the Niger flowed eastward, a fact the geographer James Rennell incorporated in a map as early as 1790. But without a living observer the report lacked credibility. 'Park's endeavours were about confirmation and not "discovery". His acclaim was to do with the credibility of direct observation, his survival and his conduct in London rather more than with the facts he secured' (Withers 2010: 207).

At this point the Association needed a plausible, presentable spokesman as well as a competent explorer. Park was both, but not without help. The Secretary of the African Association, Bryan Edwards (Member of Parliament, Jamaica planter, and author of a history of the West Indies), was delegated to help turn Park's notes into a book. Meanwhile, the well-credentialled Rennell worked on 'Geographical Illustrations'.[11] The explorer's concern to produce what his Preface calls a 'plain, unvarnished tale' (Park 2000: 45) led to leaving things out. He admitted as much to the poet Sir Walter Scott during an evening of conviviality. 'I will not shock [my readers'] credulity, or render my travels more marvellous, by producing anecdotes which however true, can only relate to my own personal escapes and adventures.' Scott, alas, could not remember the anecdotes Park shared, perhaps due to the amount of Scottish 'conviviality' flowing at the party.[12] By choosing understatement, Park succeeded in producing a runaway bestseller.

Mary Pratt calls Park a sentimental traveller, contrasting his approach with the impersonal style of many eighteenth-century travel accounts. Sentimentality in travel writing, she argues, 'both challenges and complements the emergent authority of objectivist science'. By producing a story of 'personal experience and adventure', rather than 'a narrative of geographical discovery, observation, or collection' (Pratt 1992: 75), Park followed the lead of Laurence Sterne's influential travel novel, *A Sentimental Journey* (1768) (without Sterne's irony and whimsy).[13] The explorer portrays his interactions with Africans as 'an epic series of trials, challenges, and encounters with the unpredictable' (Pratt 1992: 75). He is robbed, taken captive by hostile 'Moors', and laid low by a tropical fever. But he is also helped by a series of Africans, mostly humble people, many of them slaves (who Park claims make up three-quarters of the West African population).

Park's book makes it obvious that he is indeed a visitor, vulnerable and dependent, in someone else's home. One touching example is the 'old motherly-looking woman', spinning in a hut outside the village of Shrilla, who invites him in and feeds him leftover couscous after the town headman refuses him a handful of corn for his horse. In 'return for this kindness', Park writes:

> I gave her one of my pocket-handkerchiefs . . . Overcome with joy at this unexpected deliverance, I lifted up my eyes to heaven, and whilst my heart swelled with gratitude, I returned thanks to that gracious and bountiful Being, whose power had supported me under so many dangers, and had now spread for me a table in the Wilderness. (Park 2000: 185–6)

Marking the emotional moment with a biblical allusion, Park observes, 'in Africa, as well as in Europe, hospitality does not always prefer the highest dwellings' (Park 2000: 185).[14]

But Park also got indispensable support from European and African participants in the slave trade. The literature of African exploration has not usually been read in connection with slavery and the slave trade, largely because Britain abolished the slave trade in 1807, before much progress had been made in interior exploration (British slaves were not fully emancipated until 1838). In the 1790s, however, the slave trade was legal and lucrative, though increasingly controversial. The infrastructure created by centuries of the European slave trade, and the internal African trade that fed it, made Park's journey possible. His main contact in Africa was John Laidley, honorary consul in Pisania, a village on the River Gambia that existed solely to carry on the slave trade (Lupton 1979: 42). Laidley set him up with everything he would need to travel into the interior: a horse, two asses, trade goods including 'beads, amber, and tobacco', clean linen, an umbrella, sextant, compass, thermometer and several guns (Lupton 1979: 87). Laidley also supplied Park with human assets: his interpreter, Johnson (a well-travelled man who learned English as a slave in Jamaica), and a slave boy, Demba, who spoke Mande and another African language.

The terms in which Park promised to pay his help open a window into the West African economy. Their wages are specified in 'bars' and 'the price of . . . prime slaves' (Association for Promoting the Discovery of Interior Parts of Africa 1967: 1.307).[15] John Matthews writes in his 1788 *Voyage to the River Sierra Leone*, 'Slaves are the medium, instead of coin, for the purchase of every necessary, and the supplying of every want; and every article is estimated, by its proportion, to the value of a slave' (quoted in Festa 2006: 158). Economically and culturally, the slave trade pervaded West Africa. A credit system dependent on the slave trade let Park replenish his funds without carrying valuables that could be stolen. African slave traders in debt to Laidley pay Park in sums calculated in units of slaves. He gets shelter and information from slave traders along his route; local officials assume he is there to buy slaves. Even Johnson the ex-slave, Park's interpreter, gets involved in the slave trade: he parts ways with Park when he is offered 'half the price of a slave' to help conduct slaves to Gambia. Johnson would rather go back to his family than forge ahead with Park in Moor-infested territory, and Park does not seem to blame him (Park 2000: 180).

But as he piggybacks on the slave trade infrastructure, Park also reports on its practices – facts that slave trade opponents could cite. On his way back to the coast he encounters a coffle, or caravan, of seventy slaves bound for Morocco, 'tied together by their necks with thongs of a bullock's hide, twisted together like a rope; seven slaves upon a thong;

and a man with a musket between every seven' (Park 2000: 192). Park himself later joins a coffle headed by Karfa Taura, an African slave trader taking slaves to the coast to sell. He lands in Karfa's village of Kamalia after reaching the Niger and deciding to turn back. He promises Karfa the value of one prime slave for letting him travel under his protection. During the trip to the coast, Karfa secures his slaves using thongs like the one Park has seen. Taking no chances, he adds fetters on the captives' hands and legs, a chain around their necks, and, for those who 'evince marks of discontent', a wooden contraption for the ankles with an iron staple (Park 2000: 277).

After reaching the coast, Park crossed the Atlantic on the American slave ship *Charles Town*. The confinement of slaves on the ship was 'rigid and severe', he reports, and the mortality high. Without taking an explicit position – which would have been politically unwise, since his sponsor, the African Association, included members on both sides of the issue – Park managed to document the cruelty of both the African slave trade and the transatlantic trade. But he also benefited materially from its infrastructure. Visiting a continent scarred by European predation, the explorer describes his African hosts. Unlike many later explorers, 'Park affirms plausible worlds of African agency and experience. His relational approach to culture raises genuine possibilities of critical self-questioning' (Pratt 1992: 84). But his venture was part of a larger enterprise leading towards a very different type of European presence on the continent. Park led a second expedition in 1805, for which the African Association (buoyed by the success of his *Travels*) secured state funding – the first government-sponsored West African expedition (Marsters 2000: 8). He set out with a military escort of thirty-eight men, but died on the Niger under mysterious circumstances, leaving an ambiguous legacy.

As Park drew on the language of sensibility, other travellers incorporated in their narratives other powerful discourses familiar to educated readers. Two of these, natural history and landscape aesthetics, were specialised vocabularies describing things travellers observed or collected on their journeys. The connection between exploration and science was strong throughout the eighteenth century as students of Linnaeus hitched rides on expeditions to document new species around the globe. Cook's voyages established science as an important goal of exploration, with plant and animal species among the resources that expeditions were instructed to note in potential colonies like Australia. The benign figure of the naturalist helped to naturalise European incursions in a rhetorical strategy Pratt labels 'the anti-conquest' (Pratt

1992: 38–68). Linnaean taxonomy was a powerful conceptual engine, she argues, for transforming all of nature into a Europe-centred order: 'One by one the planet's life forms were to be drawn out of the tangled threads of their life surroundings and rewoven into European-based patterns of global unity and order' (Pratt 1992: 31).

Natural history is central to a Romantic travel book that caught the imagination of the poets Wordsworth and Coleridge. William Bartram's *Travels* describes the Philadelphia naturalist's 1770s trip around the American south-east. The language of natural history meets that of pastoral poetry in his description of a meadow or plain. It is

> encircled with high, sloping hills, covered with waving forests and fragrant orange groves, rising from an exuberantly fertile soil. The towering Magnolia grandiflora and transcendent palm stand conspicuous amongst them. At the same time are seen innumerable droves of cattle; the lordly bull, lowing cow, and sleek capricious heifer. The hills and groves re-echo their cheerful, social voices. (Bartram 1958: 119–20)

Bartram writes detailed, scientifically observant description of plant and animal species in an evocative prose whose adjectives recall eighteenth-century nature poetry. His impressions of the Native Americans (who nicknamed him 'Puc Puggy or the Flower Hunter') helped inspire Wordsworth to imagine his Lake District childhood as a natural idyll.

As travellers described unfamiliar landscapes for readers, travel writing intersected with another division of Enlightenment knowledge: aesthetics. Travel and exploration left their mark on European aesthetics. By the late eighteenth century landscape aesthetics was a prominent feature of domestic travel writing about areas of scenic beauty such as the Lake District and the Scottish Highlands. A specialised language evolved for describing natural scenery in terms of art. The best views were called 'picturesque', suitable for painting. Writers, illustrators and landscape designers developed varying interpretations of the picturesque throughout the Romantic era.[16] The exotic helped nourish picturesque taste – for example, in the Pacific (Smith 1985: 201). The concept of the picturesque expanded to include more than landscape: buildings, animals, plants, people, costumes and even customs from distant places could qualify as picturesque.

India was rich in the picturesque. William Hodges, official artist on Cook's second voyage, travelled there in 1777 and was fascinated by its light: 'The clear blue cloudless sky, the polished white buildings, the bright sandy beach, the dark green sea, present a combination totally new to the eye of an Englishman' (quoted in Archer and Lightbown

1982: 9). His spectacular aquatints render temples, pagodas and tombs alongside sprawling banyan trees, sublime waterfalls and mountain passes. Thomas and William Daniell's *Picturesque Voyage to India; by the Way of China* (1810) sums up the appropriative flavour of the Indian picturesque.

> Science has had her adventures, and philanthropy her achievements: the shores of Asia have been invaded by a race of students with no rapacity but for lettered relics: by naturalists, whose cruelty extends not to one human inhabitant: by philosophers, ambitious only for the extirpation of error, and the diffusion of truth. It remains only for the artist to claim his part in these guiltless spoliations, and to transport to Europe the picturesque beauties of these favoured regions. (quoted in Edney 1997: 61)

The geographer Matthew Edney analyses the picturesque as a disciplinary gaze, working in tandem with the scientific gaze as technologies for observing, imagining and mapping India. The picturesque evolved as a way of packaging landscape into a commodity to be enjoyed by educated, tasteful observers, trained to impose an order and structure onto nature. Such an attitude lent itself to the logic of empire: 'Most Company officials who engaged in landscape painting were concerned with examining, disciplining, and improving India. They were up-country magistrates, district revenue collectors, army officers on station, engineers building roads, and, especially, officers undertaking cartographic surveys.' The colonists' amateur art dovetailed with their professional duty to construct a 'view of India based on their power over it' (Edney 1997: 63).

Landscape is also a dominant concern in accounts of the Caribbean. Agriculture, of course, in particular slave-grown sugar cane, generated huge profits for colonists. The language of aesthetics played a part in the debate over slavery, as we see in William Beckford's *Descriptive Account of the Island of Jamaica* (1790).[17] Illegitimate scion of the richest family in Jamaica, Beckford ran plantations for a decade before going bankrupt after the 1780 hurricane. He wrote his book in debtors' prison in London. It alternates between overwrought landscape descriptions and practical advice for planters, converting 'a pictorial imperative into a gesture of self-protection that allows the colonial gaze a license to convert its ability not to see into studiously visual representations' (Suleri 1992: 76). Beckford takes his reader on a virtual tour of Jamaica's light-flooded vistas: 'gloomy dells or woody plains, ... mountain-torrents, and ... winding-streams; ... groups of negroes, herds of cattle, passing wains [wagons]' (Beckford 1790: 1.9–10). A painter could learn a lot in

Jamaica. Europe's scenery is too familiar; the West Indies can 'give scope to a new expansion of picturesque ideas' and renovate an exhausted aesthetics (Beckford 1790: 1.270, 271). Near the end of Beckford's massive book we realise it is pro-slavery propaganda. A gripping description of the hurricane tropes the apocalyptic end that Beckford predicts if Britain makes the mistake of abolishing the slave trade.

Travellers to Britain

The world came to Britain as well. London, centre of an expanding empire, drew everyone from Europeans to exotic Easterners and Native Americans. We will now consider two men who travelled to the British Isles from India and – by coincidence – met briefly in Ireland. The first is Abu Taleb, born in Lucknow, India, in 1752, son of Iranian immigrants. Like his father, he worked for the ruler (nawab) of a Muslim state, Awadh (Oudh), as an administrator and soldier. When court intrigues left him unemployed, a Scottish friend offered to pay his fare to Europe. The idea was for him to establish a Persian-language institute in Oxford or London, though this never happened. From 1799 to 1803, Abu Taleb travelled to the British Isles and back to India by way of Paris, Constantinople and Iran. He wrote an account of his journey in Persian, translated into English in 1810 by Charles Stewart, Professor of Oriental Languages at the East India Company's institute.

Abu Taleb's view is that of an outsider, a premise used by fictional satire such as Montesquieu's *Persian Letters* (1721). He became a celebrity in England: known as the Persian Prince, he was feted by London high society, met the king and queen, and attended meetings of the Royal Society, which gave him 'much mental satisfaction' (Abu Taleb 2005: 90). Six artists painted his portrait. He writes:

> Hospitality is one of the most esteemed virtues of the English; and I experienced it to such a degree, that I was seldom disengaged . . . I freely confess, that during my residence in England . . . I followed the advice of our immortal poet Hafiz, and gave myself up to love and gaiety. (Abu Taleb 2005: 63–4)

Abu Taleb's first stop in the British Isles was Ireland. In Cork he visited one Captain Baker, whom he had known in Rohilkhand, and at Baker's home met Dean Mahomed, a Bengali brought to Ireland in the 1780s by Baker's older brother and married to an Irish woman. Abu Taleb's observations on Ireland run the gamut from admiring to shocked: 'The poverty of the peasants, or common people, in this country, is such, that the peasants of India are rich when compared to them.' He enjoys the Dublin shops and is impressed with the number of coaches and carriages in the streets, all drawn by horses, not bullocks as in India: 'The only use made of bullocks here is to *eat* them' (Abu Taleb 2005: 41, 45). He censures people's 'idolatry' of stone statues: 'It is really astonishing that people possessing so much knowledge and good sense, and who reproach the nobility of Hindoostan with wearing gold and silver ornaments like women, should be thus tempted by Satan to throw away their money on useless blocks.' The fastidious Muslim is disappointed that the whole city of Dublin has just two small, cramped public baths. On a trip to the theatre he sees *The Taking of Seringapatam*, 'taken from a book recently published, containing an account of the late war in Mysore, and the fall of Tippoo Sultan'. He finds the representation 'correct' and the conclusion 'affecting' (Abu Taleb 2005: 46, 50–1).

Abu Taleb's book devotes nine chapters to an in-depth account of England: its soil, animals, roads, bridges, canals, the price of provisions, the state of the arts and sciences, the excellence of the navy, and the division of labour between the sexes. He is very impressed with the 'science of mechanics' (Abu Taleb 2005: 102). 'The manufacture of needles astonished me', he writes. He tours a 'manufactory', where 'everything appears conducted with so much regularity and precision, that a person is induced to suppose one of the meanest capacity might superintend and direct the whole process' (Abu Taleb 2005: 105). The English bring their 'passion for mechanics' to all areas of life, even the kitchen, where 'a very complete engine is used . . . to roast a *chicken*' (Abu Taleb 2005: 104). Other aspects of British culture are less attractive: the legal code (used by a tailor to defraud him) and the taxes. 'The rich are taxed for every dog, horse, and man-servant they keep; they are also obliged to pay for the liberty of throwing flour on their heads' (Abu Taleb 2005: 141). English women, he concludes, despite 'their apparent liberty, and the politeness and flattery with which they are addressed, are, by the wisdom of their lawgivers, confined in strict bondage'. But this might be a good thing: Muslim women are 'more mistresses of their conduct and much more liable to fall into the paths of error' (Abu Taleb 2005: 112).

The vices of the English include insufficient faith in religion. In the lower orders this brings a lamentable want of honesty – they will steal whatever is not nailed down. The upper ranks waste hours getting dressed and undressed, not to mention the time they spend sitting around at meals. On the up side, as well as their 'passion for mechanism', the English have a 'high sense of honour', respect merit and care about common people. They are distinguished by plain manners, sincerity, 'good natural sense and soundness of judgment' (Abu Taleb 2005: 156–7). Their slavery to fashion is a good thing because of 'the encouragement it gives to ingenuity and manufacturers of every kind' (Abu Taleb 2005: 156). After a year in London, the Muslim nobleman seems to be taking a page from Adam Smith.

Of course, Abu Taleb was no stranger to British manners and customs before he went to Europe. India at the end of the eighteenth century was a country in transition – what its Urdu poets described in melancholy terms as an *inqilab* (literally 'revolution'): 'an inversion of the existing order in which the high and noble were overthrown and the lowly rose to the top' (Ray 1998: 508–9). On the ship to Europe a fellow passenger, the aptly named Mr Grand, treats Abu Taleb with 'that overbearing insolence which characterises the vulgar part of the English in their conduct to Orientals' (Abu Taleb 2005: 16). British India's transition from commercial to territorial empire was well under way by this time. His close connections with the network of returned nabobs who host him in Britain suggest Abu Taleb is inclined to make the best of the new order.[18]

Our other traveller is of a different sort. Dean Mahomed followed his late father into the East India Company's army, and at the age of eleven formed a patronage relationship with an Anglo-Irish ensign, Godfrey Baker. As Baker rose to the rank of captain, Mahomed rose from camp follower to market master, then subaltern officer (Fisher 1996: 2). He fought in Company campaigns against the Marathas and the Rajah of Benares. When internal power struggles cost Baker his command, Mahomed, in his twenties, chose to accompany his patron to Ireland: 'a momentous decision to begin a new life in an unknown land' (Fisher 1996: 183). As an immigrant, Mahomed was unique during his lifetime (1759–1851). He fitted none of the usual categories of Indians travelling to Britain – sailors, servants, wives or mistresses of Europeans, and a few visiting dignitaries like Abu Taleb (Fisher 1996: 192).

Dean Mahomed left no written record of his impressions of the British Isles. He did, however, publish a travel book: *The Travels of Dean Mahomet, a Native of Patna in Bengal, Through Several Parts of India, While in the Service of The Honourable The East India Company, Written by Himself* (Cork, 1794). 'Written by Himself' echoes black writers such as Olaudah Equiano, who assert, against stereotypes, that persons of colour can actually be authors. In epistolary format, with the obligatory poetic allusions, his book shows Mahomed worked hard to educate himself in the English language and culture. He also worked hard to promote his book to Dublin's Anglo-Irish elite, circulating a prospectus to potential subscribers, 320 of whom advanced him half a crown. The 'very conventionality of the *Travels* ... reflect[s] Dean Mahomed's remarkable capacity, and desire, to negotiate space for himself in Anglo-Irish, and later English, respectable society' (Fisher 1996: 216, 224). The frontispiece (similar to Equiano's) portrays the author in European dress.

The *Travels* earned Dean Mahomed the title 'first Indian author in English'. Over the next half century the immigrant lived in three cities and started several enterprises to profit from his Indian identity and colonial connections. In Cork he probably worked for his patron's family, perhaps as a household manager (Fisher 1996: 237). In 1786, when he eloped with Jane Daly, he had the money to post a bond with the church rather than wait several weeks for the banns to be read. Such interracial marriages (to use today's terminology) were uncommon in the respectable classes to which Jane belonged, though more frequent among servants (Fisher 1996: 209, 220). No one named Daly subscribed to the *Travels*, nor has any trace of the Daly family been found in Mr and Mrs Mahomed's subsequent life. Godfrey Baker died without a will in 1786, so Mahomed could not have been solely dependent on him. It was at the home of Godfrey's brother, William Massey Baker, also returned from India, that he met Abu Taleb. Cork had a network of India-returned officers, in which Mahomed seems to have found a place for himself and his family.

In 1807 Dean Mahomed, with his wife and at least one child (probably more), left Cork for London; it is not clear why. He was near fifty and had lived in Ireland for over twenty years. In London he took advantage of the tastes and practices introduced by Britons returning from colonial service. Europeans had long enjoyed spices from the East, but 'by the early nineteenth century ... whole new cuisines entered the English palate'. Another area in which Britons began to look East was in the field of health and medical knowledge. Newspapers carried advertisements for nostrums such as 'Oriental Tooth Powder', something Mahomed himself would later sell (Fisher 1996: 241). Sea bathing as a medical practice was catching on at coastal spas (medicinal springs had long been popular destinations) and spa-related practices such as steam bathing and massage began to be offered to health-conscious clients. In London, Dean Mahomed discovered he could use his Indian identity to sell Britons health and pleasure (Fisher 1996: 249).

Mahomed first worked for a controversial nabob, the Hon. Basil Cochrane, who had developed a form of vapour cure and set up an apparatus in his home in fashionable Portman Square. Mahomed added a practice he would make famous: 'shampooing' (Indian therapeutic massage, rather than hair washing).[19] The treatment became popular and respected, even being described in a medical textbook (Fisher 1996: 256). By 1809, Mahomed had launched his own business. His 'Hindostanee Coffee House' was not a cafe, but an Indian restaurant and hookah bar – unique in London at the time – where Europeans returned from India could recreate parts of their experience there. Its decor included bamboo furniture, with paintings of Indian landscapes and sporting scenes on the walls (Fisher 1996: 257). But getting a tavern license was tough and expensive (taverns were identified with subversion) and wealthy returnees could have Indian food cooked at home by their servants. In less than a year Mahomed went bankrupt, a blow for his growing family. By 1813 they had moved to Brighton to begin the most successful phase of Mahomed's career.

Brighton was growing into a fashionable seaside spa. The Prince Regent, later George IV, brought additional prestige (his physician prescribed seawater for gout). His residence was enlarged, starting in the 1780s, into the Royal Pavilion, with Mughal-influenced architecture and a fanciful interior – 'a striking expression of England's rapidly expanding Eastern empire' (Fisher 1996: 271). Brighton was a ripe market for Mahomed's offerings. He managed a bathhouse, selling exotic luxuries such as tooth powder and hair dye; soon he and Jane concentrated on 'Indian' medicated baths and shampooing (massage), developing a distinctive brand. By 1815 they were included in a guidebook. Advertisements claimed that 'Mahomed's Steam and Vapour Sea Water Medicated Baths' could 'cure many diseases, particularly Rheumatic and Paralytic Affections of the extremities, stiff joints, old sprains, lameness, eruptions, and scurf on the skin ... swellings, aches and pains in the joints' (quoted in Fisher 1996: 275). In 1820 the successful healer published *Cases Cured by Sake Dean Mahomed, the Shampooing Surgeon.* Backed by a wealthy Londoner, he built Mahomed's Baths, 'the epitome of fashion in Brighton for nearly two decades', patronised by George IV and his successor, William IV. He had his portrait painted in a court costume modelled on Mughal imperial dress (though sporting an English cravat), which he reportedly wore to the horse races (Fisher 1996: 280, 294). The indefatigable immigrant marketed his Indian birth, costume and methods for a boost in a competitive field. The hybrid identity he crafted is a tribute to the creativity and savvy of this early Anglo-Asian entrepreneur.

The Rime of the Ancient Mariner

The Rime of the Ancient Mariner was the lead poem in Wordsworth and Coleridge's landmark 1798 collection, *Lyrical Ballads*. Part of what made it an enduring hit must have been its sheer weirdness. It features a ghost ship crewed by lurid apparitions called 'Death' and 'Life-in-Death', and another ship whose sailors die en masse, but return as zombies to work the rigging. Readers meet supernatural beings, from a vengeful Polar Spirit to a flock of seraphs, and are treated to other phenomena that – while perhaps scientifically explicable – seem alien and uncanny: the bizarre noises made by icebergs, which 'crack'd and growl'd, and roar'd and howl'd/ Like noises in a swound' (Coleridge 1999: ll. 59–60), and atmospheric phenomena such as the Southern Lights and St Elmo's fire. Images of phosphorescent seas and water snakes may have come from Coleridge's reading in exploration literature, or from a personal connection. His mathematics teacher at Christ's Hospital was William Wales, the astronomer who sailed with Captain Cook on his second voyage. Wales's unpublished journal, which he may have showed his pupils, describes marine phosphorescence and water snakes, icebergs, a waterspout and the aurora. Christ's Hospital, a charitable school, was a major source of boys trained in navigation for the navy, the East India Company and the Hudson's Bay Company. Coleridge had one brother in the navy and another working in India. He might have ended up there himself, had his aptitude for Greek not won him a scholarship to Cambridge.[20]

Many twentieth-century interpreters read the *Rime* as a spiritual journey. M. H. Abrams is typical: the poem's many references to religion and morality, he argues, 'invite us to take the Mariner's experience as an instance of the Christian plot of moral error, the discipline of suffering, and a consequent change of heart'. Shooting the albatross is a sin. For individualistically cutting himself off from the universal human 'community of life and love' (also represented by the wedding where the Wedding Guest is going), the Mariner is punished by isolation 'in a world in which all his companions have died and nature has become inimical to him' (Abrams 1971: 272–3). Looking back, we can recognise this as an example of what Jerome McGann (1983) calls the Romantic ideology: the belief that poetry, by its very nature, transcends historical particularity to address something more universal. Romanticism 'makes a virtue out of the displacement of sociopolitical energy into internal or spiritual energy' (Day 1996: 100). Postcolonial critics bring Romantic poetry back into the world of historical particularity. In the

Mariner's case, this is a world of deep-sea voyages, exploration and colonisation.

We can start with the poem's rather complex form, which rides the Romantic wave of interest in collecting and recording folk ballads. Coleridge gives us a ballad, but a different kind from those Wordsworth contributed. The *Rime* is 'written in imitation of the style, as well as the spirit of the elder poets' (Wordsworth 2002: 22). The archaic language – making plausible the Mariner's belief in the supernatural – situates the tale in the great European age of exploration, the sixteenth and seventeenth centuries. This is a colonial narrative, 'a supreme crystallization of the spirit of maritime expansion' (quoted in Bewell 1999: 99). Coleridge's 1817 revision added a marginal gloss that purports to aid comprehension, but on closer reading is not entirely faithful to the poem. We can separate several distinct personae or points of view: the sailor himself (perhaps illiterate, telling of his experiences); the minstrel who composes the ballad to be sung and believes in its supernatural events; and the author of the gloss, living in a somewhat later time, perhaps a ballad collector, pedantic rather than credulous. Finally, there is what we can call the implied author: a version of Coleridge himself who orchestrates and controls all the other perspectives (McGann 1990: 213). Distancing readers from the initial storyteller in this way suggests a lack of comprehension by those at home for individuals such as the Mariner, who have ventured past the edge of the known world. The poem's form figures the distorted way in which overseas experiences could enter metropolitan culture. A grubby ex-sailor with a scruffy beard and 'glittering eye' buttonholes a man on his way to a wedding, who tries to get rid of the 'grey-beard Loon', but is somehow compelled to stay and hear.

Next we come to that albatross. The Mariner tells the wedding guest how his ship sailed southward, driven by a storm, into a cold, foggy region with icebergs making weird noises. Through the fog a sea bird appears. The crew feed it and make friends with it: 'an it were a Christian soul,/ We hail'd it in God's name' (Coleridge 1999: ll. 63–4). The ice cracks, the ship makes it through, and a south wind helps it sail northward. At this point in the telling of the tale, the wedding guest reacts to the Mariner's expression:

'God save thee, ancient Marinere!
'From the fiends that plague thee thus –
'Why look'st thou so?' – with my cross bow
I shot the Albatross.

(ll. 77–80)

The Mariner never says why he committed this violent act. His ship-mates' reaction wavers. They first condemn him: 'all averr'd I had kill'd the Bird/ That made the Breeze to blow' (ll. 91–2). But then the sun breaks through the fog and they change their minds: ''Twas right, said they, such birds to slay/ that bring the fog and mist' (ll. 97–8).

Was killing the bird a crime, and if so, why? Abrams and other mid-twentieth-century interpreters, as we saw, interpret it as a symbolic sin, a kind of prideful spiritual isolation. One voice of dissent emerged as early as 1964. William Empson invokes Dickens's arch-hypocrite, Pecksniff: 'To make the poem Christian one must argue that the Mariner committed a real crime, and this has afforded many critics a steep but direct path to the heights of Pecksniffery which are their spiritual home.' Instead, Empson (not exactly a postcolonial critic) situates the deed in the concrete conditions of long-distance ocean voyages. Provisions were scarce; one result was the deficiency disease, scurvy, which killed horrific numbers of sailors. Empson reasons that the mariner shot the bird for food. A nice, fat albatross would 'make a tolerable soup which would help to keep off scurvy' (Empson 1964: 298, 301). As it happens, a close friend of Coleridge's, the physician Thomas Beddoes, published a book on scurvy in 1793.

Jonathan Lamb locates references to the symptoms of scurvy through-out the poem. Coleridge makes poetic use, Lamb argues, of the physical and psychological symptoms of this deadly disease. It becomes a meta-phor for the 'corruption of the seagoing self' – the European who leaves home to voyage afar – deplored by writers from ancient Rome up to the eighteenth century.[21] Along with deteriorating gums, blood blisters and cramps, advanced scurvy could cause depression or hallucinations. Becalmed in the Pacific, the Mariner and his crew suffer extreme thirst: 'Water, water every where,/ Ne any drop to drink' (Coleridge 1999: ll. 117–18). Things get surreal: the sailors see 'slimy things' that 'crawl with legs/ Upon the slimy sea'. At night in the rigging they see 'Death-fires' dancing, and the water seems to burn 'green and blue and white' (ll. 121–6). These could be the kind of novel natural phenomena recorded by voyagers like Wales, or they could be scorbutic hallucinations.

When the sailors hang the dead albatross around the Mariner's neck, things start getting really strange. He sees something in the sky that could be a sail. So parched with thirst he cannot speak, he bites himself in the arm and moistens his mouth with blood enough to cry, 'A sail! A sail!' (l. 153). Joyous at first, his shipmates are less enthusiastic as the vessel approaches. Lamb sees in its dice-playing crew the 'objec-tive and subjective appearances' of scurvy (Lamb 2000: 163). Death is a skeleton, his bones black, 'Save where with rust/ Of mouldy damps and charnel crust/ They're patched with purple and green' (Coleridge 1999: ll. 193–5). This and Death's laboured breathing incorporate observations of scurvy symptoms by Coleridge's contemporaries, such as Beddoes. The white skin of his companion, a leprous harlot, alludes to leprosy, a contagious skin disease rife in the Pacific and sometimes confused with scurvy. The mood swings and pathological sensory acuity attributed to the sailors are typically scorbutic. All in all, this bizarre supernatural encounter 'produces one of the most vivid representations of tropical death in British literature', as Alan Bewell writes in his magisterial study, *Romanticism and Colonial Disease* (Bewell 1999).

Coleridge's poem goes on to render a grisly statistic of early modern voyaging in the archaic idiom of the supernatural. After the ghost ship sails off, an ominous moon presides over the mass death of the Mariner's 200 shipmates: 'And every soul it pass'd me by,/ Like the whiz of my Cross-bow' (Coleridge 1999: ll. 224–5) – the weapon he used to kill the albatross. How should we interpret the 'agony' of guilt the Mariner feels? Instead of the vague Christian symbolism espoused by mid-century critics, postcolonial criticism looks to England's maritime ventures and their results: encounters with non-European peoples and, in particular, the slave trade. Back-lit by the sun, the decaying vessel is likened to a 'dungeon-grate' (l. 171). Both historically and biographically, this connection lies near at hand. The 1780s and 1790s saw intense national debate over the issue of slave trade abolition; Coleridge, a staunch lifelong abolitionist, researched the issue and even gave a public lecture about it in Bristol in 1795. Does the Ancient Mariner's guilt, then, reflect the national guilt of Britain's more than two centuries of involvement in the slave trade? Not, postcolonial critics would say, in any simple way.[22]

The Mariner personifies something else about which public discourse had been largely, disturbingly silent: the massive human cost of Britain's colonial ventures. Soldiers and sailors, from the lowest ranks of the society, paid an appalling price for their country's global activities, a price that went largely ignored. Those who did not fall victim to the enemy, or – more often – to disease, poor nutrition and crowded living conditions in camps and ships, returned traumatised, often to wander as vagrants (like so many characters in Wordsworth's poetry). The Mariner's compulsive repetition of his uncanny tale to unwilling listeners dramatises metropolitan Britons' relation to those who returned from the front lines of colonial commerce and imperial expansion. 'The *Rime* is among the first great Romantic narratives to question colonialism by interrogating not a colonised other but the "otherness" that colonialism produced within Britain itself' (Bewell 1999: 108).

Mansfield Park

No writer but Shakespeare has been made to signify Englishness as powerfully as Jane Austen. By the mid-twentieth century, through a complex process of appropriation and packaging, her novels about '3 or 4 Families in a Country Village' came to represent an 'all but lost traditional national essence' (Lynch 1996: 160). This essence is tied to a specific part of England: its rural heart, the so-called 'Home Counties'. ('Home' refers to both England as homeland and the home as domestic space, coded as feminine.) Marginal to a narrow, poetry-focused version of Romanticism, Austen is now recognised as central to a 'British agrarian Romantic canon', a 'national and nationalist creation'. Iconic for this aspect of Austen's reception is *Mansfield Park*, which Clara Tuite labels an early country-house novel (Tuite 2000: 111).

Named for the Northamptonshire estate that is its setting, *Mansfield Park* tells the story of Fanny Price, a disadvantaged niece whom the wealthy Bertrams charitably adopt. Lady Bertram's sister has married badly and borne too many children in the port city of Portsmouth, located at the outer periphery of England's green core, both a buffer from and a link to the rest of the world. Fanny is homesick, patronised by the Bertram children and tyrannised by her other aunt, the awful Mrs Norton (one of Austen's exquisitely crafted hypocrites). She grows up outwardly timid but inwardly tough. Two things catalyse the central action: the arrival of Mary and Henry Crawford, siblings and urban sophisticates, niece and nephew of the local clergyman, and Sir Thomas Bertram's extended absence. The younger generation, poorly supervised by Mrs Norton, makes mischief, putting on a play – Kotzebue's risqué *Lovers' Vows* – and (predictably) flirting and courting. Fanny observes from the sidelines, resisting pleas that she act a role in the play. Sir Thomas's unexpected return, quashing the theatricals and restoring order, also focuses more attention on Fanny, now of marriageable age. When the rich and charming Henry Crawford courts her, Sir Thomas pressures her to accept, but Fanny resists. The patriarch retaliates by banishing her to Portsmouth for an extended visit to her chaotic, déclassé family of origin. This persuades her that Mansfield Park is her true home. After Henry commits adultery with the former Maria

Bertram, now Mrs Rushworth, Fanny is free to marry Sir Thomas's younger son, Edmund, the only one who has been kind to her from her childhood, whom she has loved all along.

Mansfield Park is the book that first led postcolonial critics to debunk the critical commonplace of Austen's 'provincial isolationism' (Tuite 2000: 109). Raymond Williams quips, 'It is a truth universally acknowledged, that Jane Austen chose to ignore the decisive historical events of her time' (113). We have realised at least since the 1970s that, read with care, Austen's novels are deeply engaged with what one heroine calls 'real, solemn history' (Austen 2002: 122). Living through a revolution and a long war, she rarely alludes to these in her books. But as Williams points out, 'history has many currents, and the social history of the landed families, at that time in England, was among the most important'. This history is 'central and structural in Jane Austen's novels' (Williams 1973: 113). Crucial to the history of landed wealth is colonial money. The reason Sir Thomas Bertram leaves Mansfield Park is to visit his property on the Caribbean colony of Antigua, a tropical island where sugar is cultivated using slave labour.

Postcolonial criticism investigates the relationship between 'home' – the country estate in the green heart of England – and 'abroad' – the overseas colony whose profits underwrite the Bertrams' privileged lives. Edward Said's pioneering postcolonial analysis of *Mansfield Park* in *Culture and Imperialism* examines the role played by narrative in consolidating and resisting European empire in the nineteenth and twentieth centuries. Geographical space and spatial relationships, Said argues, are crucial to this cultural work: 'Like many other novels, *Mansfield Park* is very precisely about a series of both small and large dislocations and relocations in space', culminating when Fanny Price becomes 'spiritual mistress of Mansfield Park'. Austen locates this place 'at the centre of an arc of interests and concerns spanning the hemisphere, two major seas, and four continents' (Said 1993: 84). Though the Antigua property is seldom explicitly mentioned, it grounds a structuring principle throughout Austen's narrative: the imperative to bring what is outside, in (Said 1993: 92). As Sir Thomas, contemplating the wreck of his family, belatedly understands: 'Something must have been wanting *within*.' The immediate context points to his children's education – deficient, he realises, in teaching them a 'sense of duty . . . self-denial and humility' (Austen 1998: 314).

The larger structure of the novel, Said contends, works to connect the two outside elements that need to be brought into the English country estate: wealth from colonial possessions to supply material comfort, and a poor provincial relative – Fanny Price – to exemplify the moral vigour the proprietors lack. This structural pattern supplies an implicit moral rationale for empire: 'Austen affirms and repeats the geographical process of expansion involving trade, production, and consumption that predates, underlies, and guarantees the morality' of the reformed country estate (Said 1993: 92–3). Said's analysis of *Mansfield Park* is rooted in his belief that the novel, as a literary form, is profoundly intertwined with the history of empire. 'Without empire, I would go so far as saying, there is no European novel as we know it' (Said 1993: 69). The English novel came into being during a time of rapid imperial expansion, its arrival marked by Daniel Defoe's *Robinson Crusoe* (1719). Crusoe's aggressive 'improvement' of his island into a productive estate and later a full-scale colony signals the novel's concern with property, in particular land. *Mansfield Park* addresses the concerns surrounding landed property in a more established colonial empire. Earlier scholars read *Mansfield Park* as balancing improvement with stability or conservation, symbolically played out in debates about the fashionable practice of landscape gardening (Duckworth 1971). Sir Thomas's activities in Antigua, we can deduce, also involve 'improvement'.

Visiting the island after slave trade abolition, the slave holder presumably aims to encourage higher rates of slave survival and procreation. Sir Thomas's re-establishment of order on his return to Mansfield Park – dismantling the theatre and burning copies of *Lovers' Vows,* but also checking his stables, gardens and 'nearest plantations' and seeing his steward – imposes his values on his estate as we assume he has done in Antigua. Austen understands, Said concludes, 'that to hold and rule Mansfield Park is to hold and rule an imperial estate in close, not to say inevitable, association with it' (Said 1993: 87). One underwrites the other: 'Austen sees the legitimacy of Sir Thomas Bertram's overseas properties as a natural extension of the calm, the order, the beauties of Mansfield Park, one central estate validating the economically supportive role of the peripheral other.' Her 'narrative sanctions a spatial moral order' (Said 1993: 79).

Said's interpretation of Austen as a conservative novelist is in line with earlier critics, though they do not address the colonial connection.[23] More recent criticism questions Said's view that *Mansfield Park* upholds the legitimacy of empire. Rather than celebrate the English country estate, Susan Fraiman argues, Austen's novel actually conducts an 'inquiry into Mansfield Park's corruption that challenges the ethical basis for its authority both at home and, by implication, overseas' (Fraiman 1995: 810). Fraiman foregrounds slavery, but primarily as a trope for putting 'female flesh on the auction block' in the marriage market, as Sir Thomas does with both his daughter and, later, Fanny Price, pressuring her to marry Henry Crawford (Fraiman 1995: 812). Of course, if Austen were indeed more interested in protesting such behaviour than in questioning slavery itself, we would be justified in calling this an 'imperialist gesture' – mining slavery's usefulness as a symbol 'while ignoring slaves as suffering and resistant historical subjects' (Fraiman 1995: 813).

We can make more headway in understanding *Mansfield Park* if we reconsider a basic tenet of Said's critical method: the idea that Austen's almost total silence about slavery and colonialism is symptomatic of an inability to connect the two worlds of metropole and colony, to find a language that could encompass them both. Only with hindsight, in this view, can we see a novel like *Mansfield Park* as 'resisting or avoiding that other setting', which the high quality of Austen's art will not allow it to block completely from the reader's view (Said 1993: 96). One much-discussed passage describes how the mention of slavery in the Bertram drawing room rapidly leads to silence. Fanny and Edmund are discussing the state of Mansfield Park in the wake of Sir Thomas's return. Edmund observes:

> 'Your uncle is disposed to be pleased with you in every respect; and I only wish you would talk to him more. – You are one of those who are too silent in the evening circle.'
>
> 'But I do talk to him more than I used. I am sure I do. Did not you hear me ask him about the slave-trade last night?'
>
> 'I did – and was in hopes the question would be followed up by others. It would have pleased your uncle to be inquired of farther.'
>
> 'And I longed to do it – but there was such a dead silence! And while my cousins were sitting by without speaking a word, or seeming at all interested in the subject, I did not like – I thought it would appear as if I wanted to set myself off at their expense, by shewing a curiosity and pleasure in his information which he must wish his own daughters to feel.' (Austen 1998: 136)

How are we to interpret this silence? Said seems to generalise it to the text as a whole. But careful reading reveals that the silence is neither Fanny's (she is rebutting Edmund's accusation that she is 'too silent'), nor Sir Thomas's. It is that of Julia and Maria Bertram, to whose lack of interest in the source of their wealth Fanny is politely reluctant to call their father's attention. Their indifference is their moral failing: they are spoiled and self-absorbed, in contrast to Austen's heroine.

Postcolonial critics who situate *Mansfield Park* in a more detailed historical context realise that Austen did not need her characters debating slavery for nineteenth-century readers to know what they were talking about. The topic of slavery, the slave trade, and its abolition had been publicised for so long (since the 1770s) that reasonably well-informed readers could not have avoided knowing a lot about it. Even those who only read novels probably knew contemporary debates. 'Discussion of the West Indies and slavery was a cornerstone of even educational fiction in the late eighteenth and early nineteenth century' (Boulukos 2008: 363–4). Moreover, readers might have personal connections to slavery, as Austen did. She read Thomas Clarkson's *History of Rise, Progress, and Accomplishment of the Abolition of the African Slave-Trade by the British Parliament* (1808) as she wrote *Mansfield Park*. But she also got letters from her brother Francis, a navy officer stationed in the Caribbean and a staunch abolitionist, who specifically mentioned Antigua, the location of the Bertrams' plantation (Stewart 1993: 111).

Said makes a historical mistake in assuming Romantic fiction avoided the topics of slavery and colonialism. A related error is taking *Mansfield Park* as representative of the fiction of Austen's day. Her novels innovate in ways that have been enormously influential for the novel in English. As George Boulukos points out, her 'most influential innovations as a novelist – using free indirect discourse rather than omniscient narration or epistolary form, psychologically complex characters rather than moral exemplars – militate against offering authoritative opinions on moral and political questions'. Unlike her contemporaries, Austen refuses didacticism. She addresses moral and political issues, but she does so obliquely, 'with the . . . realistic texture that sets her narrative method apart from that of her contemporaries' (Boulukos 2008: 365, 366). Boulukos's persuasive reading aligns Austen's heroine – if not necessarily Austen herself – with a moderate, middle-of-the-road position on slavery, embraced by some abolitionists (such as Clarkson) as well as some advocates of slavery (such as the planter-historian Bryan Edwards, who coached Mungo Park on his prose). This was amelioration, the idea that slavery could be made better and more humane. It was attractive to slave owners not just because it made them feel good, but because it was politically useful in resisting demands for slave emancipation. At the time *Mansfield Park* was written, after slave trade abolition, emancipation was the next step (not achieved until 1833). Abolitionists used amelioration, perhaps disingenuously, to support abolishing the slave trade, claiming that a ban on buying new slaves would make owners treat their slaves better until slavery eventually withered away (Boulukos 2008: 362).

Austen's sparse references are consistent with an ameliorationist position: 'Fanny's decision to ask about the slave *trade* rather than slavery itself suggests that her question draws attention not to her uncle's cruelty in owning slaves, but to the actions he takes to improve their condition' (Boulukos 2008: 371). Clarkson's *History* argues that banning the trade would improve the treatment of slaves. Absentee owners like Sir Thomas who went to the colonies to implement this change could thus be seen as moral, even heroic. Fanny poses her question in a way that lets her uncle congratulate himself on his humane improvements. But if we read Fanny, and perhaps Austen (though this is far from clear), as ameliorationists, Boulukos reminds us that 'neither could be ignorant of a much more radical view of slavery – one which viewed slave holders not as potential agents of reform, but as morally inexcusable agents of oppression' (Boulukos 2008: 375). One of Austen's favourite poets, Cowper, was a radical abolitionist. Said's influential work reminded readers, out of touch with the history and culture of Austen's time, of the centrality of colonial slavery to that culture. But when we delve more deeply into this history – as postcolonial critics must – it becomes obvious that the slavery debate encompassed more nuanced positions than just 'for' or 'against'. *Mansfield Park* does not disclose, as Said suggests, widespread repression of a guilty consciousness of colonial slavery. It 'reminds us of something even more disturbing: the culturally mainstream belief of the time that, when pursuing amelioration, owning slaves – if not trading in them – was not only acceptable but even morally commendable' (Boulukos 2008: 377).

The novel's link to slavery has taken up much recent critical debate about *Mansfield Park*. A few critics examine a different kind of connection to nineteenth-century imperialism: Austen's portrayal of a particular kind of female self, the virtuous middle-class woman, with a crucial role in holding together the expanded post-Napoleonic empire. Britain took up a mode of imperialism we can call the civilising mission, justifying empire by the need to impose 'modern institutions, manners, morals, virtues, and ways of life on other cultures'. A virtuous woman such as Fanny Price – with her equally virtuous, sober mate, the clergyman Edmund Bertram – exemplifies the 'ever more efficient regulation of subjectivity' needed by imperial Britons. They had to be highly self-disciplined, not just abroad, but first and foremost at home, to sustain the 'ever more efficient and productive exploitation of property and possessions', Saree Makdisi argues (Makdisi 2008: 194, 200). Austen contrasts Fanny's virtue with the moral laxity of the younger Bertrams (except Edmund) and the Crawfords, shown by their theatrical escapades. Such behaviour threatens the well-being of the estate and must be stamped out by Sir Thomas in what amounts to an 'imperial counter-insurgency ... operation'. The series of crises that his return sets off effectively purges from the estate all the 'bad, undisciplined, unproductive, wasteful, frivolous, inappropriate, indulgent, pleasure-seeking, degenerate characters' – the Bertram daughters, the Crawfords, and even Mrs Norris – leaving Mansfield Park ruled by the sober, disciplined ethos of Fanny and Edmund (Makdisi 2008: 196).

Critics like Makdisi see Austen as a conservative writer, as did the 1970s generation, but in a new strain of conservatism shaped by two decades of war. It is a less elitist, more inclusive conservatism, with a place for formerly excluded groups such as women. During the war, activities such as sewing clothes and flags for the troops displayed the public relevance of women's domestic virtues (Colley 1992: 275). Jon Mee reads Austen as a female patriot, bringing us back to her quintessential Englishness and that of her heroine. Fanny's feeling for nature is another part of this symbolism, connecting her to the English countryside – the Home Counties – unlike the urban, sophisticated Crawfords. And perhaps unlike the Bertrams, whose colonial wealth suggests they may not be part of the traditional landed elite. Though she comes from outside, Fanny can supply that elusive something that Mansfield Park lacks: an emotional grounding in that green English centre, suggested by her shocked objection to Rushworth's cutting down the old avenue of oaks, a traditional symbol of England's strength. The novel thus sustains and strengthens a landholding family 'through an infusion of specifically female virtue from the outside' (Mee 2000: 82, 80).

How does such a reading of *Mansfield Park* deal with slavery? Mee disagrees with Said's view of the Bertrams' overseas properties as 'a natural extension of the calm, the order, the beauties of Mansfield Park' (Said 1993: 94). He sees Austen's treatment of slavery as fraught with anxiety, presenting the Antigua plantations as 'a kind of spectral double which saps [Sir Thomas's] English domestic arrangements even as it sustains them economically' (Mee 2000: 83–4, 89). This distrust extends to parts of England outside its green core, such as London, associated with the unstable Crawfords, and Portsmouth, a boundary location that brings England into contact with 'the uncertainties of the world beyond' (Mee 2000: 88). Fanny's virtue must be insulated from 'dubious and dangerous places that potentially undermine the domestic ideal'. She needs to know about them, but at a distance, fretting at home while her brother William, the navy man, protects the empire overseas. Austen gives us a similar gendered division of labour at the end of *Persuasion*, with the newlyweds' joy shadowed by the continuing danger of Captain Wentworth's naval career (Mee 2000: 87).

By the time of Jane Austen's death in 1817, the empire included roughly a quarter of the world's population and continued to expand. Being British in the Romantic era meant having an imaginative relationship to places all over the globe. Vital to that relationship was the genre of travel writing, the textual medium through which Britons strove to make sense of their complicated encounters with the rest of the world. Its vast *omnium-gatherum* encompassed beauty and violence, economics and sensibility, frankness and propaganda, and Romantic readers ate it up. Exploration and colonisation entered other literary genres as well, as they had done for centuries. Postcolonial critics put poems and novels back into the network of global connections that shaped their creation; we saw the effect of this on readings of *The Rime of the Ancient Mariner* and *Mansfield Park*. British Romantic literature is quintessentially, inescapably, a literature of empire, grounded in imperial geopolitics, even – or perhaps especially – when it seems most insular.

Notes

1. Mary Pratt's phrase (Pratt 1992: 15).
2. See Makdisi 1998, ch. 2.
3. Her remains were repatriated and buried on 2 August 2002, near her birthplace in South Africa. See Willis 2010; Crais and Scully 2009.
4. Linnaeus's student was Anders Sparrman, subject of Per Wästberg's recent novel (2010).
5. Leask (2002) discusses two important meanings of the word 'curiosity' in eighteenth- and nineteenth-century discourses of travel. One is 'bound to a negative account of the wonder aroused by distant lands . . . or . . . interest in exotic objects for commercial profit'. The other, more positive sense 'denotes an inclination to knowledge' of 'a rational, philosophical articulation of foreign singularities' (Leask 2002: 4).
6. Pratt 1992: 23; Leask 2002: 3.
7. Batten 1978: 63; Stafford 1984.
8. Goldie lists anthologies (Goldie 1989: 46). Fur trade with Europeans may have incited inter-group rivalry, though reasons for the massacre are still debated (McGoogan 2004: 149–51).
9. Fulford 2006: 188, 192. Coleridge based his ballad 'Three Graves' on Hearne's anecdotes about Copper Indian shamans (Fulford 2006: 156–65). Coleridge may have met Hearne; Hearne's biographer believes he is Coleridge's 'ancient mariner' (McGoogan 2004: 1–3). Their mutual acquaintance was William Wales, the astronomer, who sailed with Cook and taught Coleridge mathematics. Fulford thinks Wales revised Hearne's narrative.
10. By the 1760s British ships carried 40,000 Africans across the Atlantic each year (Walvin 1994: 15).
11. The book was not, as Withers points out, Park's alone, but produced by a team, including the publisher and bookseller, the Association, Edwards, Rennell

and an engraver. Proceeds: £1,050 for the first edition; three more editions by January 1800, profits reaching £2,000 and more to come (Withers 2010).
12. Withers 2010: footnote 43; Marsters 2000: 9.
13. A more recent interpretation of the relation of sentiment to empire is Festa's (2006).
14. Psalms 78: 19: 'Can God prepare a table in the wilderness?'
15. Park describes the genesis of the bar: 'In their early intercourse with Europeans, the article that attracted most notice was iron . . . iron soon became the measure by which the value of all other commodities was ascertained. Thus a certain quantity of goods of whatever denomination, appearing to be equal in value to a bar of iron, constituted, in the trader's phraseology, a bar of that particular merchandize . . . [A]t this time, the current value of a single bar of any kind is fixed by the whites at two shillings sterling. Thus a slave, whose price is £15, is said to be worth 150 bars' (Park 2000: 84).
16. See Andrews 1989.
17. Sharing a name with the author of the Oriental Gothic novel *Vathek* (1786), the author of *Descriptive Account* was his cousin.
18. See Teltscher 2000, Pettinger 1998 and Kahir 2001 on Abu Taleb.
19. 'Shampoo' anglicises the Hindi word *champi*, meaning head massage.
20. Moss 2002: 60. Lowes (1927) documents Coleridge's extensive reading in travel literature.
21. Lamb 2000: 164. Lamb is currently writing a book on scurvy.
22. Lee investigates the poem through the history of another tropical disease, yellow fever (Lee 2002a).
23. Butler 1975; Duckworth 1971. Claudia Johnson's feminist interpretation questions this view, reading *Mansfield Park* as a 'work of demystification' of the patriarchal order headed by Sir Thomas (Johnson 1988: 96, 100).

Chapter 2

Slavery and the Romantic Imagination[1]

When Jane Austen's Sir Thomas Bertram reluctantly leaves his comfortable country estate to tend to his plantations in the Caribbean, his absence initiates the novel's main action. It is no accident that this particular colony intrudes in a novel of domestic female *Bildung*. For the British Empire in Austen's day, the West Indies were no mere periphery: they drove imperial prosperity. The Bertrams' financial well-being depends – like real Britons', from peers to merchants and manufacturers, to the owners of ships and shops – on captive labour by enslaved Africans in the faraway tropics. What may seem incidental in *Mansfield Park* takes on greater significance in light of this history. Romantic Britain profited mightily by slavery. But slavery was also the source of immense guilt, controversy and struggle as more and more Britons began to question and resist it. Those who profited, predictably, fought back. The political fight over slavery dragged on for over half a century, ending in 1838 with the final emancipation of Britain's slaves. What, we might ask, does this have to do with Romantic literature? Until recently the presence of slavery and enslaved Africans in that literature garnered little attention. Even now, as Paul Youngquist and Frances Botkin note, 'studies in British Romanticism remain pretty white'. They diagnose this as 'a symptom of amnesia', revealing Romantic studies' 'institutional disavowal of the economic conditions that help make cultural production during the Romantic Era possible: the maritime economy of the Atlantic' (Youngquist and Botkin 2011: 1). Scholars have begun to address this amnesia, but much more work is needed.

Slavery and colonialism went hand in hand, though not all of Britain's colonies had slavery. It lost one slave colony, the United States, in 1783, but kept the Caribbean islands that held the vast majority of British enslaved persons. Slavery raises questions fundamental to postcolonial studies. These include the literary representation of domination – the ways in which one group exercises rule or control over another – and the cultural consequences of such power relationships. And they include the status of the human person, especially acute where many thousands of human beings are legally classified as property. What are (in Felicity Nussbaum's phrase) the limits of the human (Nussbaum 2003), and how are these culturally patrolled in British discourses about slavery? Bodies are at issue: black African bodies, often targets of grisly violence and sexual exploitation, and white British bodies supposedly in need of protection from contaminating contact with the enslaved. Postcolonial critics study theories of human variety, in particular discourses of race, in their use as ideological instruments of domination.

Romanticism has generally been studied in a national context, in conceptual terms defined by the powerful idea of the nation-state (Youngquist and Botkin 2011: 2). The eighteenth century saw the consolidation of the modern European nation state in the context of international competition over trade and colonial territories (Kaul 2009: 4). Yet the assumptions that underpin the study of national cultures limit our understanding of important aspects of Romantic cultural production: assumptions about geography – the British Isles as a national territory – and a common language as the basis of a literary culture. Paying attention to the trans-oceanic, intercontinental flows of persons, goods and ideas that circulated through the Atlantic system in the long eighteenth century and beyond opens a different perspective on Romanticism. Of course, slavery, the slave trade, and the tropical commodities produced by enslaved persons drove much of this circulation.

If we take our cue from the rising field of Atlantic studies to emphasise routes as well as roots, hybridity rather than homogeneity, Romantic cultural production starts to look different.[2] This chapter attempts a snapshot of that difference. I will discuss texts by writers who were white, black and mulatto, male and female, enslaved and free, in genres from lyric verse to the novel and autobiography. A long-standing tradition of Romantic criticism holds that the best poetry stays clear of politics or specific social comment. William Wordsworth's preface to *Lyrical Ballads*, for example, contrasts the permanent interests of the poet with the 'individual and local' concerns of the biographer or historian (Wordsworth 2002: 401). Percy Shelley's 'Defence of Poetry' similarly opposes the particular facts of the moment to poetry's eternal truth (Richardson 1999b: ix). A great deal of Romantic period verse, however, intervenes in the slavery debate. I have chosen poems that approach slavery from an especially revealing perspective: that of consumption and the commodity, namely sugar.

The history of sugar, its production and consumption, opens a window into the intricate ties binding colony and metropole, enslaved and free persons, in Britain's slave empire. One recurrent trope, which Timothy Morton calls the blood sugar topos, yields insight into the paradoxical ways in which abolitionist literature participated in what we now call racism. Abolitionists staged a boycott of slave-grown sugar using propaganda that equated consuming such sugar to eating the flesh or drinking the blood of enslaved Africans. Their well-meaning rhetoric aroused a visceral disgust that betrays abolitionists' impulse to distance themselves from the very people on whose behalf they undertook this (ultimately ineffective) exercise in self-denial. I will discuss William Cowper's 'The Negro's Complaint' and Robert Southey's sonnets on the slave trade, both of which use variants of the blood sugar topos to make their anti-slavery appeals. Like many abolitionist poems, Cowper's is written in the first-person voice of a captive African. Postcolonial critics have found it problematic for a coloniser to appropriate the voice of a colonised person in this way. The next poem I take up, William Blake's 'The Little Black Boy', does it as well, though not abolitionist propaganda in any simple sense. Recent scholarship has identified Black Atlantic connections in 'The Little Black Boy'. The poem is sometimes discussed in connection with discourses of race; my discussion will briefly survey the state of racial ideology in the Romantic era.

The dominant literary genre of Romanticism, the novel, was interwoven with colonialism from the start. I will discuss William Earle's *Obi, or, The History of Three-Fingered Jack*, which uses key formal elements of the novel tradition to tell a melodramatic story of colonial slavery. Fictionalising a 'black art' – an occult spiritual practice of African origin – *Obi* mines the material's sensational potential. The novel seems to take an overtly abolitionist stance, but on closer scrutiny undercuts this position. A central tension troubles Earle's handling of slavery: is a slave a person – a human subject – or a thing, an object, a piece of property? I will conclude the chapter with authors of African descent, few of whom gained access to print. So-called slave narratives are not contained within national borders – their authors criss-crossed the Atlantic from colony to metropole and beyond – nor in the boundaries of polite literacy. The two I will discuss, Mary Prince and Robert Wedderburn, battered denizens of the Black Atlantic, fetched up in London after involuntary or semi-voluntary journeys. Their books disclose the intimate trauma slavery inflicted on each narrator's family, childhood, body and mind. Wedderburn's *The Horrors of Slavery* and Prince's *The History of Mary Prince, a West Indian Slave* present formal and textual challenges involving the ways in which disenfranchised subjects gained access to print.

Abolitionist Verse

'I hope the slave trade may be abolished. I pray it may be an event at hand.' The ex-slave Olaudah Equiano is blunt and urgent near the close of his 1789 autobiography (Equiano 2003: 234). He did not live to see the traffic in human flesh outlawed; it would be another generation before Parliament passed a bill emancipating some 750,000 enslaved British persons and compensating their owners to the tune of £20,000,000 (Blackburn 1988: 457). Why did the British Empire, at a time when its slave colonies were turning huge profits, even consider getting rid of the slave trade and slavery?[3] Many of the factors that help us understand this conundrum are cultural ones, including abolitionist literature like Equiano's best-selling book. Numerous writers contributed to the flood of propaganda unleashed with the founding of the Society for Effecting the Abolition of the Slave Trade (SEAST) in 1787. SEAST was not a nest of wild-eyed radicals. Its members were mostly practical business-men who understood the needs and desires of their middle-class peers, and crafted political tactics accordingly. Besides lobbying Parliament, these savvy operatives leveraged the rising literacy, leisure and fashion-consciousness of the increasingly urbanised nation. Sophisticated use of the press to mould public opinion characterised SEAST from the start. Additional tactics included grassroots organising – such as Equiano's tour of the British Isles to promote his book and advocate for abolition – and a massive petition drive that in 1792 delivered to Parliament 519 petitions signed by 400,000 Britons (Oldfield 1995: 45, 114).

The abolitionists' most innovative tactic, though not their most effective, had an interesting impact on literature. This was widespread abstention from slave-produced sugar. In 1791, William Fox pub-lished his *Address to the People of Great Britain, on the Propriety of Abstaining from West India Sugar and Rum*. The pamphlet sold amaz-ingly well: 70,000 copies in four months (rising sugar prices may have helped). It inspired a nationwide sugar boycott that, at its peak, involved some 300,000 families.[4] Ineffective as an economic sanction, this did help to pry Parliament away from the long-established protectionism favouring West Indian planters (Oldfield 1995: 57–8). The symbolism of sugar in the prose and poetry of the abolition controversy has much to tell us about colonialism and slavery in the Romantic era. West Indian sugar 'became an important symbol of the proliferating chains of interdependence between England and her Caribbean colonies' (Sussman 2000: 110).

The place of sugar in British domestic life changed dramatically in a century and a half. By the late 1600s sugar had changed from a scarce import, used as a spice or condiment and sometimes a medicine, to a sweetener (used with other exotic imports, coffee, tea and chocolate). First used by the wealthy, the new beverages became part of daily life for the middle classes and later the poor. 'As the English drank more and more of the new substances, the beverages themselves became more and more English in two senses: by the process of ritualization' as well as by being produced in British colonies (Mintz 1985: 110). Coffee houses became a place to do business, air opinions and catch up on news – a material setting for what the sociologist Jürgen Habermas called the bourgeois public sphere. At home, meanwhile, the British lady presided over the tea table, a domestic setting for the civilising process (Kowaleski-Wallace 1997: 21).

Annual per capita sugar consumption in Britain rose from four pounds around 1700 to eighteen pounds by the early 1800s (Mintz 1985: 67). A transformation in sugar production had made this possible. In the 1620s England colonised the Caribbean islands of Antigua, St Kitts and Barbados. Dutch traders brought sugar-processing technology from Brazil about 1640. The British sugar industry expanded rapidly, especially after adding the large island of Jamaica in 1655. The islands still grew other agricultural products, such as coffee, cacao and indigo, but sugar dominated and would do so for centuries. Metropolitan demand kept pace with the growing supply; production and consumption were closely intertwined in the mercantilist economy.[5] The steps of this expansion:

> followed in so orderly a fashion as to seem almost inevitable. On the one hand, they represent an extension of empire outward, but on the other, they mark an absorption, a kind of swallowing up, of sugar consumption as a national habit. Like tea, sugar came to define English 'character'. (Mintz 1985: 42, 39)

But sugar meant slavery. First worked by indentured servants – criminals, political prisoners, religious nonconformists – colonial plantations soon needed more labour than these could provide. Colonists built their labour force by buying more captive Africans. The shift to a sugar monoculture led to larger plantations, whose yield justified the capital investment in technology for processing sugar cane juice. Slavery's success in Barbados and Martinique marked the beginning of 'the

Africanization of the British and French Caribbean'. Slave plantations combined agricultural and industrial features in a kind of 'agro-industry' whose features prefigured the industrial discipline later introduced in Europe: specialised skills and jobs, the division of labour into crews or 'gangs' by gender, age and ability, and an emphasis on time management and work discipline.[6] The transatlantic slave trade supplied the human commodity at the heart of this proto-industrial system.

The number of enslaved persons shipped across the Middle Passage from Africa to British colonies in the Caribbean and North America reached its height in the 1770s, when the abolitionist movement got organised. By then Britain's sugar islands were populated largely by captive Africans, outnumbering white colonists by as much as ten to one. This helps explain the relative harshness of Caribbean slavery compared to North America, where white colonists always outnumbered their human property. Slave revolt, or the fear of it, was a constant feature of life in Britain's Caribbean colonies.[7] Fear, combined with relative impunity, led to severe discipline. In 1748, the Jamaican Assembly voted down a Bill to forbid owners to mutilate or dismember their slaves without a magistrate's consent (Parry et al. 1987: 128). Killing an enslaved person was punished, if at all, by a moderate fine, and since slave testimony was not admitted in court, convictions were hard to come by. Treatment did become milder during the last half century or so of slavery, due partly to the proportional increase in Creole (island-born) persons of African descent born into slavery, and partly to political pressure from the anti-slavery movement.

An important part of the literature generated by this movement was poetry. But abolitionist poetry often fell short both as art and as propaganda. Compared to hard-hitting prose tracts such as Thomas Clarkson's *Essay on the Slavery and Commerce of the Human Species* (1786), poetry lacked 'the virtues of direct appeal and plain fact'. Anti-slavery poems have been criticised for 'vapid sentiment, stock description, stereotyped characters and situations, and patently false portrayals of Africa and of Afro-Caribbean slaves'. But abolitionist verse could also put forward incipient ideas of universal human rights and racial equality. Despite poets' habit of representing Africans as passive or suicidal, they occasionally portrayed active resistance in a positive light (Richardson 1999b: x). Perhaps the most famous abolitionist poem was William Cowper's 'The Negro's Complaint'. Cowper's abolitionist friends:

> conceiving it to contain a powerful appeal in behalf of the injured Africans, joined in printing it. Having ordered it on the finest hot-pressed paper, and

folded it up in a small and neat form, they gave it the printed title of 'A Subject for Conversation at the Tea-Table'. (Clarkson 1808: 2.153)

Here we get the flavour of SEAST's tactics to enlist the metropolitan middle classes, especially ladies. But 'The Negro's Complaint' also reached a less elite audience when it was set to music and sung in the streets.

Cowper writes in the first-person voice of a captive African, a common tactic of abolitionist verse:

Forced from home and all its pleasures,
Afric's coast I left forlorn,
To increase the stranger's treasures,
O'er the raging billows borne.

(Cowper 1999: 75)

Such ventriloquism aims for empathy through identification, but raises the question of whether the poet can access the voice and subjectivity of the oppressed legitimately – or at all. Does any attempt on the part of a metropolitan subject to speak or write in the voice of the colonised inevitably misrepresent, distort, or stereotype that person, compounding the injustice of colonialism? Or does abolitionists' 'political commitment to making visible the position of the marginalized' justify the imaginative leap the poet makes in translating a captive African's imagined sentiments into eighteenth-century poetic diction?[8] Other abolitionist poets, like the anonymous author of 'The African's Complaint On Board a Slave Ship', took ventriloquism a step farther, imitating Afro-Caribbean patois:

Here de white man beat de black man,
Till he's sick and cannot stand,
Sure de black be eat by white man!
Will not go to white man land!

(Richardson 1999a: 221)

Attempting greater realism, this well-meaning writer achieves (for modern sensibilities) a cringe-worthy condescension.

Cowper's pounding trochaic meter lends weight to his poem's bold assertion of human rights. 'Minds are never to be sold' sounds a cry of liberty. With the same forthrightness, the speaker rejects racism:

Fleecy locks and black complexion
Cannot forfeit Nature's claim;
Skins may differ, but affection
Dwells in black and white the same.

(Cowper 1999: 75)

Invoking 'affection', or emotion, as a universal human attribute to prove black people's humanity was another common abolitionist strategy (compatible with the belief that Africans needed civilising and Christianising, though this does not surface in Cowper's poem). 'The Negro's Complaint' also deploys another widespread tactic of abolitionist discourse: using slaves' bodily fluids as a metonym for their bodies:[9]

> Why did all creating Nature
> Make the plant for which we toil?
> Sighs must fan it, tears must water,
> Sweat of ours must dress the soil.
>
> (Cowper 1999: 75)

This rhetorical move makes 'a collection of fluids, rather than a coordinated body . . . the active agent in the production of sugarcane' (Sussman 2000: 117). Instead of labour, the slave's production of sugar seems to be accomplished through a process of excretion.

Abolitionist writers' fascination with slaves' bodily fluids most often focused on their blood. This is an 'aversive topos, often directed toward the female consumer' (Morton 1998: 87). Fox's pamphlet declares:

> The laws of our country may indeed prohibit us the sugar cane, unless we receive it through the medium of slavery. They may hold it to our lips, steeped in the blood of our fellow creatures; but they cannot compel us to accept the loathsome portion. (Quoted in Sussman 2000: 114)

Abolitionists' defence of slaves as 'fellow creatures' takes the form of rejecting a bodily pollution – an implied cannibalism that would defile the British consumer's pure body. Cannibalism was, of course, associated with 'barbaric' societies like those of Africa. The anti-slavery message is articulated in terms that implicitly distance British bodies from African persons and practices by invoking a visceral disgust: abolitionist ends are gained by means of colonial and racial 'othering'.

Samuel Taylor Coleridge uses another version of the blood sugar topos in his 1795 lecture on the slave trade. Coleridge, an ardent abolitionist, delivered the lecture in Bristol, a major slave-trading port. It was here that Clarkson (later Wordsworth's Lake District neighbour) began his research into the slave trade, interviewing sailors and ships' surgeons. But the city also had young intellectuals, interested in radicalism and reform (Baum 1994: 3, 7). Coleridge's approach foregrounds the Romantic imagination. Given us by our Creator so we can 'imitate Creativeness' for 'exalted and self-satisfying Delight', the imagination can be misapplied to create 'artificial Wants' – 'pestilent inventions of Luxury', leading to vice and misery (Coleridge 1969: 235, 236). 'We receive from the West Indias Sugars, Rum, Cotton, log-wood, cocoa, coffee, pimento [allspice], ginger, indigo, mahogany, and conserves – not one of these are necessary ... If the Trade had never existed, no one human being would have been less comfortably cloathed, housed, or nourished – Such is its value' (Coleridge 1969: 237). Moralists had condemned luxury since at least the early eighteenth century, though political economists believed the consumption of luxury goods helped the economy.

Coleridge exhorts his hearers to boycott sugar and rum, probably preaching to a choir of middle-class Dissenters and reformers (Morton 1998: 90, 88). Ascribing guilt for the slave trade to the consumers of slave-grown produce, Coleridge puts a Christian spin on the language of the commodity (Morton 1998: 91). If Jesus were alive in 1795, rather than change water into wine, he would:

> convert the produce into the things producing, the occasioned into the things occasioning! Then with our fleshly eye should we behold what even now truth-painting Imagination should exhibit to us – instead of sweet-meats Tears and Blood, and Anguish – and instead of music groaning and the loud Peals of the Lash. (Coleridge 1969: 247)

Since Jesus is not around to perform miracles, Christians must use their imaginations to connect luxury products to their cruel means of production. This imaginary conversion activates the connection between the site of production (the Caribbean) and that of consumption (the British Isles). The imagination, in Coleridge's formula, lets the British consumer peer across the Atlantic to the source of tropical products. Abolitionist discourse portrays the West Indies very differently than pro-slavery discourse, which tended to aestheticise tropical nature, sugar production, and even slave labour. Neither side cared very much about the hybrid, syncretic Creole culture that was actually created in the islands by the transplanted slaves (and shared with their transplanted owners).[10]

The blood sugar topos also figures in Robert Southey's six sonnets on the slave trade, published in 1797 (Southey 2011). Southey does not give us an enslaved speaker, but renders the enslaved in the third person – unlike his Botany Bay Eclogues, in the same volume, where imaginary convicts bewail their woes. Two sonnets, the third and fifth, invoke the blood sugar topos. Sonnet III gives us a colonial scene of work and punishment.

> Oh he is worn with toil! The big drops run
> Down his dark cheek; hold – hold thy merciless hand,
> Pale tyrant! for beneath thy hard command

O'erwearied Nature sinks. The scorching Sun,
As pitiless as proud Prosperity,
Darts on him his full beams; gasping he lies
Arraigning with his looks the patient skies,
While that inhuman trader lifts on high
The mangling scourge. Oh ye who at your ease
Sip the blood-sweeten'd beverage! thoughts like these
Haply ye scorn: I thank thee Gracious God!
That I do feel upon my cheek the glow
Of indignation, when beneath the rod
A sable brother writhes in silent woe.

The sonnet structure of octave and sestet splices contrasting scenes an ocean apart: labour and punishment in the colonial cane field in lines 1–9, 'ease' and refreshment in the metropolitan parlour in lines 9–14. Juxtaposing the sites of sugar production and consumption in this way is designed to get a reaction from the reader: the 'glow/ Of indignation' modelled by the first-person speaker, who hails the mangled labourer as his 'sable brother'. This alludes to the famous icon of the kneeling, chained slave that was mass-produced by Josiah Wedgwood's ceramic manufactory on brooches, bracelets, earrings and hair ornaments with the inscription, 'Am I not a man and a brother?'[11]

The adjective 'sable' describes the enslaved worker's skin colour in the elevated diction characteristic of eighteenth-century poetry (famously rejected by Wordsworth). The gesture dignifies the lowly slave, portrayed lying on the ground awaiting his beating. It is common in abolitionist poetry to find slaves in such a passive posture. (Less common is the active resistance depicted in Sonnet V, where we see the 'bold slave rear at last the Sword/ Of Vengeance' and use it to skewer his owner.) Sonnet III figures the brotherhood between the speaker and the maltreated slave through the body. The speaker's cheek in line 12, flushed with indignation, recalls the labourer's 'dark cheek' in line 2, marked with sweat or tears. Another type of bodily marking contrasts with this sympathetic glow. This is the lashing that is about to happen when the poem turns (l. 9) to apostrophise the metropolitan tea sipper, whose hand, daintily holding the cup, recalls the 'merciless hand' of the slave driver in line 2. The 'blood-sweeten'd beverage' figuratively imports to the metropole – into the teacup – the spilled body fluid of the tortured slave, ironically conflating it with the sugar he has produced. 'Southey forces the sippers to read the barbarism stirred into their luxuries, enacting this in the conventional enjambment between the sonnet's ninth and tenth lines' (Morton 1998: 101). The internal rhyme of 'ease' and 'sweeten'd' pauses in false refinement before the plain language of the last four lines raps out the truth of colonial violence and powerless sympathy.

In the fifth sonnet, as Morton writes, 'the possibility of rebellion haunts a reformist text' (Morton 1998: 98). Southey's preface sarcastically notes that after 1792 sugar abstainers slacked off, thinking 'Parliament would do all'. When the Lords failed to act, two options remained: 'the introduction of East-Indian or Maple Sugar, or . . . the just and general rebellion of the Negroes' (Southey 2011: 31, 32). At the time Southey wrote, slave revolt was a fearsome reality on Saint-Domingue (modern-day Haiti). Here Southey again turns to prosopopeia, or personification, common throughout eighteenth-century poetry. The earlier sonnet figures the exhausted labourer as '[o]'erwearied Nature' and his tormentor as 'proud Prosperity', pitiless as the tropical sun. In Sonnet V, the personified Remembrance goads the 'bold slave' to his bloody deed, assisted by 'Freedom's pale spectre', who stalks around 'with a stern smile/ Pointing the wounds of slavery, the while/ She shook her chains and hung her sullen head' (ll. 10–12).

This personified pantomime may strike us as stale by 1797. The sonnet ends with a condensed image, almost Gothic, but curiously unfocused. 'No more on Heaven he calls with fruitless breath,/ But sweetens with revenge the draught of death' (ll. 13–14). Southey's choice to use the third person rather than appropriate the enslaved man's voice gives the poem a strangely abstract effect. The blood-sweetened 'draught of revenge' recalls the toxic tea of Sonnet III, but who is the drinker? In the grisly sixth sonnet the rebel slave follows his 'tyrant lord' in death, strung up and eaten alive by a 'gorging Vulture'. Critics have questioned the motives and effects of presenting this kind of graphic violence in the guise of anti-slavery propaganda.[12] Southey frames it as a warning to those who would 'proclaim . . . Murder is legalized': the murdered slave will testify against his abusers before God (ll. 11–12). Wylie Sypher's classic study finds in several of Southey's sonnets 'a severity not un-Miltonic' (Sypher 1942: 218). Regardless of how we evaluate them as poetry, we can gain a fresh perspective on Southey's literary response to colonialism and slavery by studying its treatment of consumption and the commodity.[13]

Discourses of Race and Blake's 'Black Boy'

What was the connection, in the Romantic period, between the political debate over slavery and ideas or discourses of race? It was not as obvious as it might seem. Racial ideologies and discourses solidified during colonialism and entrenched and systematised racial hierarchies (Loomba 2005: 91). Historically, Romanticism has been seen as complicit in the development of racist ideas. Romantic aesthetics (in particular German, but also English Romanticism) emphasised the local and the particular over the global and general, seeking to understand groups of people in their geographical and historical contexts, from which their physical, mental and spiritual characteristics supposedly arose.[14] Explanations of human variety shifted significantly between 1780 and 1830. By the 1770s, not much consensus had emerged on the most salient differences among human beings and groups (Wheeler 2000: 241). Earlier in the eighteenth century, religious difference, political governance and 'manners' (shared habits and customs) were thought to differentiate peoples – a cultural approach to human variety. Visible signs of these differences were sought in clothing, habitations and trading behaviour. By 1800, however, and increasingly into the nineteenth century, human variety was described primarily in physical or anatomical terms, 'through scientific categories derived from natural history that featured external characteristics of the human body – [skin] colour, facial features, and hair texture' (Wheeler 2000: 289).

This racial science took its start from the taxonomy pioneered by the Swedish natural historian Linnaeus. His students fanned out over the globe in the mid-eighteenth century, sometimes travelling with voyages of exploration such as those of Cook. Linnaeus also classified human beings: he divided the species *Homo sapiens* into seven types, including *ferus* (four-footed, mute, hairy) and *sylvestris* (man of the woods, or orangutan) as well as *europaeus* (white, ruddy, muscular), *americanus* (red, choleric, erect), *asiaticus* (yellow, melancholic, inflexible), and *afer* (black, phlegmatic, indulgent). 'Linnaeus's static and fixed account of human variety began a trend of racial thinking that would lead to such theories as those of Robert Knox concerning the primacy of fixed racial types.'[15] The races were ordered hierarchically, with the one designated as white, Caucasian or Aryan at the top. By the mid-nineteenth century racist beliefs were widespread in England, promoted by an outpouring of 'scientific' theories such as Knox's *The Races of Man* (1850). Victorian racial theory was used to justify the imperial subjugation of non-white races. But alternatives to this taxonomical approach also emerged in the Romantic period. Sir William Jones (discussed in Chapter 4) put his Orientalist erudition behind a cultural approach to human variety, tracing racial groupings back into history through languages and customs, rather than anatomy. Johann Reinhold Forster, who sailed on Cook's second voyage, studied anatomical diversity, but also customs and beliefs, in the South Seas (Kitson 1999: x). The transition from cultural to anatomical approaches to race was gradual and uneven.

There is no straightforward relationship between slavery and racial discourse. Slavery was in place in the British colonies before anti-black racism became a prevalent ideology in England. Did race and racism develop as a rationalisation for enslaving Africans, as the historian Eric Williams famously asserted in 1944? Or did nascent racial prejudice contribute to their enslavement? Was the relationship between the two phenomena more complex, not just unidirectional?[16] It does seem probable that the political fight about slavery helped entrench positions on racial difference (Wheeler 2000: 241). The slavery controversy took place partly in literature, much of it polemical verse like that of Cowper and Southey. We turn now to a poem whose relation to the political debate over slavery is less obvious. William Blake's 'The Little Black Boy', from *Songs of Innocence* (1789), renders the voice of a colonised, presumably enslaved child. Critics disagree on whether it 'assists the philanthropic agitation' of SEAST (Erdman 1969: 132). It is clear, though, that 'a poem on such a subject, issued in such a year, must be interpreted in light of the abolition movement' (Macdonald 1994: 166). Blake is a notoriously difficult poet. Most readers, even scholars of Romanticism, do not pretend to understand his more obscure works. Saree Makdisi observes, 'Blake's work, his art, his poetry, his philosophical, religious, and aesthetic beliefs, even he himself, were in his time understood – and indeed they usually still are – as both improbable and impossible' (Makdisi 2003: 1).

Blake was also a visual artist. Through his work as an engraver for the radical publisher Joseph Johnson, he associated with leading leftists of his day: Richard Price, Mary Wollstonecraft, Joseph Priestley, Thomas Paine. He shared their distrust of the British oligarchy and their sympathy with the American and French revolutions, but Blake approached the concept of liberty differently than his fellow radicals (Makdisi 2003: 201). Like most Romantic poets, he was preoccupied with slavery and freedom in several senses. In *America: A Prophecy* (1793), he writes:

Let the slave grinding at the mill, run out into the field:
Let him look up into the heavens & laugh in the bright air;
Let the inchained soul shut up in darkness and in sighing,
Whose face has never seen a smile in thirty weary years,
Rise and look out, his chains are loose, his dungeon doors are open.
(Blake 2008: 89)

As Makdisi notes, this section of the poem – whose accompanying image in Blake's illuminated edition phenotypically suggests an enslaved African – shifts the idea of slavery away from the political, rhetorical context of the American Revolution to the more concrete arena of labour.[17] But it is not, or not just, the labour of slaves in the West Indian sugar cane fields that interests Blake: the word 'mill' is 'more readily associated with the manufactories of the early industrial period in England'. Blake's concern, Makdisi argues, is with labour as a process. Enslavement in this and other poems, such as *Visions of the Daughters of Albion* (1793), 'has to do with confinement and restriction to a particular identity and a particular role within a productive process' (Makdisi 2003: 99, 90–1). For Blake the condition of being enslaved was not restricted to those persons legally defined as property. It extended to a wide range of people caught up in the machinery of modernity, both in the colonies and in the British Isles.

'The Little Black Boy' is concerned with race or skin colour rather than (at least overtly) with slavery. On first reading the poem, one might think it purveys racist stereotypes:

My mother bore me in the southern wild,
And I am black, but O! my soul is white,
White as an angel is the English child:
But I am black as if bereav'd of light.
My mother taught me underneath a tree
And sitting down before the heat of day,
She took me on her lap and kissed me,
And pointing to the east began to say.
Look on the rising sun: there God does live
And gives his light, and gives his heat away.
And flowers and trees and beasts and men receive
Comfort in morning joy in the noon day.
And we are put on earth a little space,
That we may learn to bear the beams of love.
And these black bodies and this sun-burnt face
Is but a cloud, and like a shady grove.
For when our souls have learn'd the heat to bear
The cloud will vanish we shall hear his voice,
Saying: come out from the grove my love & care,
And round my golden tent like lambs rejoice.
Thus did my mother say and kissed me,
And thus I say to little English boy.
When I from black and he from white cloud free,
And round the tent of God like lambs we joy:

I'll shade him from the heat till he can bear,
To lean in joy upon our fathers knee.
And then I'll stand and stroke his silver hair,
And be like him and he will then love me. (Blake 1970: 9–10)

The first stanza's simile, 'white as an angel', gives whiteness a positive valence, while equating blackness with bereavement or deprivation. The child speaker seems to have internalised what Abdul JanMohamed calls the Manichean allegory: a binary, hierarchical opposition between races that transforms 'racial difference into moral and even metaphysical difference' (JanMohamed 1985: 61). In the context of the whole poem, though, this stanza reads differently. The poem's three main sections correspond with its alternating speakers: the boy himself, then his mother, and finally the boy again. The child's African mother teaches him a lesson about God, nature and human bodies, a lesson that questions in significant ways what we come to recognise as the imposed colonial mentality of the first stanza. In light of racist stereotypes of Africans as untaught, uncivilised, perhaps even un-teachable, it is important that Blake's African mother is a teacher (Richardson 1990: 239). Staging the lesson 'underneath a tree' probably alludes to reports by eighteenth-century travel writers of the African tradition of meeting under trees or in groves for purposes of worship. The ex-slave Ukawsaw Gronniosaw's autobiography, for example, presents the tree and its shade as central to African religion (Henry 1998: 77–8, 84).

Line 14 contains another important allusion. We are put on earth, the mother declares, 'That we may learn to bear the beams of love'. God's love is figured as the metaphorical beams of the sun. But why, we might ask, should one need to 'bear' sunbeams that are 'beams of love'? Real sunlight can be too hot for comfort, as in the tropics. But why speak of bearing or enduring love, which is positive in nature? Lauren Henry finds a similar ambiguity in an earlier poem by another enslaved African writer, Phillis Wheatley: 'An Hymn to the Morning' (1773). This intertextuality raises 'the interesting possibility that Blake had some familiarity with' the works of Wheatley and other Afro-British writers (Henry 1998: 67). Wheatley's neoclassical poem implores, 'Ye shady groves, your verdant gloom display/ To shield your poet from the burning day' (ll. 11–12). By the last stanza, the heat of the rising sun 'drives the shades away' and drives the speaker to end what she calls her 'abortive song' (ll. 18, 20). She complains, 'I feel his fervid beams too strong' (l. 19). As in Blake's poem, but more strongly, we see ambivalence toward the sun, whose symbolism can be traced to a complex combination of classical, Christian, and African sources (Henry 1998: 75). Like Blake's Christianised black boy, Wheatley's speaker seems to have mixed feelings about whatever the sun symbolises. Henry speculates that one reason she seeks refuge in a 'shady grove' may be Wheatley's 'conflicting feelings about Christianity' and her continuing interest in whatever African religious tradition she left behind when she was kidnapped by slave traders as a young child (Henry 1998: 76; and see Wheatley 1989).

The alliteration of 'bear the beams' formally underscores the tension or conflict between yearning for the sun of God's love and fearing it. This is resolved by the twin figures that close the fourth stanza, comparing 'black bodies' and a 'sun-burnt face' to a cloud or 'shady grove': something that intervenes between the self and the source of light and heat, protecting, but also obscuring. In this complex figure, the black body itself assumes a metaphorical or symbolic significance, standing in for all bodies or for the condition of embodiment in general. Blackness is transformed, that is, from a particular earthly condition, tying the black person to a geographical point of origin and an inferior social position, into a figure conveying the temporariness or ephemerality of all bodies, or of human beings' embodied state. The black body becomes a teaching text, as it were, for a theological doctrine heralding the ultimate irrelevance of race or skin colour to divine love. The third voice in the poem, alongside those of the boy and his mother, is that of God, 'Saying: come out from the grove my love & care,/ And round my golden tent like lambs rejoice'.

In the last two stanzas the child speaker adapts his African mother's teaching, which has so far explicitly mentioned only black bodies, to assign whiteness a place in the theological scheme. The black child takes on the instructor's role: 'And thus I say to little English boy' (Richardson 1990, 245). Line 23 figures the white body as a cloud, parallel to the cloud that is the black body, as we learned in line 16. Though both bodies are equally ephemeral, the children's roles are not identical. The black boy's relation to the white boy is ambiguous: shading him from the heat, does he act as a servant – or as a mentor, an 'older brother or protector'? The second plate of the poem in Blake's illuminated book shows the black boy 'presenting the smaller white child to Christ as a catechist presenting his pupil', Alan Richardson suggests (Richardson 1990: 244–5). The white child's pose, leaning on Jesus' knee, face raised and hands lifted, recalls the pose of the slave in Wedgwood's famous abolitionist icon, combining supplication and gratitude (Figure 2.1). How are we to interpret this ambiguous scenario?

The difficulty increases when we realise that in some versions of the

Figure 2.1 William Blake, 'The Little Black Boy', *Songs of Innocence*, Lessing J. Rosenwald Collection, Library of Congress, Copyright © 2012 William Blake Archive. Used with permission.

plate, Blake coloured the little black boy black or brown – but in others he is coloured white or pink![18] And if we read 'The Little Black Boy' alongside another poem in *Songs of Innocence*, 'The Chimney Sweeper', we might read the former differently. The latter also works with skin colour and identity, but in the context of occupation rather than race: chimney sweeps' dirty work makes them black on earth, but they turn white in the dream of heaven (Makdisi 2003: 165). Is the black boy able to use his African mother's teaching – in the manner of slaves' syncretic transformations of Christianity into a religion of liberation – to construct an identity that is positive, loving, joyful and able to teach or mentor an English child? Or must we understand the likeness between the two boys as assimilation, retaining the colonialist value of whiteness as superior and the 'ideological construction of the African as one who finally benefits from Christianity' (Mellor 1995: 359)? Blake does not make it easy for the reader to decide.

I will conclude my discussion of Blake with his work as an engraver. Hired to engrave plates from John Stedman's drawings of colonial Suriname in his *Narrative of a Five Years Expedition Against the Revolted Negroes of Surinam,* Blake seems to have imposed his own interpretive vision on Stedman's images (Lee 2002a: 99). Stedman was part of a military force hired by the Dutch government to hunt escaped slaves in the South American colony, one of the Caribbean's harshest slave societies. Several of the illustrations that Blake engraved represent cruel corporal punishment, amounting to torture; others, however, show enslaved Surinamers in relative comfort, even contentment.[19] Stedman was no abolitionist, as the book makes clear, though he often expresses sympathy with mistreated slaves (including his slave concubine Joanna). Despite their disagreement on this issue, Stedman and Blake became good friends (Bentley 2001: 115–16). The engraving 'Group of Negros [sic], as Imported to be Sold for Slaves' (Figure 2.2) directly contradicts Stedman's description of this group of captive Africans getting off a slave ship to be auctioned off for plantation labour. Stedman describes:

> a set of living atomatons, such a resurrection of Skin and bones, as justly put me in mind of the last trumpet; seeming that moment to be rose from the grave, or deserted from Surgeons Hall at the old Bailey – and of which no better discription can be given than by comparing them to walking Skeletons covered over with a piece of tand leather. (Stedman 1988: 166)

He quotes Ezekiel 37:3: 'And he said unto me Son of Man can these bones live? And I answered O Lord God thou knowest.' For the next several pages, Stedman mounts a justification of slavery, invoking arguments familiar from pro-slavery propaganda.

Blake's visual image is very different from what Stedman describes. His Africans are not skin and bones, but look reasonably healthy. A woman at the back appears to be pregnant; two others carry or lead small children. A third smokes a pipe, and a woman and a man have adorned themselves by shaving patterns into their hair. Several women wear necklaces. Two figures in the group, the man with the interesting hair and the woman in the foreground, look straight at the viewer. His gaze is challenging, hand on hip in an almost stylised pose, while her face is serene and strangely trusting. As one hand points landward, the other holds that of a small, naked child. 'Where Stedman sees lack', writes Debbie Lee, 'Blake sees plenty; where Stedman sees living death,

Figure 2.2 William Blake, 'Group of Negros, as imported to be sold for Slaves', in John Gabriel Stedman, *Narrative of a Five Years Expedition Against the Revolted Negroes of Surinam* (1796), reproduced by kind permission of the Syndics of Cambridge University Library, classmark RCS. case.b.371-372.

Blake sees spirited energy.' These people, Blake's image suggests, 'not only live in full flesh, but they will, as Stedman's text later testifies, revolt' (Lee 2002a: 99, 101).

Slavery and the Romantic Novel: *Obi*

British Romantic fiction incorporates slavery in varied ways and diverse subgenres, including sentimental, didactic, Gothic, Jacobin and even children's fiction. Notably absent is anything resembling a realistic portrait of slavery. Novels do not portray the Middle Passage, captive labour on the plantation or slave culture, African or Creole. Such 'basic aspects of life under slavery ... are hardly ever broached in a national literature that is often advertised as the inventor of sociologically realist fiction'.[20] This is less surprising if we remember that novelists representing slavery did so at a distance – from the British Isles, not the Caribbean, where British slavery was centred after 1783. The political debates over slavery mattered to its fictional representation, but not in any straightforward way. Rather than label a narrative liberal or conservative, abolitionist or pro-slavery, it is more productive to ask what desires and fears it addressed, and by what (sometimes oblique) means.

William Earle's *Obi, or, The History of Three-Fingered Jack* (1800) is unusual among fictions about slavery in being based on an actual historical incident. The man who would be known as Three-Fingered Jack came to public attention in Jamaica's Blue Mountain region in 1780–1. He was one of the numerous men and women who escaped from slavery and led a band of around sixty maroons (escaped slaves) who lived primarily by robbing travellers. The group posed a big enough threat to the colonial regime that the Jamaican Assembly offered a reward for Jack's capture. Within six months he had been killed and his band dispersed. A group of maroons, led by one John Reeder, got the reward. Dr Benjamin Moseley recorded Jack's life and death in *A Treatise on Sugar* (1799); a stage version and two prose fictions quickly followed. Thirty years later, a stage melodrama came out, which played for years in London and in British regional theatres.[21] Earle's novel elaborates Jack's story, drawing on earlier literary representations of slavery and non-fictional discourse about Africa and the West Indies, including Moseley's treatise. The novel seems at first to take an abolitionist stance when the narrator declares repeatedly, 'Jack was a man!! Jack was a hero!!!' (Earle 2005: 119). But on closer examination, Earle's narrative undermines its political impact.

His representation of Obi, or Obeah, from which the novel takes its title, is especially fraught. Historically associated with slave revolts, including the successful island-wide insurrection in Haiti (in progress at the time *Obi* was published), Obeah or Voudou was a system of spiritual power derived from African culture but syncretically developed in the New World.[22] Adepts used it for healing, personal gain, revenge, and power or invulnerability in battle. Moseley's description of this 'occult science' arises out of his discussion of yaws, a disfiguring West African skin disease (Aravamudan 2005: 34–6). Sufferers, like Earle's character Bashra, were often expelled from plantations: 'Those are the beings, who, in their seclusion, most frequently practice Obi. The more they are deformed, the more they are venerated, and their charms credited as the strongest' (Earle 2005: 119). Bashra's portrayal draws on the British stereotype of the grotesque witch or hag. Like the novel's other Obi practitioner, Feruarue, his character is complex. Both are father figures: Feruarue is the father of Jack's mother, Amri, and Bashra embraces Jack with 'the fervor of a father' (Earle 2005: 105). Earle presents their Obeah practice (unusually) as in some sense a legitimate tool of enslaved resistance (Paton 2007: 49). Feruarue, tricked into slavery, vows 'revenge, and for that purpose, studied Obi' (Earle 2005: 99). It is noteworthy that Feruarue learns Obeah not in Africa, but in the New World, where it was part of the syncretic Creole culture created by African captives.

For Romantic writers and readers, Obeah signified a threatening cultural difference. Concern with this exotic practice grew 'out of British anxieties regarding power: the fluctuations of imperial power, the power of slaves to determine their own fate, the power of democratic movements in France, in England, and in the Caribbean' (Richardson 1997: 172). Planters' anxiety about Obeah was more concrete. When it was discovered to have played a key role in Tacky's Rebellion (1760), an island-wide revolt, the Jamaican Assembly made the practice of Obeah punishable by death. Obeah could hurt planters in other ways, even giving slaves the means to poison their owners. Parliament took these issues seriously enough to conduct hearings about Obeah in 1789. Earle printed sections of Parliamentary testimony by planters and other island whites as an extended footnote to his book.

As this suggests, Earle chose a hybrid form for his novel. It is basically epistolary, told in letters from a planter, George Stanford, to a friend in England. The epistolary novel's formal element of distance – narrating events to someone absent from the scene – is charged with meaning in the colonial context. The fictional letters reporting exotic, grisly events across the Atlantic are reminiscent of business reports from administrators to absentee planters. Correspondence sutures the Empire together, but distance is its prerequisite. The material has exotic appeal for metropolitan readers because they are not inured to the everyday outrages of the slave system. Besides footnotes explaining African words and Jamaican practices, the text incorporates inset stories and even sentimental poems. These formal features suggest the novel's affiliation with both planter discourse (the conclusion is taken verbatim from Moseley's *Treatise*) and sentimental literature, a significant subset of which was abolitionist.

Letter I foregrounds the slave trade controversy. Stanford reports his 'daily altercation' with the planters:

> Jack is a noble fellow, and in spite of every cruel hard-hearted planter, I shall repeat the same to the last hour of my life. 'Jack is a negro', say they. 'Jack is a MAN', say I.
> – 'He is a slave'.
> – 'MAN cannot be a slave to MAN'.
> – 'He is my property'.
> – 'How did you acquire that property?' (Earle 2005: 70)

The conversation becomes a debate over the morality of the slave trade. The capitalised 'MAN' underscores the abolitionist tenet that slaves are persons rather than things. Stanford revisits the issue obliquely, joking that the island-wide obsession with Jack keeps him from thinking about anything else. 'Nay, there is not a *thing* called Jack, whether a smoke-jack [spit-turning device], a boot-jack, or any other jack, but . . . sets me on the fret at the bare mention of it' (Earle 2005: 70; emphasis in the original). Is a slave a person or a thing? Sarah Salih argues that *Obi* and other abolition-era narratives 'vacillate between portraying the negro as a volitional subject and . . . a "slave-thing," a vacillation that also characterizes contemporary legal constructions of the enslaved' (Salih 2007: 66). The narrator repeatedly asserts the slave protagonist's humanity, but *Obi*'s narrative arc conveys less certainty.

The main characters are introduced with broad strokes: the beautiful, wronged slave woman Amri, bent on revenge, and her son Jack, the exceptional male slave. They are 'Feloops', an African group mentioned in Mungo Park's *Travels in the Interior Districts of Africa* (1799): Feloops 'never . . . forgive an enemy. They are even said to transmit their quarrels as deadly feuds to their posterity, insomuch that a son considers it incumbent upon him . . . to become the avenger of his deceased father's wrong' (Park 2000: 76). The description of Jack recalls an earlier fictional treatment of slavery, Aphra Behn's *Oroonoko, or, The Royal Slave* (1688). Extraordinarily tall and strong like Oroonoko, Jack's facial features distinguish him from other Africans: 'his nose was not like the generality of blacks, squat and flat, but rather aquiline' (Earle 2005: 72). Letter II begins an inset narrative, 'Makro and Amri, An African Tale'. The sentimental tragedy of the captured African was standard in abolitionist discourse. It is set in a pastoral Africa rather than the barbarous, cannibal-filled continent of the pro-slavery travelogues. But this Africa is 'decultured and static . . . without any sense of real location or continuing history' (Paton 2007: 46). These Africans do not interact with other Africans, only with white Europeans, who accept their help and then betray them.

This part of the plot leans on another literary source, the story of Inkle and Yarico, popularised by Joseph Addison and Richard Steele's *Spectator* (1711).[23] Like the English merchant Inkle, Earle's villain, Captain Harrop, is shipwrecked on a wild coast and cared for by natives, Amri and her husband Makro. Unlike Inkle, Harrop civilises the Africans, teaching them to know a Christian God through the beauties of nature. He uses the sunrise to demonstrate 'the wisdom of the Creator'. The Africans fall to the ground in reverence: 'our instructor lifted us . . . we pressed him to our bosoms, and returned to our cabin, adoring the wisdom of the European, and earnestly entreating him never to leave us' (Earle 2005: 78). At the turn of the nineteenth century, when abolitionists sought to reconfigure Europe's relationship with Africa from slave raiding to benign colonisation, this aspect of *Obi* anticipates the later imperial politics of the civilising mission.

Also unlike Inkle, Harrop plots from the first to betray his hosts. A European ship appears (it happens to be his) and he hustles Amri and Makro on board. The novel's portrayal of the Middle Passage adds historically grounded elements to the melodramatic plot. Amri is chained in a 'loathsome dungeon', parted from Makro. When her chains 'gall . . . [her] ankles', a sailor laughs and rubs salt in the wound. Makro mounts a hunger strike, a tactic known to historians of slavery, and his captors try to force-feed him.[24] He calls on his wife to avenge his death and teach their unborn son 'to hate the European race' (Earle 2005: 90). A mini-oration asserts his humanity:

> I can never own a superior but my Creator. Man was his noblest work, and I am a man. He did not make slaves of one half of this globe, nor order the black to bend subservient to the white man's yoke; nor will I, a created being like them, be bought and sold, and toil like a beast of burthen, that they may enjoy the fruits of my labour. (Earle 2005: 90)

When Amri's son is born in Jamaica, she is ecstatic: '"may he not be the savior of our country! the abolisher of the slave trade!"' (Earle 2005: 95).

Earle's George Stanford, in the tradition of sentimental narrators, is self-referential and extravagant in his emotional display: 'I more than once laid down my pen, and more than once my tears floated on the page' (Earle 2005: 95). But sentiment or sensibility is, as George Boulukos reminds us, a 'plastic cultural posture', a 'cultural form without predetermined content' (Boulukos 2008: 14). It could be, and often was, used against slavery. But we also find sentiment deployed in slavery's defence, often in subtle and ambiguous ways. The conventions of the sentimental novel undercut *Obi*'s political impact by personalising Jack's resentment of slavery as individual revenge on his parents' betrayer, rather than attacking slavery as a system (Paton 2007: 54).

Jack, grown to adulthood, gets busy making his mother proud. His first move is to ask an Obi man, Bashra, for charms to help him organise a slave revolt.[25] During his childhood there have been 'frequent insurrections', all of which have failed (Earle 2005: 96). One party of rebels leads their captors 'to the cave of an Obi-Man' who turns out to be Amri's father, Feruarue. He is tortured:

> They . . . put him on the rack, he smiled at their tortures. They extended his legs and arms upon a wall, raised him from the ground about a yard, scorched the soles of his feet, and burnt him under the arm-pits; still he persevered, derided their tortures, and laughed at their preparations to agonize his frame. (Earle 2005: 98)

The trope of African stoicism, circulating at least since *Oroonoko*, lets the fiction dwell in gory detail on the torture of the insubordinate black body. Such moments present the slave as a thing – an object of torture – as well as the subject of resistance.[26] The narrative's ability to encompass both gushing sentiment and grisly violence 'resembles the legal vacillation between negro-as-subject and negro-as-object' (Salih 2007: 80).

Jack's eventual death – after his incarceration, escape to the mountains, career of depredation and dramatic recapture – extends this objectifying impulse. His body is dismembered (like Oroonoko's), his severed head and hand preserved in a pail of rum so the killers can claim their reward. His nickname reminds us that he is already dismembered, having lost fingers during an escape. This sets up a dramatic scene at Amri's execution: 'he drew another pistol, and held up his three-fingered hand to the gaze of the multitude' (Earle 2005: 147–8). The fear this inspires helps him to escape again. Earle's ending is taken largely from Moseley's *Treatise*. From subjective, sentimental narration, the text moves to a more factual mode. Salih calls this shift 'bathetic' (a 'ludicrous descent from the elevated to the commonplace', *OED*):

'Earle demotes Jack from Herculean eroticised hero into the 'thing' he always was, at least according to Jamaican slave law' (Salih 2007: 82). Like Oroonoko, Jack goes from 'noble savage' to 'savage savage', from outsized hero to half-crazed outlaw. The text's regulatory function demands this decline. The rebellious slave must be put down to allay readers' fears in the decade of the French and Haitian revolutions. But Jack's earlier incarnation as suffering hero is as necessary as his later insentience: 'power is consolidated in direct proportion to the extent of what has been crushed' (Salih 2007: 83).

The Obi of the novel's title – the spiritual power that helps Jack in his attempt to rebel – is symbolically connected to his final dismemberment. Earle's footnotes give Moseley's description of 'the Obi of the famous negro robber, Three-Fingered Jack':

> It consisted of a goat's horn, filled with a compound of grave-dirt, ashes, the blood of a black cat, and human fat, all mixed into a kind of paste.
> A cat's foot, a dried toad, a pig's tail, a slip of virginal parchment, of kid's skin, with characters marked on it in blood, were also in his Obiah-bag. (Earle 2005: 105)

The title's conjunction – *Obi, or, The History of Three-Fingered Jack* – renders Jack synonymous with this collection of 'refuse, broken pieces, fragments, partial objects' (Lee 2002b: 14). Obeah becomes a paradoxical symbol of both brokenness and power: power to heal or to kill. African remedies associated with Obeah were a primary resource for British Caribbean slaves, given the frequent neglect by owners of their slaves' health and the scarcity and often incompetence of European-trained physicians. But Obi was also linked to rebellion. It became 'a term for resistant knowledge' – feared by planters, seen by slaves as a potential cure for the condition of slavery itself (Aravamudan 2005: 33, 26). Like Jack's mutilated hand, the broken bits and pieces in his Obi horn can symbolise the homes, bodies, spirits and lives broken by slavery (Lee 2002b: 14).

Slave Narratives

The slave narrative, or abolitionist autobiography, came into being at about the time the British abolitionist movement got organised, pioneered by black abolitionists including Olaudah Equiano and Ottobah Cugoano.[27] *The Interesting Narrative of the Life of Olaudah Equiano, or Gustavus Vassa, the African, Written by Himself*, published in 1789, saw nine British editions in the author's lifetime (he died in 1797). It was an abolitionist plea wrapped in a colourful travel book, describing

Equiano's navy service in the Seven Years' War, his trip to the Arctic, an adventure in Central America and a tour of the Mediterranean with the merchant marine. The *Interesting Narrative* has been called 'the most important single literary contribution to the campaign for abolition' (Fryer 1984: 107). It gives first person testimony of the horrors of the slave trade at a time when this was invaluable to the movement. Equiano's editor and biographer, Vincent Carretta, has found evidence suggesting he was born in North America, casting doubt on his account of his African childhood.[28] We may never conclusively know, but 'available evidence suggests that the author of *The Interesting Narrative* may have invented rather than reclaimed an African identity'. If so, 'Equiano's literary achievements have been vastly underestimated' (Carretta 2005: xiv). As well as an autobiographer (archival records back his story from 1754), he may have been the first Afro-British novelist.[29] Equiano's identity as 'the African' contrasts with the bourgeois Europeanness of his dress in his frontispiece. The black gentleman, holding an open Bible, emblematises the ex-slave's remarkable upward mobility to freedom, literacy, prosperity and political influence. At his death he left an estate of £950 (about £80,000 or $160,000 in today's currency), an amazing achievement for a former slave (Carretta 2005: 366). He did not live to see the slave trade abolished.

A quarter century after Equiano's death, British slaves still laboured in the Caribbean and the anti-slavery movement was emerging from a prolonged slump. Veteran white abolitionists founded the Society for Mitigating and Gradually Abolishing the State of Slavery throughout the British Dominions in 1823. The group's approach was far from radical, beginning with modest goals such as better manumission laws, no Sunday labour and legal recognition of slave marriage and property.[30] But the anti-slavery movement also had a more radical, less respectable wing, linked to working-class politics and London's criminal underworld. A colourful figure in this rough milieu was Robert Wedderburn, born in Jamaica around 1760, son of a Scottish planter and a slave woman whom (her son claimed) James Wedderburn raped and repudiated. His autobiography, *The Horrors of Slavery* (1824), contributes to the genre of abolitionist autobiography established by Equiano and Cugoano, though there is no evidence Wedderburn knew their writings. His experiences as an immigrant in Britain resemble theirs: he served in the navy as a youth, was part of London's poor black community and had a Christian conversion experience (McCalman 1991: 3–4). But Wedderburn's radicalism, a generation later, was more extreme.

He was neither respectable nor upwardly mobile, but lived on the fringes of London artisan society. Trained as a tailor, with artisan values of pride in craft and economic independence, he was forced to scrape a living in the wartime economy patching clothes and hawking pamphlets. Late in his long life, after serving a prison term for blasphemy, he reportedly ran a brothel. 'The disjunction between his pride as an artisan and his degradation as a ragged piece-worker, beggar and thief probably goes a long way toward explaining why he . . . became a radical' (McCalman 1991: 8). Much of what is known about Wedderburn's rabble-rousing activities in tavern debating societies and his own 'chapel' (he was a registered Unitarian minister) comes from reports by government spies. The chapel was a run-down hayloft where he held debates for rowdy radical audiences. The spy reports preserve Wedderburn's raw, colloquial speech, with a touch of West Indian lilt. He seems to have been something of a performance artist, using his colour, imposing physique and gripping life story to enact themes and motifs from popular melodrama. In 1817 he published a short-lived periodical, *The Axe Laid to the Root*, whose 'most important contribution to popular radical ideology came from its sustained attempt to integrate the prospect of slave revolution in the West Indies with that of working-class revolution in England' (McCalman 1991: 23–4, 18).

The Horrors of Slavery presents Wedderburn's identity as a 'product, witness and victim of the slave system'. Slavery was 'the crucible of his being . . . [i]ts effects haunted him until his death'; his autobiography vividly conveys why this is so (McCalman 1991: 3). As an old man of sixty, he still burns with resentment for the childhood wrongs inflicted on him and his slave mother and grandmother by his father. Dr James Wedderburn was a Scottish colonist who practised as a doctor and male midwife in Jamaica and later ran a sugar plantation. He was a neighbour and friend of Thomas Thistlewood, a slave holder who left extensive diaries of his life on several plantations. One aspect of colonial culture they expose is the sexually predatory behaviour of many slave holders. He recorded his exploits with female slaves meticulously, usually in Latin. For example, on 21 June 1759: 'About 2 p.m. *Cum* Mazerine, *Sup. Terr.* Old Curing house canepiece. Gave her a bitt [small coin]. About 3 p.m. *Cum* Warsoe, in the boiling house. Stans: Backwards' (Hall 1999: 87).[31]

The Horrors of Slavery portrays James Wedderburn as lustful, but also cost-conscious (the stereotypical thrifty Scot):

While my dear and honoured father was poor, he was as chaste as any Scotchman, whose poverty made him virtuous; but the moment he became rich, he gave a loose to his carnal appetites, and indulged himself without moderation, but as parsimonious as ever. My father's mental powers were none of the brightest, which may account for his libidinous excess. (Wedderburn 1991: 46)

Citing Parliamentary testimony on planters who impregnated slaves and then sold them, Wedderburn links his personal history to the abolitionist movement. Lust for sex and greed for money converge to make the colonists' behaviour more repellent:

My father ranged through the whole of his household for his own lewd purposes; for they being his personal property, cost nothing extra; and if any one proved with child – why, it . . . might one day fetch something in the market, like a horse or pig in Smithfield. In short, among his own slaves my father was a perfect parish bull; and his pleasure was the greater, because he at the same time increased his profits. (Wedderburn 1991: 46)

Abolitionist propaganda often described slaves treated like livestock; Wedderburn inverts the trope. Wedderburn Senior schemes to get Robert's mother, Rosanna, into his possession to add her to his 'seraglio' (Wedderburn 1991: 47) – an image that assimilates the slave holder to the stereotype of the oriental despot.

Rosanna was by no means tame. She had a 'rebellious and violent temper' that she passed on, Wedderburn boasts, to her son: 'I have inherited the same disposition – the same desire to see justice overtake the oppressors of my countrymen' (Wedderburn 1991: 48). The self he presents in *The Horrors of Slavery* takes after his maternal forebears, unruly slave women whose acts of resistance the book details. Rosanna made herself so unpleasant that James Wedderburn was forced to sell her. She even got him to agree that Robert, with whom she was pregnant, 'should be FREE from . . . birth'. He proclaims: 'I thank my GOD, that through a long life of hardship and adversity, I have ever been free both in mind and body: and have always raised my voice in behalf of my enslaved countrymen!' (Wedderburn 1991: 48, 58–9). His mother had several subsequent owners. One tied her down and flogged her in front of her young son while she was pregnant. The wife of another, Dr Campbell, treated her so badly that she went on a hunger strike, 'and though a cook, abstained from victuals for six days'. At this point Campbell gave her 'leave to look out for another owner' (Wedderburn 1991: 50). Historians document slaves' creative day-to-day resistance to slavery, aimed at improving the quality of their lives in captivity.[32] Rosanna seems to have succeeded more than once in leveraging major changes.

Young Robert was sent to live with his grandmother, another remarkable woman by the name of 'Talkee Amy', as unruly as her daughter. Her name invokes the sharp tongues for which women slaves were notorious: 'that powerful instrument of attack and defence', as one colonial official wrote.[33] Amy worked as a higgler or market woman, 'retailing all sorts of goods, hard or soft, smuggled or not . . . cheese, checks, chintz, milk, gingerbread, etc.' (Wedderburn 1991: 48). The one time Robert saw his father in Jamaica was when Amy took him to ask 'if he meant to do anything for me, his son'. When Wedderburn Senior responded abusively, Amy let him have it. She 'called him a mean Scotch rascal, thus to desert his own flesh and blood; and declared, that as she had kept me hitherto, so she would yet, without his paltry assistance' (Wedderburn 1991: 49). Amy seems likely to have been an Obeah woman. It was on suspicion of witchcraft that her owner had her flogged, an atrocity that Wedderburn offers as evidence of colonial cruelty: 'upon what slight grounds the planters exercise their cow-skin whips, not sparing even an old woman of seventy years of age' (Wedderburn 1991: 50).

Formally, *The Horrors of Slavery* is hybrid, combining an account of Wedderburn's Jamaican childhood with an exchange of letters reprinted from *Bell's Life in London*, an anti-establishment newspaper. The first letter thanks the editor for his 'observations on the Meeting of the Receivers of Stolen Men' (i.e. slave dealers; the exact reference is unclear). Wedderburn offers personal testimony of his mother's rape and flogging by his father and the mistreatment endured by other slave relatives. The published letter caught the attention of 'A. Colville Esq.', James Wedderburn's son and heir, who wrote in to respond to 'this most slanderous publication' and clear his father's name. Colville's letter asserts that Robert was not actually James Wedderburn's son. He says Robert's 'troublesome' mother *could not tell who was the father* of her son (Wedderburn 1991: 53; emphasis in original) – deflecting the charge of immorality from slave holder to slave. Colville ends by threatening legal action in case of further 'slander' by the newspaper.

With the letters, *The Horrors of Slavery* reprints commentary by the editor of *Bell's Life in London*, enlisting the journal's authority on Wedderburn's behalf. The 'press is my engine of destruction', Wedderburn asserts in *The Axe Laid to the Root* (Wedderburn 1991: 96). The *Bell's* editor systematically, sarcastically destroys Colville's case, using the editorial 'we' while asserting impartiality: 'as we are of no party, our columns are as open to one part of his father's family as to another' (Wedderburn 1991: 56). The paper's editorial position is anti-slavery, though not radically so. The editor invokes the abolitionist image of the slave colony as a place very different from Britain. In response to the threat of prosecution, Colville is reminded 'that HE IS NOT in *Jamaica*, and that we are not alarmed at trifles' (Wedderburn 1991: 53). In the colony, slave holders can throw their weight around; in England, it will not work.

The Horrors of Slavery concludes with two more letters from Wedderburn to *Bell's*, restating his case and describing his visit to his father's home in Scotland five years previously. Wedderburn Senior:

> had the inhumanity to threaten to send me to gaol if I troubled him . . . nor did he deny me to be his son, but called me a *lazy fellow*, and said he would do nothing for me. From his cook I had one draught of small beer, and his footman gave me a cracked sixpence – these are all the obligations I am under to my *worthy* father and *my dear brother*. (Wedderburn 1991: 60)

Wedderburn died in poverty and obscurity around 1835, aged seventy-two. But the old man lived long enough to see a resurgence of mass radicalism that helped inspire new generations of nineteenth-century working-class leaders (McCalman 1991: 34–5). Bringing the liberationist drive gained from his experience of colonial slavery to fight working-class oppression in the metropole, he was a forerunner of future generations of colonial immigrants.[34]

The last narrative I will discuss in this chapter is *The History of Mary Prince, a West Indian Slave, Related by Herself* (1831). Like Equiano, Prince had influential white abolitionists as sponsors; like both him and Wedderburn, she was a converted Christian. Her narrative – the first by an enslaved British woman that survives – presents numerous textual and theoretical challenges, beginning with the matter of authorship. 'Related' indicates the narrative was oral, told to a white woman, Susanna Strickland, who wrote it down. The circumstances in which this took place, and the text's further fate at the hands of its editor, Thomas Pringle, as well as its reception by readers, all bear on a central question of postcolonial studies: 'Can the subaltern speak?' Posed by Gayatri Spivak in 1988, this question concerns the access – or lack of access – of those in the lowest strata of a colonial society to that society's dominant discourses. Spivak argues that overly facile claims to have recovered the voice or agency of a colonised subject risk re-colonising her in an important sense: identifying as her voice a discourse produced in her name by the very systems that oppressed her. Recent criticism is divided between those who believe they can recover Mary Prince's voice – and celebrate her as a heroine – and others more sceptical of that possibility.[35] Let us investigate this question by considering the details of Mary Prince's situation and the *History*.

Prince was born a slave in 1788 on the island of Bermuda. Her first owner was Charles Myners, who sold her as an infant to a Captain Darrel, who then gave her as a gift to his granddaughter, Miss Betsey Williams, and her parents, Captain and Mrs Williams. Mary's mother was 'a household slave in the same family ... my little brothers and sisters were my play-fellows and companions' (Prince 1997: 57). The *History* describes an idyllic childhood:

> I was made quite a pet of by Miss Betsey, and loved her very much. She used to lead me about by the hand, and call me her little nigger. This was the happiest period of my life; for I was too young to understand rightly my condition as a slave, and too thoughtless and full of spirits to look forward to the days of toil and sorrow. (Prince 1997: 57)

To modern readers, love between a slave and her owner – an owner who blithely refers to another human being as her property and as a 'nigger' – may seem implausible. The concept of the pet blurs the borderline between human and animal. Animal comparisons recur later in Mary's girlhood as she describes a vendue, or public slave auction, where she is 'offer[ed] ... for sale like sheep or cattle'. There 'strange men ... examined and handled me in the same manner that a butcher would a calf or a lamb he was about to purchase' (Prince 1997: 62).

The sentimental portrayal of Mary's idyllic childhood sets up the wrenching scene of family separation, narrated in language that emphasises the young girl's acute pain and sorrow. Slavery's effect on families was an issue that appealed to metropolitan abolitionists, in particular women. The *History* paints the auction as a scene of public humiliation, rendering Mary's response in language organised around the image of the heart:

> My heart throbbed with grief and terror so violently, that I pressed my hands quite tightly across my breast, but I could not keep it still, and it continued to leap as though it would burst out of my body. (Prince 1997: 62)

White bystanders seem indifferent to the slaves' suffering:

> Did one of the many bystanders, who were looking at us so carelessly, think of the pain that wrung the hearts of the negro woman and her young ones? No, no! They were not all bad, I dare say, but slavery hardens white people's hearts towards the blacks; and many of them were not slow to make

their remarks aloud, without regard to our grief – though their light words fell like cayenne on the fresh wounds of our hearts. Oh those white people have small hearts who can only feel for themselves. (Prince 1997: 62)

The image of the heart recurs throughout the *History* as the register of a grief and terror that is both individual and collective. But heart is also 'an alternative to the material measure of the marketplace as a measure of . . . moral and ethical sensibility' (Paquet 1992: 142). The young Mary Prince is told by her mother at their parting, and by older slave women in her master's house, to 'keep up a good heart' (Prince 1997: 63, 64). Sandra Paquet translates this as 'to be strong, resistant and conscious of self-worth in the face of extraordinary torture and brutality' (Paquet 1992: 142). The simile of cayenne pepper (an iconic Caribbean spice) applied to a wound anchors the *History's* language in a specific West Indian place, evoking the cruel punishment of rubbing salt or hot pepper into wounds after a flogging.

Paquet's is perhaps the most persuasive defence of the idea that present-day readers can recover Mary Prince's subaltern voice. She describes this voice as pre-existing the written or printed text of the *History,* but detectable through it, and distinctively Caribbean or West Indian (Paquet 1992: 135–6). A more sceptical assessment of the possibility of recovering an authentic subaltern voice from this text would focus on its highly mediated character and the circumstances, in particular power relations, surrounding its creation. At the time she told her story to Strickland, Mary Prince was living in London, working as a servant for Thomas Pringle, Secretary of the London Anti-Slavery Society and editor of her *History.* She had been sold twice more since her separation from her mother to owners who subjected her to various types of physical and psychological abuse. Her last owners, Mr and Mrs John Wood of the island of Antigua, brought her to London, where the Mansfield precedent of 1772 made it illegal to recapture an escaped slave for transport to the colonies.[36]

By Mary's account, the Woods continued to treat her badly, as they had in Antigua, forcing her to do heavy laundry though she was disabled by years of hard work and corporal punishment. A stranger to London, Prince was afraid to leave their house (she would obviously not get a good job reference). A white working-class couple, Mr and Mrs Mash, offered her shelter; Christian missionaries may have given her material aid, and abolitionists offered legal advice. Although she could remain free in England, if she were to return to Antigua – and rejoin her husband, Daniel James, a free black man – she would again be a slave. It was an excruciating choice. After trying unsuccessfully to make a living, Prince again approached the Anti-Slavery Society, and in 1829 Pringle hired her as a servant. While living at his house she dictated her *History* to Strickland; it was published in 1831 with Pringle as editor.

The form of the published narrative bespeaks Pringle's felt need to surround the slave's testimony with an apparatus to supply the authority her voice lacked for metropolitan readers. Pringle added an editor's preface, explanatory footnotes, and a Supplement – almost as long as the narrative – documenting 'circumstances connected with her case' (Prince 1997: 95). He reproduces (with scathing commentary) two letters by Wood and another by Joseph Phillips, who knew both Wood and Mary Prince in Antigua; a report by the Birmingham Ladies' Antislavery Society; a letter from seven citizens of Antigua, including Wood himself, vouching for Phillips's good character; and an excerpt from a pamphlet, 'Notices of Brazil', on abusive slave owners. Pringle added even more material to subsequent editions, notably a letter signed by his wife, Susanna Strickland, and two other ladies, testifying to the scarred appearance of Mary Prince's back (Prince 1997: 130–1). The Birmingham Ladies' Society for the Relief of Negro Slaves required this corroboration of Prince's testimony before they would send her money.

It was not unusual for persons other than educated whites to need sponsorship or verification for white readers to believe their words. A group of prominent Boston citizens grilled the African-American poet Phillis Wheatley in the 1770s to determine whether she was capable of writing the poems her owner presented as hers. To what extent does this apparatus, as it establishes the slave's credibility (and advances the cause of slave emancipation, surely one Prince supported), also function to silence her? Put another way, what is the relation between the voice the text of the *History* enables its readers to 'hear' and the historically existing nineteenth-century person who went by the name of Mary Prince (as well as Mary James, Mary, Princess of Wales and Molly Wood)? Kremena Todorova takes a sceptical stance. She invokes Homi Bhabha's concept of colonial mimicry, defined as 'the desire for a reformed, recognizable Other, *as a subject of a difference that is almost the same, but not quite*' (Bhabha 1994; 86, emphasis in original). The process of colonisation, Bhabha argues, has an ambivalent effect. It produces an appropriate or appropriated Other, but at the same time produces a threatening excess, 'a difference or recalcitrance' that both intensifies the colonising power's surveillance of the colonised subject and 'poses an immanent threat to . . . "normalized" knowledges and disciplinary powers' (Bhabha 1994: 86).

Mary Prince repeatedly meets with the suspicion that she is not quite reformed. We see this through religion. 'Ironically, everyone questions the former slave's success at becoming a good Christian' (Todorova 2001: 293). Her attackers portray her as an immoral woman, masquerading as a Christian to get abolitionist sponsorship. Even Pringle has doubts. 'Her religious knowledge . . . is still but very limited, and her views of Christianity indistinct', he concedes (Prince 1997: 116). At the end of her narrative, Prince admits that though she still hopes 'God will find a way to give me my liberty, and give me back to my husband', it is difficult sometimes: 'I endeavour to keep down my fretting, and to leave all to Him, for he knows what is good for me better than I know myself. Yet, I must confess, I find it a hard and heavy task to do so' (Prince 1997: 93). The slave's 'fretting' locates her at the margin of Christian morality – almost a good Christian, but not quite – with 'a degree of foreignness that cannot be supervised by the vigilant eye of her editor' (Todorova 2001: 294).

Jenny Sharpe also questions our access to the historically existing Mary Prince through the text of the *History*. There were certain things, Sharpe points out, that such a text just could not say and still accomplish its polemical purpose – or be published at all: 'Although Prince is a speaking subject in her testimony, she does not speak freely. The information admissible as evidence of her life is governed by the kind of woman her middle-class English readers considered a reliable eyewitness to slavery' (Sharpe 2002: xiii). One domain where we can infer that the *History* is not a full account of Mary Prince's life or character is that of sex. We know from other surviving documents that Strickland and Pringle did not include everything Mary Prince said about her sex life. Two libel lawsuits followed the publication of the *History*. The first, *Pringle* v. *Cadell*, concerned a virulent attack on Pringle and Prince published in *Blackwood's Edinburgh Magazine* by the pro-slavery propagandist James Macqueen (Cadell was his London publisher). Pringle won.

The second lawsuit was by Wood, Prince's owner, against Pringle, editor of the *History*. Mary Prince testified at both trials. At the first she said only that she had given Pringle an account of her life. At the second trial her testimony was more extensive. On cross-examination she said that before her marriage she had lived with a Captain Abbot for seven years. Before that she lived with a free black man named Oyskman, who 'made a fool of her by telling her he would make her free . . . She told all this to Miss Strickland when that lady took down her narrative. These statements were not in the narrative published by the defendant'

(Prince 1997: 147–8). Mary Prince's character became a legal issue
when her owner sued her editor for libel. Disclosing behaviour viewed
as immoral by middle-class metropolitan Britons would have discredited
the *History*. It helped Wood win his lawsuit (he got £25 in damages).
It is clear why Pringle omitted these parts of Mary Prince's life from
the published *History*, even though, as Sharpe emphasises, such sexual
arrangements were among the few resources an enslaved woman possessed, not just to strive toward freedom, but to improve the quality of
her life (Sharpe 2002: 137–40).

But this is not the only sex that was (probably) expunged from the
History. The sexual exploitation that black women endured in slavery
was also taboo. The most Mary Prince can do is elliptically allude to the
sexual advances of her third owner, Mr D—. When he buys her, she is
happy to escape the sadistic I— household in Bermuda. D— takes her
to Turk's Island, a remote 'exploitation station' where slaves pan for
salt in horrific conditions (Speitz 2011). Through this experience, Prince
comes to identify herself as a spokeswoman for fellow slaves such as old
Daniel, beaten with briars and rubbed with salt, and Sarah, dead after
being beaten and tossed in the prickly pears. 'In telling my own sorrows,
I cannot pass by those of my fellow-slaves – for when I think of my
own griefs I remember theirs' (Prince 1997: 75). Affective connections
among communities of slaves anchor Prince's narration. Ten years later
D— gets out of the salt business and retires to Bermuda, taking Mary
with him to wait on his daughters. She is happy to get off Turk's Island.

The work in Bermuda proves 'not so very bad', but Prince probably
encountered an occupational hazard that historians note as prevalent
for women domestic slaves: sexual harassment or coercion (Robertson
2003: 24).[37] Immediately preceding her elliptical description of D—'s
sexual advances, Prince narrates another violent encounter. I will quote
at length:

> My old master often got drunk, and then he would get in a fury with his
> daughter, and beat her till she was not fit to be seen. I remember on one
> occasion . . . I found my master beating Miss D— dreadfully. I strove with
> all my strength to get her away from him; for she was all black and blue
> with bruises. He had beat her with his fist, and almost killed her. The
> people gave me credit for getting her away. He turned round and began to
> lick me. Then I said, 'Sir, this is not Turk's Island'. I can't repeat his answer,
> the words were too wicked – too bad to say. He wanted to treat me the
> same in Bermuda as he had done in Turk's Island.
>
> He had an ugly fashion of stripping himself quite naked and ordering me
> then to wash him in a tub of water. This was worse to me than all the licks.

Sometimes when he called me to wash him I would not come, my eyes were so full of shame. He would then come to beat me. One time I had plates and knives in my hand, and I dropped both plates and knives, and some of the plates were broken. He struck me so severely for this, that at last I defended myself, for I thought it was high time to do so. I then told him I would not live longer with him, for he was a very indecent man – very spiteful, and too indecent; with no shame for his servants, and no shame for his own flesh. So I went away to a neighbouring house and sat down and cried till the next morning, when I went home again, not knowing what else to do.

After that I was hired to work at Cedar Hills . . . (Prince 1997: 77–8)

Prince's record of community recognition for her courageous act – 'The people gave me credit' – prefaces D—'s grudging recognition of a kind of capital, a knowledge or worldliness, that she has gained through her involuntary travel. For elite travellers, travel was a means of education (as in the Grand Tour). The definition of the traveller has not usually included involuntary travellers, such as slaves or migrant workers; we tend to think of travel as voluntary, leisured and privileged. This incident suggests a slave can be a traveller too. Knowing the difference between Bermuda, a civilised colony, and Turk's Island, a remote 'exploitation station', gives Prince the power to deflect her owner's violence with an appeal to community standards. This victory sets the stage for Prince's subsequent self-defence from D—'s 'indecency', a term that again invokes community standards. Here, too, her verbal (and possibly physical) resistance has at least limited success: hired out to others, she no longer has to work in this man's 'indecent' household. Her awareness of readers' metropolitan morality, we can infer, keeps her from going into detail about his behaviour. But she manages not to portray herself as the passive victim that abolitionist ideology would ideally demand in its drive to locate the agency for change firmly in England (Sharpe 2002: 40).

In *The History of Mary Prince,* a subaltern leaves a recorded trace that becomes part of Romantic literature and British history. Despite critics' valid doubts about the fullness or accuracy that was possible in recording such a voice, we can reasonably infer that the political project of slave emancipation, to which the *History* was designed to contribute, was a goal that Mary Prince shared with Thomas Pringle and other white abolitionists. Her testimony helps to redefine the genre of autobiography from a private statement of privileged subjectivity to a medium of collective resistance (Todorova 2001: 288). The trial of *Wood v. Pringle* is Mary Prince's last known appearance in the historical record. We do not know what became of the ageing slave after 1 March 1833.

Was she able to get back to Antigua and rejoin her husband after the Emancipation Bill? Or did she, like Phillis Wheatley, die in poverty, alone?

Romantic literature imagined slavery in a variety of ways, few of which – if any – were disinterested. Literary representations of slavery and slaves were almost inevitably engaged in the political battle over the institution of slavery that spanned the Romantic era. Those I have selected, in verse, fiction and non-fiction prose, suggest the range of representational tactics brought to bear by Romantic authors on this ideologically and emotionally fraught issue. Slavery divided the British nation; it was a source of immense profit and profound trauma. Slaves themselves, most deeply affected, were least likely to have a voice in decisions about it. The critical methods of postcolonial studies can help us sort through the pressures and priorities, silences and suppressions that went into a testament such as *The History of Mary Prince*.

Notes

1. My chapter title pays homage to Debbie Lee's important study of the same name (Lee 2002a).
2. Atlantic studies conceptualises the Atlantic world as 'one single, complex unit of analysis' (Gilroy 1993: 15), emphasising the interconnections woven by trade – in particular the slave trade – between Europe, Africa and the Americas. *The Black Atlantic*, Gilroy's influential 1993 study, designates the 'transcultural, international formation' linking Africans and members of the African diaspora in Europe and the Americas. The journal *Atlantic Studies* was founded in 2004.
3. Walvin 1994: 301. Eric Williams argued in 1944 that slavery was less profitable under mature capitalism, a controversial thesis historians continue to debate; see Solow and Engerman 1987.
4. 'Boycott' is an anachronism – the word dates to the 1880s.
5. Mercantilism is the economic theory that promoting exports (especially manufactured goods) and restricting imports to achieve a favourable balance of trade increases a nation's wealth. Colonies, in this view, existed for the good of the mother country. In the British Empire, mercantilism and protectionism gave way to free trade in the mid-nineteenth century.
6. Mintz 1985: 53, 48, 47. This insight runs counter to the assumption that modern innovations originated in the metropole and later reached the imperial periphery.
7. Parry et al. 1987: 129; see Craton 1982 on slave revolts in the West Indies.
8. Loomba 2005: 195. The context is Spivak's influential essay 'Can the Subaltern Speak?' (Spivak 1988).
9. Metonymy substitutes for a word denoting one thing (slaves' bodies) a word denoting something associated with that thing (slaves' bodily fluids such as blood, sweat, tears).
10. On West Indian Creole culture see Brathwaite 1971 and Lambert 2005.
11. The abolitionist movement created a fashion for wearing this iconic image on jewellery and hair ornaments (Oldfield 1995: 155–8).

12. See Lambert 2004, Wood 2002 and Hartman 1997.
13. Southey's early liberalism later gave way to a profound Tory conservatism, as did Wordsworth's. By 1807 he had been appointed Poet Laureate and issued a stipend. Former friends and fellow poets saw him as selling out and viciously lampooned him.
14. Bernal 1991: 206, quoted in Kitson 1999: viii.
15. Kitson 1999: x; Pratt 1992.
16. Wheeler 2000: 353, note 20.
17. Blake's images can be viewed online in the William Blake Archive at <http://www.blakearchive.org/blake/main.html?java=yes> (accessed 12 July 2012).
18. Blake coloured each book by hand as he made them. Makdisi 2003 presents as examples Copy C, plate 23, and Copy Z, Plate 10, of *Songs of Innocence and of Experience* (Makdisi 2003: 166–7).
19. Examples include 'A Negroe Female with a Weight chain'd to her Ancle' (Stedman 1988: 40); 'A Negroe Hanged Alive by the Ribs to a Gallows' (Stedman 1988: 105); 'The Flagellation of a Female Samboe Slave' (Stedman 1988: 265); and 'The Execution of Breaking on the Rack' (Stedman 1988: 548). More benign images of Afro-Surinamers include 'Family of Negroe Slaves from Loango' (Stedman 1988: 535).
20. Aravamudan 1999a: xi. Boulukos (2008) surveys Romantic representations of slavery in fiction.
21. Versions of the Three-Fingered Jack story include Moseley's 1799 *Treatise on Sugar*; William Burdett's *Life and Exploits of Mansong, Commonly Called Three-Fingered Jack*; John Fawcett's pantomime (1800); and a melodrama adapted from the latter between 1824 and 1830, in which the great African American actor Ira Aldridge played the title role. See Cox 2002 and Szwydky 2011; also Bilby on maroon oral traditions (Bilby 2005: 308–12).
22. Obi or Obeah, a West African form of sorcery or medico-religious practice traced to Ashanti-Fanti origins (Gold Coast or modern Ghana), is different from Vodou or Voodoo, which originated in the Fon and Yoruba cultures (Dahomey, modern Benin) and flourished in French Saint-Domingue (modern Haiti), playing a role in the 1791 Haitian Revolution. See Richardson 1997: 173.
23. Felsenstein (1999) documents the persistent popularity of this story.
24. Walvin 1994: 52; and see Thomas 1997: 409–30 on the Middle Passage.
25. Slave revolts were frequent in the Atlantic world, part of a continuum of resistance including day-to-day tactics, such as sabotage and malingering, and running away or marronage, as well as violent rebellions. Jamaica saw as many of these as the other British islands put together. See Craton 1982: 99 and *passim*.
26. See Lambert 2004 on problems of representation in scholarship on slavery. Hartman 1997 and Wood 2002 take opposite approaches to the voyeuristic or deadening effect of reproducing scenes of violence and torture: Hartman refuses to reproduce such scenes, while Wood's books reproduce many visual images in this vein.
27. See Blackburn 1988: 131–60 and Oldfield 1995, especially 41–69, on the early abolitionist movement, and Davis and Gates 1985 on the slave narrative genre.
28. The evidence is a 1759 London baptismal register and a 1773 ship's roster from the *Racehorse* (a ship on Phipps's Arctic expedition), listing Vassa's birthplace as 'Carolina' or 'South Carolina' (Carretta 2005: 80, 147, 149).
29. Youngquist 2005 surveys work on Equiano.
30. Blackburn 1988: 421–2, 421–72.
31. Burnard 2004 provides a full-length historical study of Thistlewood.

32. Bush 1990: 51–63; Mathurin 1975; Craton 1978.
33. Mathurin 1975: 13; Sharpe 2002: 140–6.
34. Also see Linebaugh and Rediker 2000: 287–326. James Robertson's recent historical novel *Joseph Knight* gives an unflattering portrait of the Wedderburn family in Scotland and the Caribbean (Robertson 2003).
35. On the definition of 'subaltern' see Introduction, note 4. Ferguson 1992, Paquet 1992, Larrabee 2006 and Baumgartner 2001 represent the former view; Sharpe 2002, Rauwerda 2001 and Todorova 2001 the latter.
36. Chief Justice Lord Mansfield's 1772 decision in the case of James Somerset is often erroneously interpreted to mean slavery could not exist on British soil. Its scope is narrower, forbidding owners to force their slaves to leave England: Blackburn 1988: 99–100; Ferguson 1992: 116.
37. Ferguson 1997: 10–11; Ferguson 1992: 286.

Chapter 3

Scottish Romantic Literature and Postcolonial Studies

On the island that Scotland and England share, the southern kingdom has historically dominated its northern neighbour. We can conceptualise their relationship as that of core and periphery, with the core defined as the region where a strong central government was first established, while the peripheries, or outlying regions, differ from the core in language, culture and economic organisation. The British nation was built through a process of internal colonialism, defined by Michael Hechter as 'the political incorporation of culturally distinct groups by the core'.[1] As the core grows in political and economic strength and sophistication, it expands to incorporate peripheral areas, but in ways that preserve, or even aggravate, economic imbalance and cultural bias. In England's case, this process began in the thirteenth century, when Wales became England's first colony (made part of England by Henry VIII in 1542). Scotland and Ireland followed; centuries of intermittent conflict culminated in the respective Acts of Union between England and Scotland to form Great Britain (1707) and between Britain and Ireland to form the United Kingdom (1801).

Given the distinctiveness of each nation's history of internal colonialism, I have chosen to focus just on Scottish Romantic literature and its roots in Scotland's relationship with imperial Britain. Any consideration of Scottish literature must recognise the complex and paradoxical nature of this relationship. Although they shared the experience of internal colonialism with Ireland and Wales, the Scottish people also took an active part in overseas colonisation. Different segments of the Scottish population (elite and subaltern,[2] Lowland and Highland, English-, Scots- and Gaelic-speaking) fared variously in the long process of British nation formation. To understand Scottish Romantic literature, as recent scholarship makes clear, we need different concepts and a different chronology from those applied to English Romanticism. For this postcolonial criticism and theory are indispensable. Work by Murray Pittock, Leith Davis, Ian Duncan, Janet Sorensen, Katie Trumpener and others has begun laying the groundwork for 'a more inclusive Romanticism' while critiquing the 'anglocentric underpinnings' of mainstream Romantic studies.[3]

English and Scottish Romanticism both turned to history for inspiration, but in different ways. The novel, in particular the historical novel, formed the turbulent centre of Scottish Romanticism as authors came to terms with Scotland's conflict-ridden history. I will recapitulate that history before addressing three issues essential to a postcolonial analysis of Scottish literature: the politics of language; the role of orality and the antiquarian activity aiming to fix oral literature in print; and the imagination, central to Romanticism, but differently conceived by a Scottish intellectual tradition than a familiar Coleridgean lyricism. From these considerations emerges a chronology of Scottish Romanticism that starts earlier and shapes up differently than the familiar timeline of Anglocentric Romanticism.

I will then discuss selected works by major authors. We could not imagine Scottish Romanticism without Scotland's national poet, Robert Burns, but his reception was fraught with struggle from the beginning. Burns was not the 'heaven-taught ploughman' he was patronisingly labelled, but a sophisticated poet, adept at switching linguistic registers, as his comic masterpiece, 'Tam o' Shanter' (1793), reveals. His labouring-class origins raise the issue of the intersection between class or rank and nation in the history of internal colonialism, relevant to another labouring-class author, James Hogg. But before turning to Hogg, I will pay homage to the figure whose shadow envelops Scottish Romanticism: the author of *Waverley*, Sir Walter Scott. Scott was so popular as a poet and novelist that 'other writers were compelled to accept, refuse, or work through their configuration as shades of Scott'.[4] The Marxist critic Georg Lukács famously elevated Scott as the inventor of the historical novel. *Waverley* (1814) was the first of his series of novels set in periods from the Middle Ages to the 1790s. *Waverley* treats what we might call the 'matter of Scotland': seventeenth- and eighteenth-century Scottish history. I will consider the 'account of Scott as master ideologue of internal colonialism' proposed by recent critics – an account that Ian Duncan's authoritative *Scott's Shadow* reveals as troublingly incomplete (Duncan 2007: 97, 98). Scott also wrote about Scottish participation in Britain's overseas empire in *The Surgeon's Daughter* (1827), where returning colonisers bring back to Scotland the 'spoils and contagions of empire' (Wallace 2002: 317).

Next I will consider Hogg's feisty rejoinder to Scott's genteel version of Scottish history. Hogg was a shepherd for two decades before embracing literature as a profession. The frame narrative of his novel, *The Private Memoirs and Confessions of a Justified Sinner* (1824), stages his ambivalent relationship to the Edinburgh literati. A party of these gentlemen exhume an eighteenth-century Presbyterian fanatic, Robert Wringhim. The two versions of Wringhim's story represent two divergent strands of Scottish intellectual history: the sinner's self-portrait is rooted in Calvinism, the editor's reconstruction in the Scottish Enlightenment. Hogg's intricate masterpiece forges a rough-edged Scottish Romanticism wary of domestication by an urban elite. The final author I will discuss is Thomas Pringle, who entered Chapter 2 as the editor of Mary Prince's autobiography. Pringle had previously taken part in the British colonisation of South Africa. The poetry he wrote there takes a Romantic perspective on the land and people of southern Africa and the colonists' relation to them. Pringle's poems initiated South African literature in English, opening 'possibilities . . . for the creation of a truly indigenous poetry' (Pereira and Chapman 1989: xxiii).

History

The eighteenth century saw Scotland relinquish its status as an independent country, held since 843 CE. In 1603, on the death of Queen Elizabeth I, King James VI of Scotland inherited the throne of England. However, this 'Union of Crowns' did not merge the two nations, which remained separate and distinct until 1707. In that year Scotland signed a Treaty of Union with England to form the new nation of Great Britain, a decision that would have far-reaching consequences for both nations. Not until 1999 would Scotland again have its own Parliament.[5] The merger was not inevitable. Opposed by many Scots for various reasons, it was achieved through strategic concessions by England, notably establishing the Presbyterian Church of Scotland as the state religion:[6]

> The treaty had been born out of a marriage of convenience between the governing classes in Edinburgh and London, and its successful passage through the Scottish Parliament was a close-run thing, delivered in the teeth of a good deal of popular hostility. (Devine 1999: 17)

With roughly twice Scotland's land mass, five times its population, and thirty-six times its wealth, England was obviously the dominant partner in the new nation of Great Britain. The two countries' new relationship was far from stable and harmonious; indeed, its survival was in doubt more than once in the decades after 1707.

Though Scotland lost its Parliament (gaining an agreed-upon number of members in the British legislature), its currency, and its ability to regulate trade, it kept its own system of law and courts as well as its Church. This meant a distinctively Scottish form of national and local government could continue, with the most important political decisions still made in Scotland (Devine 1999: 24). Many Scots, especially the ruling class and intelligentsia, worked hard at being British, even taking elocution lessons to lose their Scottish accents. But a distinctive Scottish identity was by no means suppressed:

> Life in Scotland was still conditioned and fashioned by intrinsically Scottish institutions: the proudly independent Presbyterian church, civil law, the parish schools and the five universities. The Scots dialect was the language not only of the most humble but also of the greatest in the land. Scottish patriotism was alive and well among the mass of the people. (Devine 1999: 29–30)

One form it took was Jacobitism: support for the exiled King James VII (of Scotland) and II (of England), who had been forced to abdicate in the 'Glorious Revolution' of 1688–9, and his son, another James. The loss of the Stuart dynasty, which had ruled Scotland since the fourteenth century, seemed to many Scots to be bound up with the loss of Scottish independence: 'in the eighteenth century and afterwards, the mythology and ideology of the Stuart cause became a kind of protest history, a self-expression of identity on behalf of those whose identity was under threat' (Pittock 1991: 5).

Between 1688 and 1745 several attempts were made to restore the Stuarts to the throne by force of arms, the most serious in 1715 and 1745. Jacobitism was a complex phenomenon, fed by the Presbyterian settlement, which Scottish Episcopalians opposed. These included most of the Highland clans, whose military prowess posed a real threat to the imperial government. Britain's European enemies, notably France, where James and his son lived in exile, supported Jacobitism. In 1715 and 1745 the Stuarts 'issued proclamations publicly committing the restored monarchy to repeal of the union ... "No Union" became a common motto on Jacobite banners' (Devine 1999: 37). Opposed to a Stuart restoration were Scotland's Presbyterians, persecuted by James II and VII in the 1680s (known as the 'Killing Time'). But Jacobitism had less support as the century wore on among Scots who profited from the Union and the imperial opportunities it brought. Glasgow's 'Tobacco

Lords', for example, made fortunes on the North American trade opened by the Union.

The year 1745–6 was a turning point for Scotland. The failed Jacobite invasion of England – the events forming the background of *Waverley* – drew massive retaliation. 'Bonnie Prince Charlie', grandson of James II and VII, took a bold gamble and almost won. France, at war with Britain (as it was for much of the century), took a renewed interest in the Stuarts and bankrolled an invasion attempt in 1744, foiled when a spy leaked the plan to the British. In summer 1745 the impatient prince landed in Scotland's Outer Hebrides with a small group of support-ers, assembled an army of 2,500 men, and marched on Edinburgh. He scored a decisive victory at Prestonpans, south of the capital. This was due not just to the military might of the Highland clans, the Jacobite shock troops, but to the weakness of the Scottish government, many of whose forces were absent on the Continent. By the time Charles marched into England the government was on alert. Expected support in Northern England did not materialise; crucially, the French were a no-show. The invaders retreated to the Highlands, pursued by the Duke of Cumberland's 9,000-strong army, and suffered a crushing defeat at Culloden, outside Inverness, on 16 April 1746. Prince Charles went into hiding for several months, aided by loyal Highlanders, before escaping to the Continent (Devine 1999: 42–5).

The British government did not repeat the mistake it had made in 1715 of leniency to defeated rebels. The Highlands were put under large-scale military occupation. 'The clans had to be broken once and for all because only their fighting skills and loyalty to the Stuarts had brought Charles close to ultimate success' (Devine 1999: 45). Cumberland's troops burned and pillaged the countryside, confiscating the Highlanders' cattle, their main source of wealth. Subsequent meas-ures banned Highland dress, a symbol of clan militarism, and carrying weapons. The British government abolished heritable jurisdiction (land-owners' private courts) and confiscated landowning rebels' estates. A system of roads and bridges, begun after the 1715 rebellion but put on hold by Continental wars, was expanded to over 1,000 miles by 1767. Fort St George, east of Inverness, was built: 'the most formidable bastion artillery fortress in Europe and a permanent physical demon-stration of the Hanoverian government's absolute determination that the clans would never rise again to threaten the Protestant succession' (Devine 1999: 46).

Language

Part of the systematic destruction of Highland clan culture in the wake of 'the '45' was an intensified suppression of the Gaelic language. Scotland in 1745 was a trilingual nation. The Lowlands, the southern half of the country, spoke largely Scots, a separate language with its own longstanding history, vocabulary and pronunciation (not a debased 'dialect' of English).[7] Highlanders in the north and the outlying islands spoke Scottish Gaelic, a Celtic language introduced by early settlers from Ireland. Scotland's third language, of course, was English. But even in England, English was not yet standardised by the mid-eighteenth century. The drive to make this happen was just beginning, with important implications for Scotland and for our understanding of internal colonialism.

Gaelic Scotland and its inhabitants had long been stigmatised as foreign and inferior. The Scottish government sponsored efforts to stamp out the language as early as 1609. After 1707, with Scotland part of Great Britain, the issue was more pressing and the stakes higher: Jacobite sympathisers were disproportionately Gaelic speakers. Half the Scottish population consisted of Gaelic-speaking Highlanders, considered by Anglo-British authorities to be barbaric, intractable and in need of 'improvement'. This was undertaken by the Society in Scotland for the Propagation of Christian Knowledge (SSPCK), chartered by Queen Anne in 1709. By 1715 the SSPCK had twenty-five schools, by 1795 (at its height), 325, with some 300,000 students (Sorensen 2000: 33). The SSPCK sponsored the creation of the first Scots Gaelic/English glossary in 1741 by Alasdair Mac Mhaighstir Alasdair (Alexander MacDonald), better known today as a Gaelic Jacobite poet.[8] As Janet Sorensen persuasively argues, MacDonald's work in spreading English literacy, intended by his employers to weaken Highland culture, actually helped foster a Gaelic national identity by standardising Gaelic as a written language (Sorensen 2000: 31). But language and literacy instruction also helped Highlanders leave the Highlands to seek their fortunes in the Lowlands or overseas, serving the empire.

Scots, the language of southern Scotland, is much closer to English than to Gaelic. It has a long history and a rich tradition of poetry going back to the Middle Ages. Many Scots speakers also spoke and wrote English, switching back and forth as convenient. The language of the British government and the wealthier, more populous part of the island, English was a key to advancement for upwardly mobile Scots. To participate fully in the unified nation, Scottish people needed to use a language that was 'acceptable to the dominant partner in the political union. Their English had to be purged of what we would now call "markers of Scottish cultural difference," but were then known as "Scotticisms"' (Crawford 2000: 18). Scottish intellectuals like the poet James Beattie and the philosopher David Hume published lists of Scotticisms to help young people purge them from their speech and writing. In England, Scots faced widespread prejudice. Stereotyped as poor immigrants or vulgar strivers, they might prefer to keep their mouths shut rather than have their origins recognised.[9]

The idea of a standard language is one we now take for granted. But for those whose language is judged incorrect or unrefined, Standard English enforces a hierarchy of education and prestige. As a national and imperial language, it works to banish regional and class 'accents', marking these as inferior. In 1746, the year of the failed Jacobite uprising, Samuel Johnson began compiling his famous *Dictionary* (published in 1755). Johnson forcefully argued the need for language standardisation; he thought Gaelic should be eradicated and all Scots forced to speak English. But behind the process of labelling vocabulary, spelling or usage 'non-standard' lies a political struggle. By comparing individual subjects' language use with one version of a national language, 'the "standard" language also constitutes them as belonging to the nation on differing terms. These hierarchized terms construct certain members as "outsiders" and inferior' (Sorensen 2000: 67). In other words, 'vocabulary and syntax distinguished the refined and civilized from the vulgar and savage' (Smith 2005: vii).

Scottish Romantic authors were sensitive to the politics of language, switching linguistic registers in ways that interest postcolonial critics. Burns's Scots poetry builds on both Scots and English literary traditions. His sophisticated register-switching frames a Scottish popular voice like Tam o' Shanter's in a dialogic construction that both 'produces the language of the peasant and distances us from it'. The effect is to question the Romantic practice of reducing 'orality's ... elusive nature to the dimensions of cultural codification and collection' (Pittock 2008: 155). Walter Scott makes extensive use of Scots in his novels, staging Scotland as a multicultural nation. The Scots-speaking voices of minor characters in Hogg's *Justified Sinner* serve as a kind of chorus, contrasting with the follies and excesses not just of the sinner himself, but of his enlightened, metropolitan editor.

Orality and the Ossian Controversy

Language in its oral form, spoken or sung as folk tales or ballads, took on special significance for Scottish Romanticism. Eighteenth-century Scotland combined a highly literate population, due to its strong system of parish schools and flourishing universities, with a rich oral culture in Scots and Gaelic. The project of capturing oral heritage in written form garnered widespread interest among Romantic intellectuals. Collecting oral poetry served different purposes in different parts of the British Isles. For Scotland as an internally colonised nation, putting orality into print could be a form of cultural resistance to the dominance of the English language and imperial Britain. By evoking Scottish orality, antiquarians, novelists and poets, including Burns, Hogg and Scott, 'challenged political and aesthetic presumptions regarding the imagined superiority of the English language and the homogeneity of the British nation' (Davis and McLane 2007: 125, 128). For Britain's peripheries, including Wales and Ireland as well as Scotland, the oral poet or bard came to symbolise the role of literature in defining national identity as a response to British internal colonialism (Trumpener 1997: xiii).

The controversy surrounding Ossian, the ancient Celtic bard supposedly translated by James Macpherson in the 1760s, illustrates the stakes of such symbolism. The Ossian poems were hugely popular, not just in Britain but throughout Europe. Romantic novelists including Ann Radcliffe, Sydney Owenson and Walter Scott drew on Macpherson's image of Celtic Scotland, with its misty mountains, legendary heroes and melancholy singers. Napoleon commissioned paintings of Ossian's heroes, Goethe inserted bits into *The Sorrows of Young Werther*, and the Romantic critic Hazlitt ranked Ossian with Homer and Dante among the world's greatest poets (Stafford 1996: vi). The Ossian vogue stimulated tourism in the Highlands, where enraptured tourists recited the poems beside waterfalls or on mountaintops (Andrews 1989: 202). This was part of a reaction against urban sophistication and mounting consumerism in an increasingly prosperous Britain. Primitivism – a 'refusal to validate the contemporary social world' (Butler 1981: 16) – led educated Britons to search for a time or place that modern values had not yet penetrated (Stafford 2005: 416). Travel writing about primitive cultures, such as Cook's Tahitians, fed this urge. Scottish Enlightenment philosophers and historians joined Rousseau in pondering human society's remote origins, often contrasting them favourably with the modern world (Butler 1981: 23). This dovetailed with a classicism that admired the vigour and directness of early mankind: Homer (another bard) was an outstanding example (Stafford 2005: 417).

Such a primitivist poetics marked an important shift in literary aesthetics. Hugh Blair, Professor of Rhetoric and Belles Lettres at Edinburgh University from 1759 to 1783, writes in his *Critical Dissertation on the Poems of Ossian* that although the 'productions of uncultivated ages' may be 'unpolished', they have 'that enthusiasm, that vehemence and fire, which are the soul of poetry' (Macpherson 1996: 345). Blair's enthusiasm is fuelled by Scottish nationalism, celebrating a language and culture more ancient than anything in England. But locating Ossian's heroic Celtic culture in a distant past could also reassure English readers. Defeated and isolated, the blind bard was a safe symbol of a Highland culture no longer a threat to its southern neighbour. By 'lamenting the superseded', Macpherson's primitivism displayed 'the dominance of the [English] reader's own society' (Stafford 2005: 418).

James Macpherson was born in a Gaelic-speaking area of the Highlands in 1736. Nearby stood a British barracks, built in the 1720s as part of the imperial government's response to the 1715 Jacobite rebellion. As a boy Macpherson soaked up Scotland's Gaelic folk legacy. He was too young to fight in 1745, but his uncle, the clan chief Macpherson of Cluny, was 'out' and suffered the consequences when Cluny Castle was razed and the community terrorised by the victorious British. Cluny was in hiding for nine years. His nephew 'lived through scenes of appalling violence, and saw his home and family under ... constant threat as the imperial government carried out its harsh measures to wipe out the Highland way of life and pacify the region forever' (Stafford 1996: ix).

Entering the University of Aberdeen in 1752, Macpherson was immersed in a different side of eighteenth-century Scottish culture. The Scottish Enlightenment was in full swing. Macpherson's tutor, William Duncan, translated Caesar's *Commentaries*; Caesar's adversaries, 'the German tribes, with their strength, physical courage and austere lifestyle', appealed to Scottish intellectuals as an antidote to civilised refinement and luxury. It must have been eye-opening for the young Highlander to discover that intellectuals could admire a 'primitive' culture rather like the one in which he had grown up (Stafford 1996: x–xi). In 1759 Macpherson met an Edinburgh author, John Home, with a passionate interest in Scottish folklore. Home asked Macpherson to translate something and showed his work to other members of Scotland's literary elite, including Blair, who sponsored the publication of *Fragments of Ancient Poetry, Collected in the Highlands of Scotland,*

and Translated from the Galic or Erse Language (1760). Blair helped
sponsor a trip to the Highlands to collect further material (Trevor-Roper
2008: 91–6). The Scottish intelligentsia's enthusiasm for the project had
a nationalist edge; the young Macpherson had ambitions and smelled a
way to pursue them.[10]

Macpherson's style sharply distinguishes the Ossian poems from
other mid-eighteenth-century poetry. It is a poetic prose that emphasises its status as 'translation' with an inverted word order modelled
on that of Gaelic. Its 'paratactic breathlessness' – a lack of transitions
or smooth flow – telegraphs the ancientness of the material (quoted
in Stafford 2005: 419). We see these qualities in this passage from the
Fragments:

> By the side of a rock on a hill, beneath the aged trees, old Oscian sat on the
> moss; the last of the race of Fingal. Sightless are his aged eyes; his beard is
> waving in the wind. Dull through the leafless trees he heard the voice of the
> north. Sorrow revived in his soul; he began and lamented the dead.
>
> How hast thou fallen like an oak, with all thy branches round thee!
> Where is Fingal the king? where is Oscur my son? where are all my race?
> Alas! in the earth they lie. I feel their tombs with my hands. I hear the river
> below murmuring hoarsely over the stones. What dost thou, O river, to
> me? Thou bringest back the memory of the past.
>
> The race of Fingal stood on thy banks, like a wood in a fertile soil. Keen
> were their spears of steel. Hardy was he who dared to encounter their rage.
> (Macpherson 1996: 18)

The blind bard, lamenting his lost race of heroes in a melancholy natural
setting, is an apt symbol for a Scottish nation whose martial prowess
had been so recently shut down by its southern neighbour.

Suspicions as to whether Macpherson had translated the poems or
written them himself set off a literary feud. The issue is not as straightforward as it might seem: 'The poems which appeared as *The Works of
Ossian* are neither literal translations from an easily identifiable Gaelic
manuscript, nor a fantasy creation conjured up by James Macpherson'
(Stafford 2005: 419–20). He drew on genuine sources, collected in the
Highlands. His characters are established in Celtic legend, rooted in
the Gaelic culture that the Scottish Highlands and Islands shared with
Ireland. Since Macpherson's sources were largely oral, and many of his
informants aged, evidence of their authenticity was harder to get as time
passed. The London Highland Society carried out an eight-year investigation, publishing its results in 1805; its findings were inconclusive.
They could not find a single Gaelic text on which Macpherson's productions were obviously based, but they noted that much Ossianic poetry

was still in oral circulation. Fifty years earlier there would have been more (Stafford 2005: 420). The debate continues to this day.

At the crux of the controversy is the status of the oral. Macpherson's most strident detractor was Samuel Johnson, a man of the written word, who travelled to the Highlands and Islands in 1773 with his Scottish biographer, James Boswell, and in 1775 published *A Journey to the Western Islands of Scotland*. Johnson labels Gaelic, or 'Earse', 'the rude speech of a barbarous people, who had few thoughts to express, and were content, as they conceived grossly, to be grossly understood' (Johnson and Boswell 1984: 116). He scorns unwritten languages, in which few 'have opportunities of hearing a long composition often enough to learn it, or have inclination to repeat it so often as is necessary to retain it; and what is once forgotten is lost for ever' (Johnson and Boswell 1984: 117). With this attitude, rooted in beliefs about language and the progress of civilisation, Johnson had to label Macpherson a fraud. His judgement (along with other slurs on Scotland and Scots) drew indignation from north of the border. Johnson's linguistic imperialism is consistent with his interpretation of Scottish history: 'what the Romans did to other nations, was in a great degree done by Cromwell to the Scots; he civilized them by conquest, and introduced by useful violence the arts of peace' (Johnson and Boswell 1984: 51). Any civilisation Scotland possessed, in this view, was imposed from outside. Johnson's *Journey* all but ignores the intellectual ferment of Edinburgh and the other Scottish universities, focusing instead on Scotland's most 'primitive' areas.

Rather than label Macpherson a fraud in the absence of a written original, a postcolonial perspective lets us understand the Ossian poems as 'a sophisticated attempt to mediate between two apparently irreconcilable cultures' (Stafford 1996: viii). The translation Macpherson undertook was a cultural one: he transformed scattered pieces of Gaelic poetry, painstakingly collected from oral sources, into something 'suitable for displaying the genius of the Celts to an international audience' (Stafford 2005: 420). From this perspective he certainly succeeded. Macpherson was both a Highlander and a university-educated gentleman. As a Highlander, rooted in oral tradition, he was free to draw on this body of knowledge and generate his own variants, as oral storytellers had always done. As a university man, he wanted Scotland's early poetry to resemble the prestigious legacy of Homeric Greece, so he amalgamated the fragments and called them an epic (Stafford 1996: xv). In short, 'Macpherson's act of restoration may be more legitimate than it has sometimes seemed' (Stafford 2005: 422).

Critics disagree about the political valence of the Ossian poems.

Trumpener sees them as part of a bardic resistance to internal colonialism (Trumpener 1997: 8). In her view, antiquarian scholarship like
Macpherson's (and that of Burns, Hogg, Scott and others) challenges
imperialist assumptions that societies naturally develop toward the *telos*
of the metropolitan centre. Nationalist histories use oral traditions to
resist imperial pressure (Trumpener 1997: 29, 33). Leith Davis, on the
other hand, sees the poems' subversive character 'compromised by their
promotion of British hegemonic values'. Proposing a mythic Caledonia
as the cradle of an island-wide civilisation, Macpherson creates a
'homogenized nation that prefigures the homogenization he desires in
the present' (Davis 1998: 76). Macpherson's work made it attractive
for Lowlanders to identify with the Highlands as a symbol of national
pride. But although the reputed forgeries helped Highland, Lowland
and English readers find a common identity, their focus on a distant past
diverted attention from contemporary Gaelic culture 'at a time when, in
fact, there was a renaissance in Gaelic poetry, a rejuvenation of Gaelic
culture in the midst of political and economic changes' (Davis 1998: 83,
82).

Imagination

The Anglocentric version of Romanticism commonly taught to under-
graduates revolves around the Romantic imagination. Its 'fetishization
of creative subjectivity' (we might call it an ' "inner processes of the interior mind" model of Romanticism') elevates poetry, in particular five or
six canonical poets (Pittock 2008: 4, 5). This dimension of Romantic literature is clearly available and important, but it is not all there is. Recent
scholarship questions the hierarchy of genres with poetry on top as it
re-maps Romanticism with increased attention to Britain's peripheries.
Scotland's spectrum of languages and legacy of oral poetry, music and
tales forged a distinctively Scottish Romanticism. Cairns Craig argues,
in an important essay (Craig 2004), that the imagination itself looks
different to Scottish Romanticism. Samuel Taylor Coleridge is commonly considered the great theorist of the Romantic imagination. His
Biographia Literaria presents an imagination that is organic, resisting
the mechanical or mechanistic models of mind current in Enlightenment
thought and mechanistic aspects of the social and technological developments leading towards the Industrial Revolution. Coleridge's Romantic
aesthetics drew on German Idealist philosophy, developing these ideas
partly by disputing the theories of the English philosopher David
Hartley. But behind Coleridge's quarrel with Hartley lies a 'repressed

... effort to marginalize the influence of the most significant British thinker of the eighteenth century' – the great Scottish empiricist David Hume (Craig 2004: 25).

The difference between Coleridge's and Hume's models of the imagination is as vast as the gulf between idealism and empiricism, or theism and atheism. For example, take the concept of the poetic symbol (important to scholars of Romanticism). Poetic symbols are sensory stand-ins for ideas, which for Coleridge (as for Plato) are more real than anything else. Ideas are 'transcendental truths of eternity', underwritten by the divine truth of Christ Himself (Craig 2004: 31, 32). For Coleridge, the imagination is our human link between the realm of the senses and that of ideas. For Hume, in contrast, the imagination has no such metaphysical foundation. It is nonetheless our only means of discovering a stable world. In reality, alas, the world is a fiction – one that inevitably falls apart under scrutiny. Luckily, most people, in ordinary life, are not paying very close attention.

Hume's empiricist aesthetics behaves very differently from Coleridge's idealist aesthetics. In a Humean model, aesthetic experience arises from the way the mind works: its structure, its tendencies, its storehouse of associations built up from experience. Aesthetic experience is 'the experience of a profound sense of contingency, of the random and the accidental, of the fragility by which we are bound to the object of our aesthetic contemplation'. But it is not merely subjective: we can all access a common fund of memories. These are what unites that elusive entity, a nation (Craig 2004: 33, 34). The national dimension of Romanticism is one important thing missing from its Anglocentric version, even though many political theorists believe modern nationality came into being during the Romantic era (Pittock 2008: 6). The 'fragility of those communal memories' occasions 'the anguish that afflicts Romantic nationalisms in their desperate effort to maintain the associative power of their common culture'. The pathos of Scott's last minstrel or Macpherson's blind bard dramatises this condition (Craig 2004: 34).

All the factors I have discussed – history, language, orality and theories of the imagination – point toward a chronology for Scottish Romanticism that is markedly different from the standard timeline of Anglocentric literary history, with 'rhythms of continuity, change, and disjunction quite different from the English model to which it has been subordinated' (Duncan et al. 2004: 3). Such a chronology begins well before 1798 (*Lyrical Ballads*) or even 1789 (the French Revolution). As parameters, Pittock suggests 'Enlightenment arguments over the nature of the imagination', the 'individuated, subject-driven language of sensibility' and

Primitivism's heroic elevation of a safely distant past (Pittock 2008: 29). These put us around the mid-eighteenth century: for example, 1761, the year Macpherson published his first volume of Ossian poems. Rather than posit 'Enlightenment' and 'Romantic' cultural moments as sequential, we should understand them as, in Scotland, 'symbiotically intertwined' (Craig 2004: 21). A postcolonial perspective understands Scotland as 'part of a larger political, economic, and cultural geography, encompassing not only "Britain" . . . but Europe, North America, and an expanding world-horizon of colonized and dominated territories' (Duncan et al. 2004: 10). Far from backward-looking and trapped in nostalgia, Scottish Romanticism is vitally engaged with the modern conditions of cultural hybridity, colonial domination and commodified textuality.

Robert Burns

Burns, son of an Ayrshire tenant farmer, drew condescension from his elite contemporaries. The novelist Henry Mackenzie called him a 'Heaven-taught ploughman', suggesting his poetic achievement came from naïve inspiration, not wide reading and skilful craftsmanship (McGuirk 1985: 63). Since his death, distorting assumptions have clouded Burns's legacy. It is no surprise that the conservative reaction during and after the French wars made Burns a mascot for a contented Scottish peasantry. His 'Cotter's Saturday Night', a portrait of a happy farming family, was trotted out as a 'post-Burkean account of a peasant world of piety, humility and, hence, hierarchical loyalty' (Noble and Hogg 2001: lxiii). Such an image was in tune with the times, but also convenient for British internal colonialism: the Union's junior partner as a nation of contented peasants.

The bard lives on worldwide, after a fashion, celebrated each January at Burns Suppers rife with tartan, haggis, lovely lyrics and sentimental toasts (including two in 2012 in Eugene, Oregon). Burns clubs and societies flourish. His works are sold in train stations and airports and translated into over fifty languages, including a Chinese version published in 2005 to help increase whisky exports (Pittock 2008: 145; McGinn 2011). But Burns is less visible in recent literary histories of Romanticism. As recently as the mid-twentieth century he was counted among the major Romantics, but by the 1960s his critical stock began to decline. By 2000 'articles on Burns had sunk to one-sixth of those devoted to Shelley, the least popular of the "Big Six"' (Pittock 2008: 145). What is going on?

Whatever the cause, this movement replicates Wordsworth's strategic decision to render the 'language of men' as a homogeneous English unmarked by regional difference. The language of men could not be Cumbrian dialect, despite the local ambience of so many of Wordsworth's poems. Part of his ambitious project – an imperial one in this sense – involved overwriting local and national differences 'to create an assimilated nation of participants in the British cultural realm' (Davis 1998: 107). A homogenised language, purified of local markers, is best for unifying a nation (and an empire) under the banner of poetry.[11] Burns's increasing marginalisation by mainstream literary history reflects the persistence (or resurgence) of Anglocentric attitudes valuing 'pure' English as supposedly universal and inclusive. We should replace this, critics like Pittock suggest, with a more inclusive Four Nations Romanticism valuing literature written in all the languages of the British Isles, including Burns's Scots as well as Scots Gaelic, Irish Gaelic and Welsh.

Burns wrote in Scots, Standard English and a spectrum of variations in between that he devised for specific poetic purposes. If students of literature in English can wade through Chaucer's Middle English and consult footnotes on Shakespeare's puns, they should be able to appreciate Burns's language (though North Americans may need audiotapes to follow the pronunciation). Postcolonial criticism has aided recent efforts to retrieve Burns from neglect, sentimental misreading or ignorant condemnation. In particular, the 2001 publication of *The Canongate Burns*, with extensive introduction and critical commentary on individual poems, debunks such misappropriation. Burns was a radical, endangering his government post with the Excise through (justifiable) suspicion of Jacobinism (Mackay 1992: 521–3). He was a Scottish nationalist, deploring the Union in 'Fareweel to a' our Scottish Fame':

> What force or guile could not subdue
> Thro' many warlike ages,
> Is wrought now by a coward few
> For hireling traitors' wages.

(ll. 9–12)

Burns was a vicious satirist and a frank, vulgar realist when he wanted to be, as well as an extraordinarily gifted Romantic lyric poet.

Postcolonial studies afford new insight into one of Burns's most famous poems, 'Tam o' Shanter' (1793). Burns wrote it in response to a request by the English antiquary Francis Grose for ghost stories about Alloway Kirk, a picturesque local ruin, to put in a book of Scottish antiquities (Burns 2001: 261). (Burns too was a collector, contributing songs – original as well as traditional – to George Thomson's *Select Collection of Original Scottish Airs* and James Johnson's *Scots Musical Museum*). Grose wanted 'a popular tale that would represent the Scottish nation as a Gothic, superstitious Other for English readers' (Davis 1998: 120). Burns complied, but in a way that good-humouredly calls the whole enterprise into question. If the antiquarian commits cultural colonisation – 'ideological appropriation of the lived life of the Scottish people into the collective ordering of antiquarianism' – then 'Tam o' Shanter' turns a satirical gaze back on the coloniser, challenging 'Anglocentric notions of value' in this 'great poem of Romantic resistance to antiquarian collection', as Pittock argues (2008: 155, 159, 163).[12]

Burns wrote a humorous poem about Grose, 'An Address to the People of Scotland': 'A child's amang you takin notes,/ And, faith, he'll prent it' (ll. 5–6). The poet's affectionate caricature of his fat friend piles up clichés about haunted Scotland:

> Ilk ghaist that haunts auld ha' or chamer,
> Ye gipsy-gang that deal in glamour,
> And you, deep-read in hell's black grammar,
>   Warlocks and witches;
> Ye'll quake at his conjuring hammer,
>   Ye midnight bitches.
>
> (ll. 19–24)

'Glamour' is here used in its original sense of 'magic, enchantment, spell'. We might say that 'Tam o' Shanter' represents the revenge of Scotland's 'midnight bitches' on metropolitan readers who gawk at their revels or call them picturesque.

If 'Tam o' Shanter' is about antiquarian collecting, it is more fundamentally about pleasure and its relation to respectable morality, 'the Kirk's and the state's prescription of self-denying, prudent "virtue" as the peculiar duty of the rural poor' (McGuirk 2007: 174). This attitude is embodied by the voice of the poem's narrator. The poem mocks such a mindset, most obtrusively in the tale's tacked-on moral (ll. 221–6). But it also:

> comments on the process of imagining a community, either one's own or another, because it represents the Scottish nation not as a holistic community but as a split image. Both the familiar, comfortable world of the pub and the unsettling satanic community constitute a picture of Scotland . . . Rather than attempting to delineate the nation with one representation, Burns offers a picture of an imagined community ghosted by its *unheim-*

lich Other. In doing so, he works against the attempt to write a cohesive national identity.[13]

What ties the poem's split image of Scotland together is illicit pleasure, defying official morality. Tam and the nubile witch Nannie (in her 'Cutty Sark', or too-short shift) are kindred spirits. The poem is a narrative of boundary-crossing from one magical place of pleasure to another. Tam starts out in his cosy local pub, getting drunk with his 'drouthy [thirsty] neebors', in particular his best buddy, Souter [Cobbler] Johnny. He'll eventually have to ride home past the old church, though he prefers not to think about this for the moment. Burns's narrator introduces Tam from the point of view of his wife, Kate, who spitefully prophesies that her 'blethering, blustering, drunken blellum [idle talker]' of a husband will end up 'catch'd wi' warlocks in the mirk/ By Alloway's auld, haunted kirk' (ll. 19–20, 31–2). She is proved wrong when Tam survives a hair-raising ride through the stormy night and an encounter with a witches' Sabbath, including the Devil himself.

The narrator sets up Tam's wild ride by switching from Scots to English – indeed, to an elevated poetic diction – in lines 59–67. Diction is at the heart of Burns's poetic achievement here and elsewhere in his *oeuvre*. A bilingual, bicultural poet, Burns makes full and brilliant use of the wide spectrum of language available to him. In Pittock's words, his 'control of register and its implications is not only double, but polyglossic' (Pittock 2008: 155). 'Register' is defined as 'variety or level of usage, especially as determined by social context and characterized by the range of vocabulary, pronunciation, syntax, etc. used by a speaker or writer in particular circumstances' (*OED*). 'Polyglossia' refers to the character of language embodied in particular instances of its use, each one carrying a particular 'socio-linguistic point of view' that ties it to not just a nation but a class, a locality, a particular milieu. Mikhail Bakhtin has suggested that all language registers an ongoing struggle among such localised perspectives.[14] In 'Tam o' Shanter', Burns's diction shifts back and forth along a spectrum ranging from pure standard English to broad Ayrshire Scots, with synthetic varieties of 'light Scots' in between. This register-shifting, or code-switching, helps develop the relationship between Burns's unstable narrator and the wayward Tam.

Robert Crawford calls this linguistic synthesis 'British' because it brings together language from the whole island of Britain. Using in poetry 'the mixed speech which is the language of Scotland' was not new in 1793. The Scottish poet Allan Ramsay, a contemporary of Pope, championed the union of the two tongues. Drawing on both English and Scots 'makes our Tongue by far the completest', he writes (quoted in Crawford 2000: 105). A bilingual poet has richer resources and more options than a monolingual one. This is not the same idea of Britishness championed by Burns's elite contemporaries, Edinburgh literati such as Hugh Blair and Adam Smith. Politically, Burns questioned the fairness of the Union (as had earlier Scottish writers such as Tobias Smollett).

> Yet if we say Burns is a British poet, in the sense that he fully utilized the spectrum of British language, then it is clear that he did this precisely because he was a Scottish writer. His deployment of a mixture of Scots and English is fully consonant with the characteristic delight of his imagination in combining high and low, little and large. It represents a mingling of the low, dominated Scots language with the high, dominant language of 'proper English'. (Crawford 2000: 106)

We see this in famous Burns lyrics such as 'To a Mouse' and 'To a Louse'. Burns's is a resistant Britishness, pitted against the homogenising drive represented by his contemporary Wordsworth. In 'Tam o' Shanter', the use of Scots resists Grose's antiquarian project of rendering what Pittock calls 'the hidden old Scotland' accessible to metropolitan connoisseurs – drawing a 'deliberate if partial veil over the tale' for readers not fluent in Scots (Pittock 2008: 162, 156).

Lines 59–67, with their abrupt switch to standard educated English, throw a wet blanket on Tam's 'glorious' drunken mood (l. 57), signalling his eviction from the cosy pub into the harsh realm of reality and respectability:

But pleasures are like poppies spread,
You seize the flower, the bloom is shed;
Or like the snow falls in the river,
A moment white – then melts for ever;
Or like the borealis race,
That flit ere you can point their place;
Or like the rainbow's lovely form
Evanishing amid the storm.

(ll. 59–67)

The stack of similes, comparing pleasure to flowers, snowflakes, butterflies and a rainbow, is incongruous in more ways than one. Their elegant evanescence contrasts with the earthiness of the main storyline. Playing to metropolitan readers' taste, they do not fit the labouring-class Scottish milieu; their inappropriateness subtly ridicules anyone tone-deaf enough to think they do. Pittock reads these lines as an attempt by the narrator, an outsider, to control the language of representation – an attempt that manifestly fails (Pittock 2008: 158). It is cut short by a homely Scots proverb and a simple, literal truth: 'Nae man can tether time or tide;/ The hour approaches *Tam* maun ride' (ll. 68–9).

The word 'hour' recurs three times in three lines, putting time and change in the foreground as Tam leaves the fireside for the stormy night. Burns's metaphor for the fateful hour fits the moment of boundary crossing: 'That hour, o' night's black arch the key-stane,/ That dreary hour he mounts his beast in' (ll. 70–1). Near the end of the poem, Tam encounters another arch and keystone as he crosses the bridge over the River Doon to safety (ll. 208, 211). The arch and keystone in line 70 mark the crossing from inside to outside, light to dark, but also the linguistic crossing from literary English to Scots and the incongruity it generates. Burns's prose introduction to 'Tam o' Shanter' (written in English for Grose's metropolitan readership) contains a related image: 'When he had reached the gate of the kirk-yard, he was surprised and entertained, through the ribs and arches of an old gothic window which still faces the highway, to see a dance of witches merrily footing it round their old sooty blackguard master' (Burns 2001: 262). The window is a picturesque frame for tasteful readers, setting off the grotesque scene inside. The image provides a visual equivalent in the introduction to the poem's linguistic code-switching after lines 59–67, when the delicate similes are overwhelmed by the power and directness of the Scots verse narration. Burns takes advantage of the wide linguistic spectrum available in his bicultural milieu to satirise the antiquarian collector's colonial relationship to his folkloric material.

The narration again switches to English to appeal to metropolitan taste with the sublimity of the stormy night: 'The lightnings flash from pole to pole;/ Near and more near the thunders roll' (ll. 99–100). At the church, aestheticised nature gives way to supernatural mischief. Burns describes the 'unco [strange, wondrous] sight' he sees there in Scots, the thickest of it reserved for the dance itself:

> They reel'd, they set, they cross'd, they cleekit,
> Till ilka carlin swat and reekit,
> And coost her duddies to the wark,
> And linket at it in her sark!

(ll. 149–52)[15]

The 'crossed alliterations and internal vowel rhymes in the second couplet', Thomas Crawford notes, 'suggest the figures of a Scottish country dance' (Crawford 1960: 232). Sexual excitement mounts in lines 181–90 as three male gazes, the narrator's, Tam's and the Devil's, watch Nannie dance in her scanty shift. The climax consists of Tam's spontaneous outburst – the only words he speaks in the entire poem – which alert the dancers to his presence and force him to run for his life: 'Weel done, Cutty-Sark!' (l. 191):

> Tam for one moment wrests the narrative from the narrator, returning it to oral immediacy; he is Tam the Chanter (the pipe part of the bagpipes), calling out his appreciation of the dance played before the Deil, likewise excited and piping on Scotland's native instrument ... [T]he residue of writing's record of orality is inflamed, if only for a moment, by the intervention of Tam's delighted and abandoned contact with the hidden world revealed by his ride. (Pittock 2008: 162)

The form the Devil takes is that of a 'tousie tyke [shaggy dog], black, grim, and large' (l. 121). Like other Romantic poets, Burns is of the Devil's party; this Devil clearly expresses 'the animal in us' (Crawford 1960: 230). The other animal with a key role to play is Tam's horse, Maggie, who carries him to safety, leaving her tail in Nannie's hand. Tam gets off scot free, as it were; the narrator's moralistic warning – 'Remember Tam o' Shanter's mare' (l. 226) – rings hollow. The poem gives us Burns's Scotland as 'an imagination of freedom, projected out of an unspoken milieu of oppression' (McGuirk 2007: 176). The 'Scottish peasant voice triumphs' (Pittock 2008: 163), but it is only one of the multiple voices and linguistic registers deftly navigated by Scotland's great Romantic poet.

Walter Scott's *Waverley*

The figure of Sir Walter Scott – antiquarian, poet, novelist – casts a commanding shadow over Scottish Romanticism. Prolific and hugely popular, Scott dominated Edinburgh's literary scene for decades. His series of anonymously published historical novels, launched in 1814 with *Waverley*, out-sold all other novels combined. They have been credited (erroneously) with inventing the historical novel and (more plausibly) with ushering the novel into the nineteenth century as 'a genre that realizes its modernity in a discursive reckoning with history, from which it seizes – to make its own – the narrative of modernization'.[16] Robert Crawford reads *Waverley, or, 'Tis Sixty Years Since* as a 'multicultural novel', mediating Scotland's cultures for English readers with the aim of strengthening the Union (Crawford 2000: 130, 123). Saree Makdisi views it less charitably as an imaginative 'colonization of a Highland past', helping to invent 'a new Highland reality' (Makdisi 1998: 71). The novel's fictional events surround the decisive defeat of Scottish Jacobitism.[17] Published the year Britain finally won the war with Napoleonic France, *Waverley* revisits the 1745 rising as a turning point in the modernisation of the Highlands, essential for the nineteenth-century Empire to flourish (Mack 2006: 5). Scott represents the pre-modern culture of the Highlands as exotic, glamorous and doomed. Ian Duncan calls *Waverley* a modern historical romance, defining 'the condition of romance as modernity's vision of worlds it has superseded, charged with a magic of estrangement, peril and loss: a cultural uncanny' (Duncan 1992: 9).

Like Burns, Scott was bicultural, though from a different class. Son of a solicitor, he was born in Edinburgh, but spent parts of his childhood in the rural Scottish Borders. He was educated at Edinburgh University, followed his father into the law, and was later appointed Sheriff (judge) for the Scottish county of Selkirk. But he earned his reputation and wealth by writing: first a string of popular narrative poems, including *The Lay of the Last Minstrel* (1805) and *The Lady of the Lake* (1810), and after 1814 the anonymous *Waverley* novels (which he did not acknowledge as his until 1827). Scott was also an antiquarian and a collector of Scottish oral poetry, publishing in 1802–3 a three-volume set entitled *The Minstrelsy of the Scottish Border*. This interest in cultural preservation entered his fiction as well.

In the novel, a young English officer, Edward Waverley, stationed at a British military post in Scotland, takes a leave of absence to visit his uncle's Jacobite friend Baron Bradwardine at his Lowland manor, Tully-Veolan. From there he travels north into the Highlands right at the time (though he does not know it) when the 1745 rising is about to begin. He meets a Highland clan chief, Fergus Mac Ivor, committed to the rebellion, and his equally fanatical sister Flora, who together engineer the young Englishman's political seduction. Combining nefarious misrepresentation with an appeal to Waverley's romantic imagination, the two persuade him to switch sides and join Bonnie Prince Charlie's army. Plot twists rescue the naïve youth from the consequences of his treason so he can make peace with the British government and marry the sweet Scottish girl Rose Bradwardine, re-enacting the Union in domestic life. The historical novel as a genre turns on this 'key homology' between public and private: it 'identifies a collective process of social change with an individual process of psychological, sentimental, and moral development' as 'national history and bildungsroman mediate one another' (Duncan 2006: 175).

Waverley's journey north resembles both ethnographic fieldwork and tourism. Like the ethnographer, he (and with him the reader) starts as an outsider. His ignorance functions heuristically as those around him are forced to explain their culture and translate their language. Moving forward in space, Scott's protagonist seems to go back in time in a representational strategy characteristic of colonialist ethnography. The anthropologist Johannes Fabian calls this 'denial of coevalness': representing a 'primitive' society as a kind of throwback to an earlier stage of world history, stuck in a different temporal order from the one inhabited by the perceiver'.[18] Waverley's first impressions of Scotland suggest an underdeveloped region. In the Lowland village near Tully-Veolan, the 'houses seemed miserable in the extreme, especially to an eye accustomed to the smiling neatness of English cottages . . . on each side of a straggling kind of unpaved street . . . children, almost in a primitive state of nakedness, lay sprawling' (Scott 2007: 34). Scott's narrator interjects a tentative judgment: 'The whole scene was depressing, for it argued, at the first glance, at least a stagnation of industry, and perhaps of intellect' (Scott 2007: 35). But this is not the immutable stupidity of the truly primitive. There is potential here: 'It seemed . . . as if poverty, and indolence, its too frequent companion, were combining to depress the natural genius and acquired information of a hardy, intelligent, and reflecting peasantry' (Scott 2007: 36).

The novel's cultural mediation is inseparable from its historical setting 'sixty years since'. Waverley's impressions of Tully-Veolan and the rest of pre-modern Scotland constitute the 'before' picture of a set that is completed by the novel's 'Postscript, Which Should Have Been a Preface'. Here we get a snapshot of a modernised Scotland:

> There is no European nation which, within the course of half a century, or little more, has undergone so complete a change as this kingdom of Scotland. The effects of the insurrection of 1745, – the destruction of the patriarchal power of the Highland chiefs, and the abolition of the heritable jurisdictions of the Lowland nobility and barons, the total eradication of the Jacobite party, which, averse to intermingle with the English, or adopt their customs, long continued to pride themselves on maintaining ancient Scottish manners and customs, – commenced this innovation. The gradual influx of wealth, and extension of commerce, have since united to render the present people of Scotland a class of beings as different from their grandfathers, as the existing English are from those of Queen Elizabeth's time. (Scott 2007: 363)

Looking back from the standpoint of successful modernisation, Scott's narrator frames the rebels' violent defeat and its aftermath as necessary evils. Their brutality is minimised in the novel, whose hero manages to miss the bloody battle of Culloden. The narrator's satisfaction with the Union status quo is tempered by the nostalgia that marks Scott's representation of the proto-feudal societies of the Jacobite Lowlands, and especially the Highlands, throughout the novel.

The novel's work of cultural mediation is especially concerned with Scotland's language cultures. Waverley first enters the Highlands with a Gaelic-speaking guide, Fergus's clansman Evan Dhu Maccombich.[19] '[Y]ou never saw such a place in your life, nor ever will, unless you go with me or the like of me', Evan proclaims (Scott 2007: 80). They climb a steep pass 'up a chasm between two tremendous rocks' beside a precipice. Through a 'narrow glen' they reach 'a black bog, of tremendous extent, full of large pit-holes, which they traversed with great difficulty and some danger, by some tracks which no one but a Highlander could have followed' (Scott 2007: 81, 82). The sublime, scary terrain makes a fit setting for the linguistic incomprehension that ensues when the English-speaking Evan Dhu leaves Waverley in the care of another Highlander with a battleaxe and 'very little English'. Scott renders this man's speech as a kind of pidgin that Crawford calls 'translatorese' (Crawford 2000: 127): '"Ta cove was a tree, four mile; but as Duinhé-wassal was a wee taiglit, Donald could, tat is, might – would – should send ta curragh"' (Scott 2007: 83). The effect is an 'intelligible foreignness' (Buzard 1995: 41). 'This conveyed no information. The *curragh* which was promised might be a man, a horse, a cart, or a chaise' (Scott 2007: 83). It turns out to be a boat, which carries them to 'The Hold of a Highland Robber' (which is the title of the next chapter). Unfamiliar landscape and unintelligible language convey the pre-modern Highlands to the English reader with an aura of romance.

Often cited as the epitome of this romance is the scene where the attractive Flora Mac Ivor takes Waverley to one of her 'favourite haunts', a sublime waterfall. She sings him a song she has translated from the Gaelic of 'the family *bhairdh* [bard]' (Scott 2007: 112, 105):

> I have given you the trouble of walking to this spot, Captain Waverley, both because I thought the scenery would interest you, and because a Highland song would suffer still more from my imperfect translation, were I to produce it without its own wild and appropriate accompaniments. To speak in the poetic language of my country, the seat of the Celtic Muse is in the mist of the secret and solitary hill, and her voice in the murmur of the mountain stream. He who woos her must love the barren rock more than the fertile valley, and the solitude of the desert better than the festivity of the hall. (Scott 2007: 114)

This elaborate sequence combines 'the language of Ossian, early tourism, and theorists of the picturesque to create what might be termed a "union landscape"': an aestheticised rendering of the Celtic North in terms accessible and attractive to the English readers for whom the novel mediates this 'earlier unfamiliar world' (Pittock 2008: 192–3). For David Blair, the sequence exemplifies Scott's creation of an imaginary, non-specific space: a part of Scotland that

> can function ideologically as a hothouse of Fergus's and Flora's Jacobitical rejection of His Majesty and all he stands for . . . Flora's fierce Jacobitism and Edward's dreamy Romanticism are linked as forms of delusive narrative and delusive self-imaging, permitted by the way in which the space in which they are nurtured lies beyond the reach of [imperial] cartography. (Blair 2006: 97)

The waterfall is a kind of bower, a 'generative centre of the voice and figures of romance, tended by a female genius'. But it is also a clever stage for political seduction, and Flora's song 'a Jacobite call to arms', though Waverley ignores its political content. This scene captures the relationship between the novel's two modes of romance and history, 'their fateful collapse into one another' (Duncan 1992: 81–3). Waverley escapes the implosion unscathed as his author manoeuvres him through the minefield of the rebellion back to the safety of private life. Scott's adroit handling of setting and genre glamorises this chapter of Scotland's history of internal colonialism while justifying its outcome from the vantage of six decades on.

Scott handles the representation of place very differently when he gets to the Jacobite army's occupation of Scotland's capital. By describing the army's encampment from the spatial perspective of an 1814 map of Edinburgh, Makdisi argues, the novel manages to make it seem 'as though a Highland host were actually descending on the Edinburgh of Scott's own time . . . as the ghostly apparitions of the "primitive" existence of the past'. The army, in particular, 'represents the irruption of the past into the present' (Makdisi 1998: 90). Poorly armed Highland peasants have descended on the city:

> Here was a pole-axe, there a sword without a scabbard; here a gun without a lock, there a scythe set straight upon a pole; and some had only their dirks, and bludgeons or stakes pulled out of hedges. The grim, uncombed and wild appearance of these men . . . created surprise in the Lowlands, but it also created terror. So little was the condition of the Highlands known at that late period, that the character and appearance of their population, while thus sallying forth as military adventurers, conveyed to the

> south-country Lowlanders as much surprise as if an invasion of African Negroes or Esquimaux Indians had issued forth from the northern mountains of their own native country. (Scott 2007: 228–9)

Comparing the Highlanders to exotic colonised peoples overseas underscores the idea that societies from different stages of world history are confronting each other in present-day Scotland. In the wake of the French Revolution an armed peasantry held another kind of terror for genteel readers, despite the feudal overtones of Scott's description of the Jacobite leaders. The gritty detail with which he describes these Highland 'Helots' (Scott 2007: 228) lends an additional urgency to the need to contain or exorcise the rag-tag invasion.

By the end of the novel, Scott has accomplished just that. If,

> at the beginning of the novel, the border between the Lowlands and the Highlands defines a boundary between different spaces and times, this border is afterwards set in motion, like a shoreline during the sweep of the tide. By the end of the novel, the borderline has been pushed back out of sight. (Makdisi 1998: 92)

Even Tully-Veolan, the nest of Lowland Jacobites, is dramatically cleansed. Laid waste by British troops and confiscated by the government as the penalty of its owner's treason, the estate is then bought by the English officer Colonel Talbot, whose life Waverley has saved in battle. Talbot restores Tully-Veolan and its gardens and gives them back to the Baron, who is stripped of his feudal jurisdiction and made into plain Mr Bradwardine. '[S]ymbolically and politically cleansed by an almost ritualistic passage through the modern economic system of the market', the manor is now just one more 'grand country house in the English tradition' (Makdisi 1998: 93).

The process of imperial modernisation advanced by the 1745 uprising and its aftermath was by no means over in 1814, as Makdisi points out. Nor was its outcome as benign as Scott's postscript suggests. The Highland Clearances – the mass dispossession and displacement of much of northern Scotland's population in the late eighteenth and early nineteenth centuries – were still happening when Scott wrote. The most notorious of the Clearances took place between 1807 and 1821 on the Sutherland estate, when the Countess of Sutherland moved between 6,000 and 10,000 tenants from the interior to new settlements on the coast.[20] *Waverley* mentions none of this. The novel 'has virtually nothing to say about the Highlands of its own time', carrying out what Makdisi calls a 'textual repression of the Highland present', which Scott overwrites with his romanticised Highland past (Makdisi 2008: 71–2).

Waverley's romanticised Highlands made an influential contribution to the rather bizarre process by which the area – earlier looked down on as backward, even barbaric – was adopted as the symbolic identity of Scotland as a whole. Misty mountains and lovely lochs, tartans and bagpipes still telegraph Scotland's brand for the tourism industry (McCrone et al. 1995). Another factor in the 'tartanisation' of Scotland was the Highland regiments' contribution to the British Empire, starting as early as the Seven Years' War but especially visible in the Napoleonic Wars – partly an ironic result of the bleak conditions that drove so many Highlanders from their homes. All this had its apotheosis in 1822, when King George IV visited Edinburgh, an event stage-managed by Scott himself, including plentiful pageantry based on 'fake Highland regalia and . . . mythical customs and traditions'. His Majesty decked his ample form in a Highland outfit of kilt, plaid and bonnet, complete with custom-made pink satin underwear, for the occasion.[21]

Such a modern production of the past – an invented tradition – appears in the novel in the form of the painting that hangs in the dining room of the refurbished Tully-Veolan:

It was a large and animated painting, representing Fergus Mac-Ivor and Waverley in their Highland dress, the scene a wild, rocky and mountainous pass, down which the clan were descending in the back-ground. It was taken from a spirited sketch, drawn while they were in Edinburgh by a young man of high genius, and had been painted on a full length scale by an eminent London artist . . . [T]he ardent, fiery, and impetuous character of the unfortunate Chief of Glennaquoich was finely contrasted with the contemplative, fanciful, and enthusiastic expression of his happier friend. Beside this painting were hung the arms which Waverley had borne in the unfortunate civil war. The whole piece was generally admired. (Scott 2007: 361)

This aesthetic distillation of Highland romance commemorates a convicted traitor whose head hangs over the 'Scotch yate' of Carlisle castle. But the scene in the painting never took place. Makdisi and Duncan disagree about the painting's significance. For Makdisi, even though the novel does not advance the painting's version of the past as accurate, but emphasises its artificiality, the symbolic claim it stakes nonetheless '"becomes' real": that is, it takes on political, cultural, and symbolic significance on its own terms . . . The portrait's invention of the past is . . . an allegorical restatement of *Waverley*'s own production of the past.' The novel, in other words, does the same thing as the painting: 'it reifies and ossifies history, commodifying both' (Makdisi 1998: 97). Duncan, on the other hand, sees Scott's 'persistently ironical narration' as establishing a critical distance between this type of representation and the alert reader. 'Scott exposes the imperial production of this work of art, across the metropolitan sites of Edinburgh and London . . . Only if we are reading badly . . . can we acquiesce in its nostalgia, or mistake it for the narrative that frames it' (Duncan 2006: 175). Scott's storytelling lends itself to multiple modes or levels of reading. As middlebrow entertainment, it sold better than anything else in the Romantic era; as self-reflexive cultural commentary it rewards postcolonial critics' efforts.

The Surgeon's Daughter

Scott's novels, in particular *Waverley*, are central to debates about internal colonialism. He also wrote, though less often, about Scottish participation in the overseas empire. By the late eighteenth century Scots were pursuing opportunities in all areas of the empire, 'from commerce to administration, soldiering to medicine, colonial education to the expansion of emigrant settlements' (Devine 2003: xxvi). Scotland's status as a relatively poor peripheral region and the political upheavals of the seventeenth and eighteenth centuries contributed to massive emigration away from the region and resulted in a significant Scottish presence throughout the empire: in North America, the Caribbean, India, South Africa, Australia and New Zealand. The second Waverley novel, *Guy Mannering* (1815), features a military veteran, returned from India, whose colonial experience (and not just his fortune) helps him to interpret and navigate the world back home. A much later work, *The Surgeon's Daughter*, part of Scott's *Chronicles of the Canongate* (1827), asks what motivates young Scots to seek their fortunes abroad. In this novella three of them end up in India, and it ruins their lives.

Richard Middlemas is the illegitimate son of a mysterious, wealthy man (his wealth, we later learn, was gained in India), who leaves him to be raised by a village doctor or surgeon in the rural Lowlands. Menie Gray, the surgeon's daughter, falls in love with Middlemas instead of with Adam Hartley, her father's other apprentice and a worthier character, who is in love with her. Hartley reluctantly heads for India as a ship's surgeon. Middlemas, dissatisfied with his limited prospects in Scotland, is envious:

'happy dog – to India! . . . Oh, Delhi! Oh, Golconda! . . . India, where gold is won by steel; where a brave man cannot pitch his desire of fame and wealth so high, but that he may realize it, if he have fortune to his friend!' (Scott 2000: 198)

Middlemas's romantic sensibility succumbs to the rhetoric of a local youth, Tom Hillary, who has been in India and returned to recruit soldiers for the East India Company. Scott's narrator, Chrystal Croftangry, comments ironically in a 'multi-layered narrative voice which requires careful reading even as it carries the reader along its swift and exciting currents' (Wallace 2002: 314):

> [Hillary's] merits were thought the higher, when it was understood that he had served the honourable East India Company – that wonderful company of merchants, who may indeed, with the strictest propriety, be termed princes. It was about the middle of the eighteenth century, and the directors in Leadenhall Street were silently laying the foundation of that immense empire, which afterwards rose like an exhalation, and now astonishes Europe, as well as Asia, with its formidable extent, and stupendous strength. Britain had now begun to lend a wondering ear to the account of battles fought, and cities won, in the East; and was surprised by the return of individuals who had left their native country as adventurers, but now appeared surrounded by Oriental wealth and Oriental luxury, which dimmed even the splendour of the most wealthy of the British nobility. (Scott 2000: 201)

Attentive readers may catch Scott's allusion to the creation of Satan's headquarters, Pandemonium, in *Paradise Lost*: 'Anon out of the earth a fabric huge/ Rose like an exhalation' (quoted in Lamont 2003: 39). 'At the outset of an imperial narrative, we find expressions of doubt' (Lamont 2003: 39). Like *Waverley*, *The Surgeon's Daughter* is a historical novel, set in the 1770s, roughly half a century before its publication. The narrator looks back from the vantage point of Britain's achieved domination of the subcontinent. But the mood is not complacent. By the mid-eighteenth century the East India Company was on the defensive, accused of exploitation and bad behaviour. A few chapters later the narrator notes that that the Company is having trouble signing up soldiers: 'the military service of the King was preferred, and that of the Company could only procure the worst recruits, although their zealous agents scrupled not to employ the worst means' (Scott 2000: 219). Croftangry's earlier description of the directors as 'princes' is thus either naïve or satirical. Reports about India, the alert reader learns, need careful evaluation, which they may not get, depending on listeners' attitudes and desires (Wallace 2002: 314).

The Surgeon's Daughter bears interesting similarities to *Waverley*, as Lamont notes. Both are historical novels, set half a century or more before the time of their publication. Each follows a young man over a mountain pass to a more traditional society. Here the pass is in the southern Indian mountains; the society is Mysore, ruled in the 1770s, when the story takes place, by Haidar Ali. This Muslim sultan was a staunch opponent of British expansion, along with his son, Tipu Sultan. The first Anglo-Mysore War was fought to an uneasy truce in 1767–9; a second was to begin in 1780. (A third and fourth would be fought before Tipu's decisive defeat in 1799.) As in *Waverley*, 'those beyond the pass are about to erupt violently in protest at the threat to their own self-rule and identity' (Lamont 2003: 41). Both books are notably reticent about the crushing defeats each traditional society would suffer at the hands of the imperial power. The end of *The Surgeon's Daughter* sees the British in a position of material as well as moral defeat, with little inkling that Mysore's fortunes will turn after Haidar Ali's death in 1782 (Lamont 2003: 43).

The plot of the novel turns on Richard Middlemas's base betrayal of his fiancée and his country. Kicked out of the East India Company after a duel, he goes to work for a woman, the cross-dressing Begum Montreville, who sides with Mysore's rulers against the British. Middlemas makes a deal with Tipu Sultan, characterised as a woman-iser, who is attracted to the miniature portrait of herself that Menie has given Richard. He lures Menie to India, ostensibly to join him, really to turn her over Tipu for his harem or zenana. In the end Adam manages to save her; Haidar Ali – no fan of his son's behaviour – orders Richard crushed to death by an elephant:

> Curling his long trunk around the neck of the ill-fated European, the monster suddenly threw the wretch prostrate before him, and stamping his huge shapeless foot upon his breast, put an end at once to his life and to his crimes. (Scott 2000: 284)

This lurid denouement is in keeping with the extravagance of Richard's imperial dreams and the aura of hyperbole that has clung to India throughout the narrative. An

> insistence on the reality of imperial fantasies constructs the imperial identity; narrative creates character, which then generates lurid text, in a circular and degenerative motion. Richard Middlemas tries to replicate his father's dream of finding fame and fortune in India, but finds instead disgrace, disappointment, and the worst impulses of his own mind. (Wallace 2002: 322)

Nor do the surviving characters find happiness together. Hartley dies of a tropical disease and Menie lives out her life in Scotland as a boring spinster in this dystopian imperial yarn.

Hogg's *Confessions of a Justified Sinner*

If *Waverley* redacts Scotland's rebellious past to lay it to rest and assimilate Scotland to a unified Britain, James Hogg's *The Private Memoirs and Confessions of a Justified Sinner* (1824) is a very different kind of Scottish historical novel. Here '"union" is an impossible condition at every level of the representation' (Duncan 2006: 271). Hogg's novel is formally disjunctive, giving us two very different versions of the story of one Robert Wringhim. The unlucky protagonist is born in the late seventeenth century of an ill-assorted marriage that mirrors Scotland's theological and political schisms. A jovial Tory groom marries a fanatical Calvinist bride; 'completely at variance' over religion (Hogg 2010: 5), they partition their house to give each separate quarters – emblem of a divided nation (Duncan 2010: xxvi). Improbably, the couple produces two sons, opposites in every way. The first, George Colwan Junior, is his father's son, robust, likeable, fond of sports and parties. The second absorbs the extreme Calvinism of his mother and her spiritual mentor, the Revd Robert Wringhim, whose name he is given. This includes antinomianism, the belief that God's 'justified' elect are exempt from normal moral laws. As Wringhim Senior tells his namesake, 'no bypast transgression, nor any future act of [his] own, or of other men, could be instrumental in altering the decree' (Hogg 2010: 88). No one really believed this; in fact, the Presbyterian Church of Scotland considered antinomianism heresy.[22] But it drives the novel's bizarre central premise: a mysterious stranger called Gil-Martin manipulates Calvinist theology to convince the devout Wringhim to kill his own brother and mother. The tormented protagonist flees through the Scottish countryside in an increasingly chaotic, demented and despairing finale that culminates in a suicide pact.

Hogg frames the two narratives, Wringhim's and the editor's, with the grisly scenario of an opened grave. In it – along with a decaying corpse – the editor finds 'the very tract which I have here ventured to lay before the public' (Hogg 2010: 188). The found manuscript was a well-known convention of the Gothic novel, starting with Walpole's *Castle of Otranto* (1764). In the half-century to follow, scholars and antiquarians actually did find numerous manuscripts (Ferris 2008: 268). Romantic novels call attention to the relation between these retrieved texts and their modern editors. In *Confessions* – as in Maria Edgeworth's Irish tale *Castle Rackrent* (1800) – the editor takes the condescending position of an educated, enlightened observer in relation to the unenlightened author of the narrative he edits. But Hogg, like Edgeworth, subtly exposes his editor's blind spots until we end up with two unreliable narrators and no means to adjudicate between them. Wringhim's narrative and the editor's represent two strands of Scottish intellectual history, seventeenth-century Calvinism and eighteenth-century Enlightenment, which 'don't talk to one another' (Ferris 2008: 280). 'I do not understand it', the editor finally admits (Hogg 2010: 188). The Scottish past remains alien and inassimilable, making *Confessions* one of a number of Romantic-era narratives that question the novel's capacity to convey individuals' histories across space and time.[23]

But Hogg's grave-robbing scenario also literalises 'the central metaphor of modern antiquarian romance revival: the recovery of "remains", "reliques", or "fragments" of a departed organic culture' (Duncan 2007: 285). Such antiquarian revival, central to Romantic ideas of national culture, here conspicuously fails to 'replenish the ruined imaginative life of modernity'. Instead it is subjected to a 'grisly burlesque' (Duncan 2007: 213), with the grave robbers snipping off bits of the corpse's clothes to give to acquaintances as 'natural curiosities' (Hogg 2010: 182). Douglas Mack reads Hogg's exhumation as in part a response to his sometime friend and patron Scott, whose use of Scottish history and culture as literary material could look like the same kind of cultural souvenir-hunting pursued by Hogg's editor (Mack 2006: 83). The fictional editor is connected to *Blackwood's Edinburgh Magazine* and one of its contributors, John Gibson Lockhart, Scott's son-in-law, who turns up as a character to accompany the editor to the grave. They first hunt up one James Hogg, from whose letter to *Blackwood's*, reprinted as part of the novel, the editor supposedly found out about the grave. Hogg's cameo appearance in his anonymously published novel has him gruffly declining to guide the city visitors to the grave, located in his home district of Altrive. The Ettrick Shepherd, as he was known, has better things to do than 'ganging to houk up hunder-year-auld banes' (Hogg 2010: 183). Scholars read this interaction as 'a riposte to some of the metropolitan condescensions of *Blackwood's*', with whose editors Hogg had a somewhat troubled relationship (Garside 2001: xli).

This tongue-in-cheek scene opens a window on a central fault line of class and geography in Scottish Romanticism. Like Burns, Hogg came from the labouring class, son of a tenant farmer in the Scottish Borders. He worked long years as a shepherd before turning to literature as a profession. Hogg was also rooted in Scottish folk tradition; his mother, a shepherd's daughter, was famous in her region as the last person to converse with the fairies. She had 'her mind stored with tales and songs of spectres, ghosts, fairies, brownies, voices, &c'. Hogg first met Scott on one of the latter's collecting expeditions in 1802 when he came to the Hoggs' cottage to hear Mrs Hogg chant a ballad (Garside 2001: xiii, xvii). Hogg had an intimate personal relationship to the oral folk tradition that came to the city-born Scott in a more mediated, literary manner.

Orality, folk tradition, and subaltern voices preside over the breakdown of both the Scottish intellectual traditions represented by the novel's two versions of Wringhim's story. Soon after the editor narrates the suspicious death of George Colwan Junior, his voice gives way to that of Bell Calvert, an Edinburgh prostitute who has witnessed the night's events. Bell swears she saw young Wringhim and his shape-shifting companion kill the young laird. 'We have nothing on earth but our senses to depend on: if these deceive us, what are we to do?' she asks (Hogg 2010: 62). But her senses testify to events inexplicable by logic and science. This is one of the ways in which Hogg's novel tracks the fall of Humean empiricism or scepticism 'into a bottomless irony', with Wringhim's fanaticism as its 'monstrous double' (Duncan 2007: 251). Both the Wringhims' Presbyterian sect and the editor's enlightened metropolitan circle are estranged, Duncan argues, from the 'customary culture of naturalized belief' described by the moderate Presbyterian minister Blanchard, who becomes the first victim of Wringhim and Gil-Martin's killing spree (Duncan 2007: 252). The novel shows us this culture, and the Scottish rural society where it has its roots, under destructive pressure from the metropolitan cultures of internal colonialism.

Wringhim's mental state deteriorates as people accuse him of terrible deeds that he cannot remember, 'acts of cruelty, injustice, defamation, and deceit' (Hogg 2010: 145). 'I was a being incomprehensible to myself', he writes despairingly. His servant, Samuel Scrape, an 'honest blunt fellow' and very talkative, provides Wringhim – and the reader – with folk wisdom: 'od saif us, sir, do you ken what the auld wives of the clachan say about you? . . . they say the deil's often seen gaun sidie for sidie w'ye' (Hogg 2010: 145–6). Scrape passes on a story told by an old wife, Lucky Shaw, about the town of Auchtermuchty and the fanatics who live there. As the townspeople enthusiastically welcome a new preacher, the old 'cunning man' Robin Ruthven hears some 'corbie craws' talking about their plan to 'gull the saints of Auchtermuchty'. He sneaks into the revival, yanks up the preacher's gown, 'and behold, there was a pair o' cloven feet!' (Hogg 2010: 149–51). The folk tale gives Wringhim 'a view of my own state'. Not that he suddenly realises his friend is the devil, but he is compelled to judge his own deeds by the golden rule, the old wife's guide to detecting the cloven foot: the gospel principle of 'do as you would be done by'. None of Wringhim's actions, of course, can pass this test (Hogg 2010: 152).

Finally, though, folk wisdom is not enough to rescue the sinner from the abyss of solitude and self-doubt. 'The suicide's grave swallows author and reader as well as narrator and editor', Duncan concludes. Collecting, cataloguing and editing the artefacts of oral culture, turning them into text, Romantic intellectuals are saving and losing them at the same time:

> [T]extuality, in Hogg's novel, marks a lethal alienation from common life in its original condition of a traditional community, which, as the medium of natural belief, cannot be recovered in the commodity form of a fiction. For Hogg, as for ourselves, there is no access to that lost world except through another text. (Duncan 2007: 286)

Wringhim's lifetime coincides with key events in Scottish national history: the 'Glorious Revolution' of 1688–9, which pushed the last Stuart off of the English throne, and the 1707 Union with England. As does Salman Rushdie in *Midnight's Children*, *Confessions* 'synchronises its protagonist's story with the founding of the modern state – meaning, in this case, not the birth but the demise of an independent nation' (Duncan 2010: xxv). Hogg's psychological Gothic renders Scotland's modernisation by internal colonialism through the disintegration of the protagonist's mind. The rough-hewn voices of Samuel Scrape, Lucky Shaw and the fictional James Hogg form a kind of Greek chorus, performing 'a shrewd resistance to authority in the form of a resistance of Scots to English' (Duncan 2010: xxiii), but incapable of halting Wringhim's lethal decline.

Thomas Pringle

We met Thomas Pringle in Chapter 2 as the editor of Mary Prince's slave autobiography and Secretary of the London Anti-Slavery Society. Before that, though, Pringle and his family were part of the Scottish colonial diaspora, helping Britain colonise South Africa. Born on a Scottish farm, Pringle attended Edinburgh University and began a literary career that stalled during an economic recession. Other family members had dispersed: one brother was working in England, another in America. In 1819 the British government advertised for colonists for South Africa's Eastern Cape. Pringle and his party were chosen among 40,000 applicants, partly thanks to a recommendation from Sir Walter Scott, to whom Pringle later dedicated his *Poems Illustrative of South Africa*

(1834).[24] After helping start the family settlement, nostalgically called Glen-Lynden, Pringle took up a post (also secured with Scott's help) at the new government library in Cape Town. But his activities as a journalist and his liberal politics got him in trouble with the Tory governor, Lord Charles Somerset, and he returned to London in 1826.

Pringle's South African poems apply Romantic forms and preoccupations to South African material. One way they work through the settler's relationship to an unfamiliar place is with landscape description. Pringle's *Narrative of a Residence in South Africa* (1835) claims an advantage for Scottish settlers:

> the sublimely stern aspect of the country, so different from the rich tameness of ordinary English scenery, seemed to strike many of the *Southron* [English] with a degree of awe approaching to consternation. The Scotch, on the contrary, as the stirring recollections of their native land were vividly called up by the rugged peaks and shaggy declivities of this wild coast, were strongly affected, like all true mountaineers on such occasions. (Pringle 1966: 7)

His poem 'Evening Rambles' performs a 'metonymic displacement of one landscape into another', as David Bunn argues, finding reminders of Scotland in a South African scene (Bunn 1994: 139):

> The sultry summer-noon is past;
> And mellow Evening comes at last,
> With a low and languid breeze
> Fanning the mimosa trees,
> That cluster o'er the yellow vale,
> And oft perfume the panting gale
> With fragrance faint: it seems to tell
> Of primrose-tufts in Scottish dell,
> Peeping forth in the tender spring
> When the blithe lark begins to sing.
>
> (ll. 1–10)

The 'mellow' evening light lets the colonist narrator blur the distinction between home and colony, positing a 'transitional landscape' that manages to combine the two (Bunn 1994: 139). The effect is unstable and transitory, though, leaving the speaker to confront the full unfamiliarity of his surroundings:

> But soon, amidst our Lybian vale,
> Such soothing recollections fail;
> Soon we raise the eye to range
> O'er prospects wild, grotesque, and strange.
>
> (ll. 11–14)

One thing that helps the speaker come to terms with this strangeness is the unimpeded movement of the eye over the landscape, familiar from eighteenth-century landscape poetry like that of Thomson (another Scot). Pringle combines seeing with naming, inserting Dutch vernacular designations into his English text: 'There the spekbom spreads its bowers/ Of light-green leaves and lilac flowers' (ll. 25–6) ('spekbom' literally means 'bacon tree'). By the end of the descriptive sequence he has achieved 'a powerful image of synthetic reverie ... a Wordsworthian flash of sympathy between self and landscape' (Bunn 1994: 140): 'With the deep green verdure blending/ In the stream of light descending' (ll. 33–4). The colonist's Romantic imagination has succeeded in familiarising the 'wild, grotesque, and strange' South African landscape, making it a safe place for his 'rambles', the word itself connoting a leisure and security inconsistent with settler life on the colonial frontier (Bunn 1994: 139).

Other poems in the volume explore colonial relationships, complex and often violent, with the land and its indigenous people. Pringle was aware of the injustices inflicted by colonial policy. As a settler himself, he also – unavoidably to some extent – participated in these (Pereira and Chapman 1989: xvi). He ventriloquises South African voices, as in 'The Captive of Camalú', the lament of an African shepherd whose family have been slaughtered by whites. The poem ends with an address to 'UTIKO', 'Of every race the Father-God', praying for Europe to rescue Africa and 'prove indeed her Christian Friend' (ll. 59, 64, 80). 'The Forester of the Neutral Ground, a South-African Border-ballad' narrates in the voice of a Dutch settler the story of his interracial marriage, defying his father, to 'Brown Dinah, the bondmaid who sat in our hall' (l. 32). When the patriarch sells Dinah into slavery, her lover rescues her and takes her to live in the desert:

> Then tell me, dear Stranger, from England the Free,
> What good tidings bring'st thou for Arend Plessie?
> Shall the Edict of Mercy be sent forth at last,
> To break the harsh fetters of colour and caste?

(ll. 89–92)

Again Pringle turns to the metropolitan centre for relief from the injustice of colonial life. His editors credit him with 'a rare respect for the customs and aspirations of the indigenous inhabitants'. They locate his enduring contribution to South African literature in 'his intellectual and emotional quest, within the possibilities and constraints of his time, for progressive conduct and action in a severely divided landscape' (Pereira and Chapman 1989: xxvi).

Another South African critic, Matthew Shum, takes a different view of Pringle's legacy. His postcolonial analysis of 'The Bechuana Boy' highlights the disjunction between Pringle's literary self-presentation and his actual behaviour. The poem tells, from the first-person perspective of a settler, the story of a 'swarthy Stripling' (l. 6) who shows up one day with a tame springbok fawn and tells the settler his 'hapless history' (l. 24). Pringle's note on the poem identifies the story as that of an 'orphan boy' who 'came accidentally under [Pringle's] protection' (conceding that the part about the pet fawn is 'poetical license'; Pringle 1989: 78). In the poem, the boy tells of his capture by the 'Bergenaars' (with their 'wolfish howl of joy', l. 27) and sale into slavery:

And there, like cattle from the fold,
By Christians we were bought and sold,
'Midst laughter loud and looks of scorn –
And roughly from each other torn.

(ll. 69–72)

Living as a slave among Boers, the boy makes a pet of the fawn, which he rescues from 'wolfish wild-dogs' (l. 108). When his owner takes away his pet to give to his own child, the boy escapes with the fawn to the desert, ending up at Pringle's door:

Because they say, O English Chief,
Thou scornest not the Captive's grief:
Then let me serve thee, as thine own –
For I am in the world alone!

(ll. 141–4)

The fantasy of the indigenous worker volunteering his services to the colonist is at least as old as Robinson Crusoe and Friday. Of course the settlers take him in:

And One, with woman's gentle art,
Unlocked the fountains of his heart
And love gushed forth – till he became
Her Child in every thing but name.

(ll. 149–52)

The sentimental ending implies a quasi-familial relationship between the white settlers and the black orphan.[25] Shum calls attention to the parallel between the boy's adoption of the wounded animal and the Pringles' adoption of the boy. This doubling recalls the well-established association between slaves and pets, familiar from Restoration and eighteenth-century paintings in which a smartly dressed black child counterpoints the beauty of the portrait's subject. The effect in the poem, Shum argues, 'is, paradoxically' – given the poem's sentimental tone – 'to diminish the boy's humanity' (Shum 2009: 306).

Pringle's note tells how he and his wife took the boy, Hinza Marossi, to England with them, where he was baptised in 1827 and shortly thereafter 'died of a pulmonary complaint under which he had for many months suffered with extraordinary meekness' (Pringle 1989: 78). Shum points out a similarity between Hinza Marossi and Pringle's later protégée, Mary Prince: both function as what Gayatri Spivak calls 'native informants'.[26] They can be represented in print only to the extent that they conform to European norms of selfhood and experience, functioning as ideal subjects of readers' sympathy. The native informant exists 'only under the erasure of his or her identity, since to become an informant means to relinquish, or to be severed from, autochthonous forms of selfhood'. Only in this way can a black subject be eligible for 'admission into the repertoires of modernity' (Shum 2009: 318).

We will never know how Hinza Marossi experienced his time with the Pringles in South Africa and England. We do know Pringle was disingenuous about how the boy came into his possession. Domestic labour was scarce in 1820s South Africa. Historians disagree as to what caused the influx of refugees into the Cape Colony from the north at that time, but it is clear that they were absorbed into the colony's labour pool with an indeterminate status somewhere 'between slave, serf, and "free" labourer' (quoted in Shum 2009: 295). Letters from Pringle survive, requesting that the government allot some of these refugees to his party. He wrote to a friend, 'I have got a little . . . orphan boy for Mrs. P about 5 years of age. My father and brothers have also got a few of these poor creatures, till it is to be decided what is to be done with them' (quoted in Shum 2009: 296). Shum concludes 'there is little doubt' that Pringle's practice 'was complicit in borderline forms of slave ownership', as well as that he knew 'the circumstances under which he gained possession of both the boy and other juvenile labourers would be damaging to his humanitarian credentials, and . . . sought to suppress these facts' (Shum 2009: 297). The disjunction between Pringle's poetic narration in 'The Bechuana Boy' and the prosaic process of colonial settlement should not discredit the larger achievement of his poetry, though it should remind us of the unbridgeable distance between colonial realities and metropolitan sensibilities.[27]

I have tried to suggest the ways in which reading Scottish Romantic literature with attention to the colonial relationship between Scotland and England makes a difference to how we understand British Romanticism.

Emerging from Scotland's history of internal colonialism, Scottish Romantic literature was engaged with that history, including the 'armed contestation of British supremacy' as recently as 1745 (Pittock 2008: 16). Presenting Scotland as a nation in its own right and not a mere periphery, this literature pushes back against ongoing efforts to subordinate Scottish culture and Scottish languages to a hegemonic Standard English. And presenting Scotland as a multicultural, multilingual nation, Scottish Romantic writers explore the fault lines within that nation, making its internal diversity and conflict the theme of some of its richest works, such as the novels by Scott and Hogg discussed above. Scottish Romantic literature is a resolutely social literature, not a literature of inwardness and retreat. Appreciating this must lead us toward a more inclusive Romanticism, one not limited by that 'fetishization of creative subjectivity' and those 'inward processes of the interior mind' that for twentieth-century critics defined the essence of Romanticism (Pittock 2008: 4, 5).

Notes

1. Hechter 1975: 32, 4–5. The term 'Celtic fringe', assimilating Wales, Scotland and Ireland together, assumes too much homogeneity among these diverse areas, as Linda Colley notes (Colley 1992: 14; and see Sorensen 2000: 17).
2. Douglas Mack applies the concept of the subaltern to the Scottish context (Mack 2006: 1–13). For a definition see Introduction, note 4.
3. Pittock 2008: 7; Duncan et al. 2004: 2.
4. Duncan, *Scott's Shadow* (Duncan 2007: xii and *passim*).
5. The seventeenth century was a bloody one for the British Isles; see Devine 1999, Lynch 1996. As I write, Scottish leader Alex Salmond has proposed a referendum on Scottish independence to take place in 2014, while British prime minister David Cameron is making a case for preserving the Union.
6. Devine 1999: 12.
7. The Scottish journalist Francis Jeffrey wrote in 1809: 'We beg leave … to observe, that this Scotch is not to be considered as a provincial dialect, the vehicle only of rustic vulgarity and rude local humor. It is the language of a whole country, – long an independent kingdom, and still separate in laws, character and manners. It is by no means peculiar to the vulgar; but is the common speech of the whole nation in early life, – and with many of its most exalted and accomplished individuals throughout their whole existence' (quoted in Davis 1998: 125).
8. See Mack 2006: 91–2.
9. Crawford 2000: 56. Anti-Scottish feeling hit its peak during the 1762–3 administration of Lord Bute, the Scottish prime minister, accused of favouring his countrymen.
10. After publishing several more volumes of Ossian's works, Macpherson bought a seat in Parliament (from Cornwall) and a Highland estate. He wrote two histories, worked as agent for the Nabob of Arcot (southern India), and died far from his humble beginnings (Murphy 1993: 9).

11. I am referring to Wordsworth's famous declaration in the 1802 Preface to *Lyrical Ballads* that 'the language of such Poetry as I am recommending is, as far as is possible, a selection of the language really spoken by men' (Wordsworth 2002: 398). Note the qualifying phrases: 'as far as is possible', 'a selection'. He goes on to assert that when this selection 'is made with true taste and feeling', it 'will entirely separate the composition from the vulgarity and meanness of ordinary life' (Wordsworth 2002: 399).
12. The case of Francis Grose complicates the idea of the antiquarian as coloniser (Leask 2010: 257 ff.). Antiquarianism was actually a fringe subculture in England, though often aligned with cultural nationalism in Scotland, Ireland and Wales. See also Butler 1999.
13. Davis 1998: 120–1. Benedict Anderson famously defines the nation as an imagined political community, one of the means of whose creation was print capitalism, including newspapers and novels as well as other print media, such as Burns's verse. On *Unheimlichkeit*, or unhomeliness, see Bhabha 1994: 9.
14. Bakhtin 1981: 273. The term Bakhtin uses in this essay, 'Discourse in the Novel', is actually heteroglossia, which I take to mean approximately the same thing Pittock means by polyglossia. For the applicability of Bakhtinian theory to Burns's poetry see Morris 1987, but also McGuirk's cautionary response (McGuirk 1991). Jeremy Smith (2009) also addresses Burns's linguistic choices.
15. 'Cleekit' = clasped one another; the rest is roughly 'every witch sweated and steamed, cast off her clothes for the work and set to it in her shift'.
16. Duncan 2007: xi; Duncan 2006: 173.
17. Scott claimed to have started the novel in 1805 (sixty years after 1745), laid it aside, and finished it in 1814.
18. Buzard 1995: 36; Makdisi 1998: 81; Fabian 1983: *passim*.
19. Evan's behaviour at his leader's treason trial touchingly exemplifies loyalty unto death (Mack 2006: 8–11).
20. Devine 1999: 177; see 170–95 for more on the Clearances.
21. Devine 1999: 235; and see Duncan 2007: 3–8.
22. It 'seems to have been a bugbear invoked in internecine doctrinal disputes more than . . . a position actually professed by anyone' (Duncan 2010: xxix).
23. Heydt-Stevenson and Sussman 2008: 25. Other novels that do this include Maturin's *Melmoth the Wanderer*, Mary Shelley's *Mathilda* and Mary Wollstonecraft's *Maria, or, The Wrongs of Woman*.
24. Pringle came to Scott's attention with his 1816 verse epistle, 'The Autumnal Excursion', an imitation of Scott's style that Hogg included in his collection *The Poetic Mirror*. Scott graciously said he 'wished the original notes had been as fine as their echo' (Pereira and Chapman 1989: xiii).
25. Shum (2009) points out that the poem draws on the aesthetics of sympathy elaborated by the Scottish Enlightenment thinker Adam Smith in his *Theory of Moral Sentiments*.
26. Spivak 1999: *passim*.
27. Pringle's recently published letters (Pringle 2011) shed additional light on his relationship to Hinza Marossi and his rhetorical intent in 'The Bechuana Boy'.

Chapter 4

Romantic Orientalisms

> India yet holds a mythologic mine,
> Her strength may open, and her art refine:
> Tho' Asian spoils the realms of Europe fill,
> Those Eastern riches are unrifled still.
> William Hayley
> *Essay on Epic Poetry* (1782)

Well before the Romantic era, British writers found it worth their while to mine exotic romances from the East. The Frenchman Antoine Galland started the fashion for such literary Orientalism with *Mille et une nuit* (1704–17), translated from Arabic and Englished by 1706 as *The Thousand and One Nights*. Its popularity brought plenty of imitations to Britain's expanding print market: Turkish, Persian, Chinese, 'Mogul' and 'Tartarian' tales. British and French authors used Eastern tales as vehicles for social, political and philosophical comment, from Voltaire and Montesquieu to Oliver Goldsmith and Samuel Johnson (Richardson 2002: 4–5). But Britain's commercial and diplomatic ties to the East yielded material benefits as well: imported silks and spices, porcelain and enamel, ivory and gems. The centre of empire avidly consumed the East 'in the shape of products, objects, visual experiences and literary texts' (Saglia 2002: 76). The *Arabian Nights* spread stereotypes of 'the Oriental' as despotic, irrational and sex-obsessed, but it also injected elements of magic and the marvellous into European fiction. It was an antidote to neoclassical sterility and boring realism, and it caught the imagination of Romantic writers such as Coleridge and De Quincey early in their lives.

The 1780s saw a significant change in British literary treatment of the East. Leaving eighteenth-century 'pseudo-Orientalism' behind, many Romantic writers aimed for a more scholarly, carefully documented presentation of works about the East. William Beckford's novel *Vathek*

(1786), published with copious footnotes by the scholarly Reverend Samuel Henley, inaugurated this new approach.[1] This development arose from two key changes in Europe's, and in particular Britain's, relationship to Asia. The first is what Raymond Schwab, in his classic 1950 study, calls the 'Oriental Renaissance' (Schwab 1984), comparing the arrival of Sanskrit texts in Europe to that of Greek texts in Europe in the fifteenth century. The Frenchman Anquetil-Duperron's 1771 translation of the *Avesta* from the Persian opened the door. Then in 1784 Warren Hastings, Governor General of Bengal, and Sir William Jones founded the Asiatic Society of Bengal, whose journal, *Asiatic Researches*, brought to the British Isles the fruit of groundbreaking linguistic, literary and legal scholarship done in India by colonial administrators and civil servants. These included Charles Wilkins's 1785 translation of the *Bhagavad-Gita,* as well as Jones's numerous translations from Sanskrit, Persian and Arabic. His version of Kalidasa's drama *Sakuntala* captured the imaginations of Romantic writers from Shelley to Goethe (Leask 2005: 141).

The Asiatic Society was made possible by Britain's dramatically expanding commercial and colonial presence in India. The British East India Company controlled Bengal by 1765; its other two bases on the subcontinent were Madras on the east coast and Bombay in the northwest. Rapidly expanding its territory around each of these sites through wars of conquest against the Mughal Empire and other local powers, the Company would control almost the whole subcontinent by the 1820s. From a trading company, it had become a colonial state. The Company's limited staff and administrative inexperience with such a large population of non-European subjects left it reliant on the infrastructure put in place by the Mughal Empire (one of the three powerful Islamic empires that dominated Asia in the seventeenth and eighteenth centuries, along with the Persian Savafid and Turkish Ottoman Empires). The Mughals spoke and wrote Persian, which was the official language of British India until 1835 (Leask 2005: 139). British officials' interest in Sanskrit, the language of classical texts and older Hindu religious writings, grew out of their perception that they could not fully trust the Indian authorities on whom they had to depend to manage lands and collect revenue. As a matter of policy, the colonisers decided to govern the Indians by their own laws. This approach would be reversed by the end of the Romantic era, as we will see. India's new rulers worked hard to associate themselves with indigenous legal and religious authorities (Bayly 1988: 114). A 1781 Act of Parliament recognising Hindu and Muslim legal customs made the British colonial judiciary dependent on indigenous legal experts, known as pandits. Jones, an accomplished linguist working in India as a supreme court judge, translated both Hindu and Muslim legal codes (Teltscher 1995: 195–7). Such linguistic and legal scholarship was instrumental to British colonial power.

The postcolonial critic Edward Said, drawing on the thought of Michel Foucault, famously theorised the interconnection between colonial knowledge and power in *Orientalism* (1978). According to Said, there is no such thing as disinterested knowledge: all knowledge, even the most seemingly abstruse, serves the interests of those in power. He offers three main definitions of Orientalism. The first includes scholars such as Jones and the other members of the Asiatic Society: anyone 'who teaches, writes about, or researches the Orient . . . is an Orientalist'. This designation, no longer in use, survived in academia well into the twentieth century. Second, for Said, 'Orientalism is a style of thought based upon an ontological and epistemological distinction between "the Orient" and . . . "the Occident"' – between East and West as fundamental ways of being in and knowing the world (Said 1978: 2). This perceived dichotomy between Europe and its 'others', Said asserts, was central to the formation of modern European culture and to Europe's colonial expansion (Loomba 2005: 43). Said's third definition articulates the connection between knowledge and power: Orientalism is 'the corporate institution for dealing with the Orient . . . by making statements about it, authorizing views of it, describing it, by teaching it, settling it, ruling over it: in short, Orientalism as a Western style for dominating, restructuring, and having authority over the Orient'. After the late eighteenth century, he claims, no one could write, think, or act on the Orient 'without taking account of the limitations on thought and action imposed by Orientalism . . . [B]ecause of Orientalism the Orient was not (and is not) a free subject of thought or action' (Said 1978: 3). Numerous critics have found Said's theory overly monolithic and insufficiently historical. Moreover, as Nigel Leask points out, Said 'overestimates the confidence and unity of purpose of European imperialists and writers, failing to register adequately the anxiety, not to mention the critical scruples, which often underwrite orientalist texts' (Leask 2005: 139).[2] But none of this negates Said's central point: that representations of the East cannot be properly understood outside the context of imperial power.

Recent work by scholars of Romantic literature has developed Said's insight in ways that will inform my discussion. All but one of the works I have chosen are set in India, the site of massive imperial expansion in the Romantic era and the source of much of the scholarly knowledge of Asia circulating in the metropole. I begin with the writings of Sir William Jones, whose work, vital to the East India Company's colonial government, also mediated Hindu culture for British readers. Besides legal translation, Jones wrote poems based on his study of Persian, Turkish and Arabic poetry and critical essays on these literatures. Bringing the culture of the imperial periphery back to the metropole, Jones contributed to the development of Romantic literature in ways literary historians have not often acknowledged. His work also influenced a later generation of Romantic writers. Before turning to some of these, I will briefly consider the visual art produced in romantic India. A number of painters travelled there starting in the 1750s, attracted by the profits to be made from the patronage of prosperous 'nabobs', the term for men who made huge fortunes working for the East India Company. Two very different portrayals of colonial families, by the painters Francesco Renaldi and Johann Zoffany, will illustrate the shift in the Company's approach to colonial government and Indian culture taking place gradually between the 1780s, when Jones flourished, and the 1830s. From an approach that respected and incorporated Indian culture – though admittedly to a limited extent and in an instrumental manner – the Company moved toward a drive to impose British language, laws and values upon its colonial subjects.

One important step in this transition happened in 1813, when Parliament renewed the Company's charter, inserting a controversial 'pious clause' allowing Christian missionaries access to Company-controlled areas. Romantic writers intervened in the debate leading up to this decision, including the poet Robert Southey, whose Hindu verse romance *The Curse of Kehama* (1810) portrayed Hinduism as 'a cesspool of monstrous gods and demonic devotees' in need of Christian enlightenment (Franklin 2006: 18). Other writers disagreed. Sidney Owenson's novel *The Missionary* (1811), deeply influenced by Jones's work and sharing his attitude of interest in and respect for Eastern religions, presents Hindu society as highly resistant to Christian conversion. Owenson's story of chaste longing and tragic punishment, inflected by the 1790s genres of the Gothic and Jacobin novel, as well as by the Romantic genre she helped create, the national tale, caught the imagination of Percy Shelley. His 1816 quest romance *Alastor* is set partly in Kashmir, the exotic backdrop of *The Missionary*; the 'visionary maid' who appears to his protagonist in a dream recalls Owenson's heroine. But *Alastor* deliberately eschews scholarly footnotes like those used by Southey and Owenson, signalling an inward, allegorical turn. Postcolonial criticism helps us read Shelley's enigmatic poem as an exploration of imperial desire. The last work I will discuss, Byron's *The Giaour* (1813), is set not in India but in the Ottoman Empire. However, significant features connect it to the work of Jones and Owenson. Byron, too, uses footnotes (though his sometimes take a sardonic tone). More importantly, he shares Jones's 'open-minded receptiveness to other cultures' and 'hostility to Eurocentrism' (Franklin 2000: 66, 65). His poem can also be read as a riposte to the evangelical enthusiasm of the religious right of his day.

Sir William Jones

Born in Westminster in 1746, the Welshman William Jones would die in Calcutta, several thousand miles to the east, in 1794. In his relatively short career he mastered Persian, Turkish, Hebrew, Arabic and Sanskrit, as well as Greek, Latin and French. His scholarship on Indian law earned him a knighthood and a judgeship in the Supreme Court of Bengal in 1783. The following year he founded the Asiatic Society of Bengal. Jones's accomplishments had a lasting impact on British literature and colonial rule. His work of translation both opened Hindu literature to metropolitan readers and helped 'legitimize British rule in an Indian idiom' (Majeed 1992: 22). *Orientalism* situates Jones as an early participant in the project 'to gather in, to rope off, to domesticate the Orient and thereby turn it into a province of European learning'. Jones's goals, according to Said, were to 'rule and to learn, then to compare Orient with Occident . . . with an irresistible impulse always to codify, to subdue the infinite variety of the Orient to "a complete digest" of laws, figures, customs, and works' (Said 1978: 78). This view drastically oversimplifies Jones's achievement, though I agree with Said that we must always bear in mind the scholar's commitment to colonial rule: he worked for the British government of Bengal. As Jones wrote, 'I have the delight of knowing that my studies go hand in hand with my duty' (quoted in Teltscher 1995: 198). His legal translations, including *Al Sirajiyyah, or, The Mohamedan Laws of Inheritance* (1792) and the *Institutes of Hindu Law, or, The Ordinances of Menu* (1794), were motivated by his mistrust of Indian legal experts. In a 1788 letter to Governor General Cornwallis, Jones advocated for the creation of a 'Digest of Hindu and Mohammedan laws' so that the pandits and maulvis would not 'venture to impose on us when their impositions might be so easily detected' (quoted in Majeed 1992: 19). The colonial judge could not bear to be at the mercy of indigenous authorities in the performance of his duty. Such codification tended to skew the interpretation of Hindu and Muslim law in a conservative direction; judicial practice was more flexible before the letter of the law was spelled out in English. Jones's digests thus promoted 'a more stratified and rigid system of castes ... and a more homogeneous religious practice' (Majeed 1992: 28). Orientalist scholarship had a lasting impact on the social order of colonised India.

Jones studied Persian, Turkish and Arabic poetry at Oxford, and in 1771 published a grammar of the Persian language, which the East India Company adopted for its employees. The book used poems as examples, including the first published English verse translation of a Persian poem. It would introduce generations of creative writers to Persian poetry: 'Romantic Orientalism [was] born ... within the pages of a Persian grammar' (Franklin 1995b: 9). In Bengal, Jones became more familiar with Hindu mythology and composed a series of hymns celebrating Hindu deities. These poems emphasise creativity and the nature of perception; they feed the Romantic fascination with these themes. Jones's hymns introduced European readers both to Hindu mythology and to a syncretic approach to religion and culture (Franklin 1995a: xxvi). The way in which Jones presented Hindu mythology to metropolitan readers can be viewed either as thoughtful cultural translation or as an 'exercise in poetic appropriation', in Kate Teltscher's words (1995: 208). Drawing on post-Augustan literary conventions, Jones excised the most suggestive bits of his originals. Love-bites and fingernail-wounds, for example – valued in Sanskrit poetry as marks of distinction – were unlikely to endear Hindu mythology to genteel Britons. Thus, for 'Inflict arrow-wounds with your sharp nails!' Jones substitutes the Petrarchanised 'grant me death from the arrows of thy keen eyes' (Franklin 1995b: 107). Is he exercising appropriate tact in rendering culturally alien material for a domestic audience? Or do his changes distort the original and 'muffle . . . notes of cultural dissonance' (Teltscher 1995: 215)?

Jones's 'Hymn to Lacshmi' (1788) celebrates the 'Ceres of Hindustan', goddess of fortune, prosperity and fertility and consort of Vishnu. Teltscher traces the way the poem moves through different personae or speaking positions. A prose preface or 'Argument' fills readers in on the various names of the deity and myths of her origin, ending with a pragmatic justification for studying Hindu mythology: readers who might prefer Greek and Roman myths should remember that:

> the allegories contained in the Hymn to LACSHMI constitute at this moment the prevailing religion of a most extensive and celebrated Empire, and are devoutly believed by many millions, whose industry adds to the revenue of *Britain*, and whose manners, which are interwoven with their

religious opinions, nearly affect all *Europeans*, who reside among them. (Jones 1995: 154)

Here Jones speaks from the perspective of an administrator, valuing knowledge for its contribution to colonial authority.

As the poem opens, the speaker is positioned within Hindu culture, addressing Lakshmi as a worshipper: 'Thee, Goddess, I salute; thy gifts I sing' (l. 5). Following two stanzas of second-person praise of the goddess – 'Thy bounties I survey' (l. 11) – the speaker takes up a third-person narrative of her life, from 'sacred infant' (l. 37) to wedded consort of Vishnu. The poem's middle stanzas describe Lakshmi's powers of rewarding human virtue with natural abundance and punishing vice with flood, drought or famine (Teltscher 1995: 218). The hymn concludes with another second-person address, but with a difference. Here the speaker seems to take up the role of a sort of advisor to the deity on colonial affairs:

Oh! bid the patient Hindu rise and live.
His erring mind, that wizard lore beguiles
        Clouded by priestly wiles,
To senseless nature bows for nature's GOD.
Now, stretch'd o'er oceans vast from happier isles,
He sees the wand of empire, not the rod:
Ah, may those beams, that western skies illume,
        Disperse th' unholy gloom!
Meanwhile may laws, by myriads long rever'd,
Their strife appease, their gentler claims decide;
So shall their victors, mild with virtuous pride,
To many a cherish'd grateful race endear'd,
        With temper'd love be fear'd:
Though mists profane obscure their narrow ken,
They err, yet feel; though pagans, they are men.

(ll. 238–52)

The perspective here, unlike in the body of the poem, is anchored in Christian religion and occidental condescension to the 'patient Hindu', deluded by 'priestly wiles'. The British Empire appears as the benevolent saviour not only of the Hindus, but of 'many a cherish'd grateful race' across the globe, who reciprocate with a strange combination of love and fear. 'Here word-play ('wizard'/'wand') and punning ('lore'/'laws') combine to suggest the neat inevitability of British rule. Enlisting Lakshmi's aid for the successful continuance of colonial authority, Jones situates himself within two cultures at once' (Teltscher 1995: 219). By the end of the poem, however, the speaker again speaks from outside

Hindu culture. We know this from the word 'pagans' – a single word that aligns the speaker and readers together as different from, and superior to, India's non-Christian population. To introduce Hindu mythology to British readers, Jones uses strategies that draw on the familiar repertoire of neoclassical poetry: poetic diction, classical analogies and allusions, and European decorum. These choices 'convey a sense that Hindu culture cannot be transmitted directly, but must be mediated or Europeanized. Jones implies European cultural primacy in his very advocacy of Hindu culture' (Teltscher 1995: 219).[3]

The Orientalist's zeal as a cultural mediator changed the course of history in two additional ways. Jones's 'Third Anniversary Discourse' to the Asiatic Society articulated a famous insight that laid the foundation for Indo-European comparative grammar and modern comparative linguistics: the idea that the classical languages of India and Europe descend from a common source, a language that no longer exists (Franklin 1995b: 90). But Jones's thought had another, more specifically literary impact. His 1771 *Poems Consisting Chiefly of Translations from the Asiatic Languages* (published before he went to India) contains two critical essays, 'Essay on the Poetry of the Eastern Nations' and 'An Essay on the Arts, Commonly Called Imitative'. M. H. Abrams's *The Mirror and the Lamp: Romantic Theory and the Critical Tradition* (1958) credits the latter with 'the first explicit codification of an expressive theory of poetry' (Sitter 2008: 385).[4] It is a critical commonplace since Abrams's study that the late eighteenth century witnessed an epochal shift in literary aesthetics from art as imitation, or mimesis, to art as expression – the 'spontaneous overflow of powerful feelings', as a later Romantic would put it (Wordsworth 2002: 393). But literary historians who credit Jones with helping to catalyse this change seldom mention the venue in which his essays appeared: a collection of Eastern poetry. Zak Sitter argues that this signals 'orientalism's implication in a seminal moment in Romantic poetics'. The 'Romantic break', he contends, 'depends crucially on a geopolitical as well as an aesthetic logic' (Sitter 2008: 386).

Jones urged Europeans to look to Oriental literature as an alternative to the prevailing tradition of mimetic aesthetics. Geographical difference – specific cultural and historical conditions – enabled Eastern poets to produce a tradition of poetry centred on poetry's 'true principle, which is also its origin: the expression of passion' (Sitter 2008: 398). The Arabians, Jones writes, 'being perpetually conversant with the most beautiful objects, spending a calm, and agreeable life in a fine climate, being extremely addicted to the softer passions, and having ... a language singularly adapted to poetry', were 'naturally excellent poets', something their manners and customs also promoted (Jones 1995: 325–6). The European ancients composed their poetry in similar conditions of close access to nature and creative originality. Jones compares the tenth-century Persian poet Ferdusi to Homer: 'both drew their images from nature herself, without catching them only by reflection . . . and both possessed, in an eminent degree, *that rich and creative invention, which is the very soul of poetry*' (Jones 1995: 334; emphasis in original).

In his 'Essay on the Arts, Commonly Called Imitative', Jones uses the example of an anti-imitative poetic tradition that he finds in Eastern poetry as a basis to question the neoclassical truism that all art is mimetic:

> [T]hough *poetry* and *musick* have, certainly, a power of *imitating* the manners of men, and several objects in nature, yet . . . their greatest effect is not produced by *imitation*, but by a very different principle; which must be sought for in the deepest recesses of the human mind. (Jones 1995: 338; emphasis in original)

Because Islam stigmatises imitation (as Jones generalises from its prohibition of some kinds of pictorial imitation), yet produces great poetry, the true source of its greatness must lie elsewhere. Getting to know the art of a very different culture, yet one that shares ancient roots with our own, can give Europeans a new and truer understanding of what art really is. 'Jones's essays denaturalize imitation as the inevitable foundation of all representation and localize it in time and space as a modern, European aberration' (Sitter 2008: 401).

With his fellow members of the Asiatic Society, Jones undertook a comprehensive study of Asian culture. Their object was nothing less than 'MAN and NATURE; whatever is performed by the one, or produced by the other' (*Asiatic Researches* 1799: xii–xiii). The introduction to the inaugural issue of *Asiatic Researches* makes clear the connection, in this ambitious enterprise, between scholarly knowledge and colonial power:

> [A] mere man of letters, retired from the world and allotting his whole time to philosophical or literary pursuits, is a character unknown among *Europeans* resident in *India*, where every individual is a man of business in the civil or military state, and constantly occupied either in the affairs of government, in the administration of justice, in some department of revenue or commerce, or in one of the liberal professions; very few hours, therefore, in the day or night can be reserved for any study, that has no immediate connection with business. (*Asiatic Researches* 1799: iii)

The members of this new learned society spent their days at work on the business of empire: colonies could not afford full-time philosophers. Nonetheless, the knowledge produced in these colonial soldiers', merchants' and judges' spare time did not '*simply* follow the priorities of colonial conquest and administration', in Fulford's words. By giving metropolitan readers unprecedented access to the complexity and sophistication of Hindu culture, the work of Jones and his fellow researchers changed Romantic literature's representation of the East. Jones 'studied Indian tradition *both* in order to facilitate colonial rule *and* because he was delighted by a culture that, in several respects, he thought superior to that of Britain'. His Orientalism did not just reinforce imperial authority, though it did that. It also afforded a basis for questioning that authority by opening an alternative tradition of aesthetic and moral value (Fulford 2008: 186).

Changing Attitudes and Colonial Painting

The work of cultural translation done by Jones and others was essential to the mode of governance practised in India under the rule of Warren Hastings, Governor General from 1773 to 1785. As the East India Company metamorphosed from a business enterprise to a full-scale colonial government, it undertook to rule Indians by their own laws, or at least their laws as interpreted by British scholars. Historians refer to this as an 'Orientalist' approach (yet another definition of the word). The 'anglicist' approach that eventually replaced it assumed that Britain, a more advanced civilisation, should impose its culture, laws and religion on India. James Mill's *History of British India* (1817) exemplifies the latter view. Mill spent eleven years producing this massive work, though he never went to India. Analysing Indian civilisation through a Scottish Enlightenment paradigm of progress, the *History* judges India as barbaric and 'rude' (a word Mill uses frequently). He sees no evidence of improvement: 'It is in no quarter pretended, that the Hindu superstition was ever less gross than it now appears' (Mill 1975: 241). To Mill, this is a static, stagnant civilisation. 'As the manners, institutions, and attainments of the Hindus have been stationary for many ages; in beholding the Hindus of the present day, we are beholding the Hindus of many ages past' (Mill 1975: 248). The only way India will ever progress, in this view, is if the British impose European civilisation upon it.[5]

Mill's contempt for Indian civilisation was shared by more and more of those involved in the colonial enterprise, especially evangelical Christians, who were keen to persuade Parliament to let Christian missionaries into India. William Wilberforce, the anti-slavery crusader, backed this initiative, along with Charles Grant, author of the influential memorandum, 'Observations on the State of Society among Asiatic Subjects of Great Britain, Particularly with Respect to Morals' (1793). Hastings's high-profile impeachment for imputed corruption marked a turning point in British rule. His trial dragged on from 1788 until 1795, his attackers including such prominent statesmen as Edmund Burke and Charles James Fox.[6] Though Hastings was finally acquitted, subsequent Governors General took an anglicist path. In the Charter Act of 1813, which renewed the East India Company's royal charter for twenty years, Parliament took greater control of India. Evangelical Christians got included in the Act the so-called 'pious clause', opening India to missionaries and requiring the Company to help fund the material and moral improvement of India.

This change in colonial attitudes and practices was gradual and uneven in its implementation, but profound in its eventual consequences. The case of India formed part of a broader shift, observed by the historian Christopher Bayly, between Britain's so-called first and second empires. The loss of the American colonies coincided with the expansion of British imperial interests in the East, in particular India. The massive expansion of imperial dominion during the French Wars accompanied a wave of conservative patriotism and militarism in the British Isles: evangelical Protestantism, nationalism and empire grew more closely linked (Bayly 1989: 138). In India, Governor General Cornwallis (formerly the losing commander of British forces in the American war) instituted reforms to disentangle East India Company employees from the Indian commercial classes with whom they had worked closely, often in conditions fostering the corruption publicised by Hastings's trial. The Cornwallis Code, implemented in 1793, regulated Company administration in pursuit of an ideal of moral 'independency', seen as a guarantee of honesty and civic virtue. But as Bayly points out, this notion was also 'crucial to the development of British racial stereotypes and racial exclusiveness' (Bayly 1989: 152). Corruption or depravity came to be seen as characteristic of Indians in general, a reason for British colonists to keep their distance. An emerging racial hierarchy ranked various groups by innate virtue, with Europeans, of course, at the top. The admiration for Indian civilisation characteristic of Jones and his fellow Orientalists gradually gave way to the disdain exemplified by Mill's *History* (Bayly 1989: 148–52). Along with this came an increasing disapproval of racial mixing. In this new 'climate of opinion . . . liaisons with Indian women and gross peculation were no longer admired' (Bayly 1988: 78).[7]

Figure 4.1 Francesco Renaldi, *The Palmer Family*, 1786 (oil on canvas), British Library, London, UK/ The Bridgeman Art Library.

We can recognise signs of this momentous shift in some of the visual art produced in British India. In metropolitan Britain, wartime conservatism fostered a cult of domesticity, centred on a wife and mother whose virtue and nurturance elevated and sustained her family.[8] The two paintings reproduced here (Figure 4.1 and Figure 4.2), though executed at approximately the same time, portray two very different images of Anglo-Indian domesticity. Francesco Renaldi's *The Palmer Family* (1786) records an arrangement common among European men travelling to the colonies without their wives: common-law marriage to a native woman (or in Major Palmer's case, two women).[9] Palmer joined the East India Company's army in 1766 and held various posts in his long career, including aide-de-camp to Governor Hastings, commander of a battalion of sepoys (Indian troops), and Resident at the Maratha Peshwa's court at Poona. He died in India in 1816 (Archer 1979: 282). In Renaldi's unfinished conversation piece, Palmer is comfortably ensconced amid his Indian family of two wives, three children and three servants. He gazes fondly at his senior wife, Faiz Bakhsh, a Muslim

Figure 4.2 Johann Zoffany, *Colonel Blair with his Family and an Indian Ayah*, 1786/7, Tate Images, UK.

lady of the royal house of Delhi. She is seated on the ground with her baby boy, Hastings, flanked by her two toddlers, William and Mary. Palmer's younger wife (also a princess, according to his great-granddaughter) leans against his leg. 'Renaldi's idyllic rendering of domesticity . . . conveys the maternal tenderness of Bibi Faiz Bakhsh, the paternal concern of Major Palmer, and the conjugal affection . . . between Palmer and his bibis.' To European eyes – especially prudish Evangelical eyes – this colonial household would have looked like that lascivious Oriental institution, a harem, with a British officer in the role of Oriental despot. 'Palmer's contented gaze acts as an affront to the cult of domestic femininity and to the evolving ideology of British womanhood', writes Beth Fowkes Tobin in her study of colonial painting (Tobin 1999: 114, 115). Renaldi's painting and others he made of British colonists' bibis record a historical moment when British men working in India lived with Indian women, adopting Indian customs and family arrangements, and sometimes Indian clothing as well.[10]

Such cultural crossing would meet with increasing disapproval in the years and decades that followed. A second family conversation piece,

Johann Zoffany's *The Blair Family* (1986/7), looks ahead to a different mode of coexistence between British colonists and their Indian subjects. Like a number of European artists, Zoffany travelled to India to try his fortune at a time when his reputation in Britain was on the wane.[11] He stayed for six years, painting numerous portraits (including one of Hastings) as well as landscapes and action pictures, such as the spectacular crowd scene in *Colonel Mordaunt's Cock Match* (1784/6). The Blair family appears in proper British dress, like the subjects of other Zoffany conversation pieces such as *The Auriol and Dashwood Families* (1783–7) and *The Morse and Cator Families* (1784). In the former, family members take their tea outdoors under a jackfruit tree, served by Indian servants. The latter painting contains no hint of India in its composition, presumably at the subjects' request. Two couples play the piano and cello, surrounded by other icons of European culture, such as a classical column. In *The Blair Family*, the couple and their two daughters relax on the veranda of their house in Cawnpore. Colonel William Blair, in uniform, holds hands affectionately with his wife. Their older daughter, Jane, plays the piano, while her younger sister Maria tickles the chin of a cat held by an Indian child. In a humorous touch (characteristic of Zoffany's work), the cat seems alarmed by the attention of the spaniel at lower right. The family could almost be gathered in an English drawing room.

Besides the child servant, India enters the picture through the paintings hanging on the wall above the family's heads. Rather than copies of actual paintings, these were probably simulated from sketches Zoffany made on his travels around Bengal (Webster 2011: 525). Their subjects are significant. The large middle painting is a landscape including a native hut, travellers with an elephant and a Muslim tomb. It is flanked by two smaller paintings whose subjects may not be obvious in our reproduction. Both of these portray Indian customs that the British considered bizarre or barbaric. The one on the left shows wood being piled up in preparation for *sati*, the burning of a Hindu widow on her husband's funeral pyre. After his return to England, Zoffany painted at least three scenes of *sati*, capitalising on its grisly allure for British viewers. This ritual of self-sacrifice by a virtuous wife was especially fascinating in an age of sensibility, attuned to ideals of virtue and sensitive to human suffering. *Sati* figured in numerous travel accounts, including the artist William Hodges' *Travels in India* (1793). A debate went on for decades over whether the British government should ban the practice (a ban was enacted in 1829). The painting on the right depicts the ceremony of *Charak Puja* or hook swinging, in which devotees from the untouchable caste had hooks inserted between their shoulder blades and were whirled in the air from a rope on a high yardarm to propitiate the goddess Kali (Webster 2011: 526). Zoffany's compositional device, miniaturising these alien customs and framing them for display behind a scene of prosperous British domesticity, powerfully conveys the dominance of European cultural values and customs over those of the colonised peoples of India.

Romantic literature actively intervened to change British attitudes toward India. Robert Southey published a long narrative poem focused on each of India's main religions. His Islamic quest romance, *Thalaba* (1801), narrates the magical adventures of a boy brought up as a Bedouin herdsman. *The Curse of Kehama* (1810) also features a protagonist of low social rank: a Hindu peasant, Ladurlad, cursed by an evil rajah, Kehama. Southey's preface describes 'the religion of the Hindoos' as 'of all false religions ... the most monstrous in its fables, and the most fatal in its effects' (Southey 2011: 117). The poem portrays an India in which humble people like Ladurlad and his daughter are at the mercy of a barbaric religious law. Southey enlists the reader's sympathy on behalf of the poor against an evil despot, who obviously figures the hated Napoleon. The poet – in his youth (like his fellow Lake Poets Wordsworth and Coleridge) an idealistic radical – was by 1810 very much a Tory, soon to be named Poet Laureate. Marilyn Butler calls Southey's portrayal of Hinduism 'powerful propaganda – Grant popularized and sensationalized', serving the religious right of his day (Butler 1994: 416–17). But Southey's aim in writing the poem was by no means primarily propagandist. He looked to Hindu mythology to inject new energy into a European genre, the epic, which he saw as exhausted. His extensive scholarly footnotes to his poems (relying heavily on the work of Jones as well as travel narratives) opened a detailed view of the East to his readers, including other poets such as Coleridge, Shelley and Byron.[12] By treating Eastern culture 'as a subject-matter, belief system, and poetic style as appropriate to the epic as were Trojan wars to Homer', *The Curse of Kehama* actually practised an Orientalism akin to that of Jones, using the East to call Western cultural superiority into question. As his preface makes clear, however, Southey was highly ambivalent about this endeavour. If his poetic imagination drew him into Jones's India, his conservative politics and religion uneasily resisted (Fulford 2008: 188).

The Missionary

Though its reviews were mixed and its sales mediocre, *Kehama* drew indirect responses from liberal writers such as Sydney Owenson (Lady Morgan). Her Romantic novel *The Missionary* (1811) approaches Hinduism very differently. Owenson's *The Wild Irish Girl* (1806) was so popular that the author came to be identified with its heroine, the dispossessed Irish princess Glorvina (Wright 2002: 11). Her liberal politics did not prevent the best-selling author from being lionised by London high society; she went to parties in *faux* antique Irish dress and played Celtic airs on her harp. Owenson composed *The Missionary* during extended visits to her friend the Marquis of Abercorn and his lady at their mansions in northern Ireland and southern England, reading aloud after dinner for aristocratic guests including the Duchess of Wales and Lord Castlereagh, Secretary of State for War and the Colonies. Rhapsodic and implausible, Owenson's novel met the performative expectations of celebrity authorship while also contributing to the national debate on colonial policy (Franklin 2006b: 163). *The Missionary's* numerous footnotes reveal that she had done her homework. In particular, she knew Jones's work well (Drew 1987: 240–58). Like Southey's poems, Owenson's novel participates in the 'new realism of orientalist description' made possible by the pioneering Orientalist scholarship of Jones and others (Leask 2005: 142). Though her style of narration is far from anything we would call 'realist', she is clearly concerned to anchor her portrayal of Hinduism in scholarly detail. She thanks the Dublin barrister Sir Charles Ormsby for letting her use his '*Oriental Library*': 'Your Indian histories place me upon the fairy ground you know I love to tread ... and you have contributed so largely and efficiently to my Indian venture, that you have a right to share in the profits'.[13] Unlike earlier eighteenth-century Orientalism, this new strain aimed at authenticity. It strove to be 'a form of knowledge which incorporated the iconography and mythology of Britain's Asiatic subjects into the nation's image repertoire, in precisely the manner demanded by William Jones' (Leask 2005: 143).

Owenson's choice of setting was strategic. An Irish patriot, she had written about Ireland and would do so again. But in 1811 the Irish question was considered settled, while India remained very much subject to debate (Wright 2002: 29). Pressure was building to let the missionaries in. *The Missionary* is set in India, but emphatically not British India, and in the seventeenth rather than the nineteenth century. The Portuguese colony of Goa on India's west coast was the first European beachhead on the subcontinent, established in 1510. But Portugal was also in the news at the time Owenson wrote, with the Duke of Wellington campaigning to liberate it from Napoleonic Spain. It had been ruled by Spain from 1580 to 1640, the period when *The Missionary* is set. The novel thus maps sites of colonial domination onto one another (with Ireland always in the background). Displacing the issues of colonisation and religious conversion onto seventeenth-century Portuguese India defuses their political sensitivity and allows debates about colonialism to be generalised.

A related strategy of displacement characterises a Romantic genre on which Owenson drew: the Gothic novel, in particular Ann Radcliffe's Gothic. Set in the past, in France or Italy rather than England, Radcliffe's bestselling 1790s novels work through issues of gender, patriarchy and power under cover of unthreatening fantasy. The Radcliffean Gothic also drew extensively on travel writing; aestheticised landscape forms part of its stylised treatment of cultural otherness. The other 1790s genre in which *The Missionary* participates is the so-called Jacobin novel, or polemical novel of ideas.[14] Staging philosophical debates about culture and religion, toleration and intolerance, through a star-crossed intercultural love affair, Owenson practices what Katie Trumpener calls the 'Jacobin-feminist national tale' (Trumpener 1997: 138). But the national tale typically ends with a marriage between partners who allegorically embody their respective nations and cultures. Glorvina, for example, marries an Englishman who comes to love Ireland as well as its princess. Though *The Missionary*'s protagonists are similarly allegorical, a Hindu priestess and a Catholic priest cannot marry. Bound to celibacy, they are obviously not headed for a happy ending.

The novel opens in Portugal, where Hilarion, scion of a noble family, is a priest with an 'insatiable thirst for the conversion of souls' (Owenson 2002: 77). He sails to Goa and travels to Lahore to study languages with a local pundit. A celebrated Brahmin guru comes to town to host a theological debate among local scholars; on the pundit's advice, Hilarion attends the gathering to preach Christianity. There he sees the Guru's granddaughter Luxima, 'the most sacred of vestals, the Prophetess and Brahmachira of Cashmire' (Owenson 2002: 90). Owenson establishes Luxima's allegorical character along with her exotic beauty: 'she looked like the tutelary intelligence of the Hindu mythology, newly descended on earth, from the radiant sphere assigned her in the Indian zodiac' (Owenson 2002: 92). It is a vision heavily indebted to Jones's work on Hindu mythology. The helpful pundit has another suggestion: if Hilarion can convert this priestess to Christianity, 'her example will operate like a spell on her compatriots, and the follower of Brahma would fly from the altar of his ancient gods, to worship in that temple in which she would become a votarist' (Owenson 2002: 98). Testing this theory will lead the missionary down a dangerous path.

It leads to Luxima's home, the 'delicious vale' (Owenson 2002: 103) of Cashmire (Kashmir) in India's far north. Owenson culled her description of Kashmir from the travel narrative of François Bernier:

> Surrounded by those mighty mountains whose summits appear tranquil and luminous, above the regions of clouds which float on their brow; whose grotesque forms are brightened by innumerable rills, and dashed by foaming torrents, the valley of Cashmire presented to the wandering eye scenes of picturesque and glowing beauty, whose character varied with each succeeding hour. (Owenson 2002: 105)

You can see why Romantic readers, including Percy Shelley, loved this stuff. Hilarion sets up camp in a 'wild and sequestered' cave, the fabulous *'grotto of congelations'* (Owenson 2002: 107) that Bernier heard about but was unable to visit. Luxima performs her daily worship nearby, at the confluence of two streams, a site 'sacred to the followers of Brahma', as Owenson's footnote informs readers. Her description of the first meeting between Hilarion and Luxima broadcasts her characters' allegorical significance:

> Silently gazing, in wonder, upon each other, they stood finely opposed, the noblest specimens of the human species, as it appears in the most opposite regions of the earth; she, like the East, lovely and luxuriant; he, like the West, lofty and commanding: the one, radiant in all the lustre, attractive in all the softness which distinguishes her native regions; the other, towering in all the energy, imposing in all the vigour, which marks his ruder latitudes: she, looking like a creature formed to feel and to submit; he, like a being created to resist and to command: while both appeared as the ministers and representatives of the two most powerful religions of the earth; the one no less enthusiastic in her brilliant errors, than the other confident in his immutable truth. (Owenson 2002: 109)

The tableau epitomises the hoary gendered stereotype of East as feminine and West as masculine. Balachandra Rajan traces the history of this feminisation of the Orient in English literature in *Under Western Eyes: India from Milton to Macaulay*. He sees *The Missionary* as participating in 'two discourses: a literary discourse of world humanism, for which William Jones provides an Indian scholarly foundation, and an imperial discourse gendered so as to offer India the enlightenments of feminine submission to Western overlordship' (Rajan 1999: 135–6). In this view,

Owenson takes up the gendered stereotypes of the latter discourse partly in order to create a platform for the discourse of world humanism, or religious tolerance. Her text opportunistically deconstructs the gendered East–West binary but never completely supersedes it. For example, Hilarion uses his 'towering' intelligence in the service of denial, hiding his attraction to Luxima. She meanwhile proves both more reasonable and less languid that the stereotype would predict, becoming a character with motives and agency of her own.

Hilarion cultivates Luxima's acquaintance, intent on converting her. The novel takes a perspectivist approach to religion: Hinduism is characterised as 'impious', 'idolatrous', and so forth (Owenson 2002: 100, 120), but this is clearly Hilarion's perception. He realises that Luxima sees Christianity in the same way: 'in the same light as the infidel appeared to him, in such had he appeared to her; alike beyond the pale of salvation, alike dark in error' (Owenson 2002: 113–14). But she does not share his zeal for conversion: 'to see thee prostrate at the shrine of Brahma, I would not see thee changed from what thou art – for thou belongest to thy sublime and pure religion and thy religion to thee' (Owenson 2002: 141). As the two grow closer, Hilarion uses emotional blackmail – the threat of leaving – to get Luxima to declare herself a Christian. But as soon as they share their 'first look of love acknowledged and returned' (Owenson 2002: 172), things begin to fall apart. Someone sees them together, and she knows exposure will get her 'excommunicated', as Owenson terms it (the author's strategy of using Christian terms to denote elements of Hinduism works to erode the differences between the two faiths (Wright 2002: 46)). The lovers decide on 'immolation', or sacrifice – having no more contact so as to stay true to their respective religious vows. They agree to meet just one more time to say goodbye. Luxima shows up dressed as an outcast, shunned by her Hindu community. Hearing a religious procession, they flee to a 'terrific cavern', which turns out to be a Hindu temple, described in a colonial Gothic mode, like something out of *Indiana Jones and the Temple of Doom* (Wright 2002: 38): 'Idols of gigantic stature, colossal forms, hideous and grotesque images . . . This sanctuary of the most awful superstition, worthy of the wildest rites of a dark idolatry, was . . . wrapt in . . . gloom' (Owenson 2002: 185–6). They watch from behind a pillar as Luxima's traumatised grandfather, the guru, pronounces sentence: shunning for her, execution by burning for him (punishments drawn from Jones's translation of the Hindu legal code, the *Ordinances of Menu*).

To escape, Hilarion persuades Luxima to travel with him to Goa ('as my disciple only') and to be baptised (Owenson 2002: 191). But she draws the line when he tries to make her shed her 'muntra, or Brahminical rosary':

> Oh! thou wilt not deprive me of these also? I have nothing left now *but these*! nothing to remind me, in the land of strangers, of my country and my people, save only these: it makes a part of the religion I have abandoned, to respect the sacred ties of nature; does my new faith command me to break them? (Owenson 2002: 193–4)

Here Owenson's novel of ideas takes up its polemic, making the important point that when religion forms part of a cultural continuum, conversion is unlikely to succeed and damaging to individuals when it does. Hilarion realises as much and makes no attempt to proselytise during their journey:

> Withheld less by a principle of self-preservation than by his fears for the safety and even life of his innocent proselyte; he also felt his enthusiasm in the cause weakened, by the apparent impossibility of its success; for he perceived that the religious prejudices of Hindostan were too intimately connected with the temporal prosperity of its inhabitants, with the established opinions, with the laws, and even with the climate of the country, to be universally subverted, but by a train of moral and political events, which should equally emancipate their minds from antiquated error, in which they were absorbed, and destroy the fundamental principles of their loose and ill-digested government. (Owenson 2002: 196)

The ambiguous suggestion is that without radical social and political change, religious conversion will not succeed. What 'train of moral and political events' would accomplish such a dramatic change? Is it advisable, or even possible? Owenson's narrator does not say.

On their way out of Kashmir, Luxima and Hilarion pause on a mountaintop for 'a last view of her native Eden', like 'the first pair, when they had reached the boundary of their native paradise' (Owenson 2002: 206–7). Religious intolerance is the snake in their fragile Eden. After implausible adventures, they join a caravan whose travellers form an image of subcontinental hybridity and multicultural coexistence:

> Mogul pilgrims, going from India to visit the tomb of their prophet at Mecca; merchants from Thibet and China, carrying the produce of their native climes, the Western coasts of Hindostan; Seiks, the Swiss of the East, going to join the forces of the rebelling Rajahs; and faquirs and dervises, who rendered religion profitable by carrying for sale in their girdles, spices, gold-dust and musk. (Owenson 2002: 223)

Also travelling with the caravan are a few Europeans, including some Jesuit monks. A conversation Hilarion has with one of them marks how far he has come from his former zealous attitude. This becomes the occasion for Owenson to comment incisively on colonialism. The Jesuit accuses the missionary of 'languor in zeal' for not preaching Christianity everywhere he goes (Owenson 2002: 225). The word 'languor' invokes the stereotype of the languid Oriental, earlier applied to Luxima. Is the missionary turning into his opposite? In his defence he cites Hinduism's resistance to proselytism for the reasons canvassed above.

The Jesuit retorts, '[H]ad its disciples been always thus moderate, thus languid, thus philosophically tolerant, never would the cross have been raised upon the remotest shores of the Eastern and Western oceans!' Hilarion's answer is an anti-colonialist set piece:

> Too often has it been raised under the influence of a sentiment diametrically opposite to the spirit of the doctrine of him who *suffered on it*, and who came not to *destroy*, but to *save* mankind. Too often has it been raised by those whose minds were guided by an evil and interested policy, fatal to the effects which it sought to accomplish, and who lifted to Heaven, hands stained with the blood of those, to whom they had been sent to preach the religion of peace, of love, and of salvation; for even the zeal of religion, when animated by human passions, may become fatal in its excess, and that daring fanaticism, which gives force and activity to the courage of the man, may render merciless and atrocious, the zeal of the bigot. (Owenson 2002: 225)

For Owenson's British contemporaries this would have called to mind the so-called Black Legend of the Spanish colonisation of the New World, often deployed to make British colonialism look benevolent by contrast. Her strategic choice of setting thus frees her to employ this strong rhetoric. Hilarion adds a sardonic crack:

> the religion we proffer them is seldom illustrated by its influence on our own lives. We bring them a spiritual creed, which commands them to forget the world, and we take from them temporal possessions, which prove how much we *live for it*. (Owenson 2002: 226)

A footnote reports the small number of converts produced by two centuries of missionary activity – an estimated 12,000 out of 100 million Hindus, 'almost entirely *chancalas*, or outcasts' (Owenson 2002: 226). Driven by rhetoric and backed by data, Owenson's polemic gives a serious dimension to this extravagant, exotic Romantic novel.

The Jesuits turn out to be from the Spanish Inquisition. They arrest Hilarion and Luxima and take them to Goa for execution. The city's population is restless: 'it was rumoured, that the power of the Spanish government in Portugal and its colonies was on the point of extinction, and it was known by many fatal symptoms, that the Indians were ripe for insurrection' (Owenson 2002: 241). Here Owenson inserts her only footnote referring to contemporaneous British India: 'An insurrection of a fatal consequence took place in *Vellore* so late as 1806 . . . supposed to have originated in the religious bigotry of the natives, suddenly kindled by the supposed threatened violation of their faith from the Christian settlers' (Owenson 2002: 241). A later, more serious revolt, the 1857 Mutiny, was also generally attributed to anger at British disrespect for indigenous religion. It is no coincidence that Owenson chose to republish *The Missionary* in 1859.

The novel's denouement is a scene of intense drama and symbolic resonance: Hilarion's auto-da-fé, or execution by burning at the stake. Such a death by fire would certainly have called to mind for educated Britons the controversial Hindu custom of *sati*. At the beginning of *The Curse of Kehama*, Southey imagines a double *sati*: two widows of the slain Prince Arvalan burn with his corpse. 'They force her on, they bind her to the dead' (l. 172). In Southey's poem, *sati* appears inhuman, as well as hypocritical in pretending that widows want to die. At the time Owenson wrote, the debate over whether the colonial government should ban *sati* was ongoing, part of the larger debate over the extent to which the colonial government should intervene in Indian culture. *Sati* could be used to justify expanding the scope of the colonial government: 'white men protecting brown women from brown men', as Gayatri Spivak puts it in her famous essay, 'Does the Subaltern Speak?'[15]

When Luxima (broken out of prison by the perennially meddling pundit) reaches the place of execution, Owenson again renders her as an icon, but one whose significance varies with the observer's beliefs:

> A form scarcely human, darting with the velocity of lightning through the multitude, reached the foot of the pile, and stood before it, in a grand and aspiring attitude; the deep red flame of the slowly kindling fire shone through the transparent drapery which flowed in loose folds from the bosom of the seeming vision, and tinged with golden hues, those long dishevelled tresses, which streamed like the rays of a meteor on the air; – thus bright and aerial as it stood, it looked like a spirit sent from Heaven. (Owenson 2002: 248)

Christians see the cross on her bosom (given her by Hilarion) and think they are witnessing 'a miracle wrought for the salvation of a persecuted martyr'. Hindus see a 'Brahmin mark' on her forehead and think they behold the '*herald* of the tenth *Avatar*, announcing vengeance to the enemies of their religion'. Hilarion himself sees 'only the unfortunate he had made – the creature he adored – his disciple! – his mistress! – the Pagan Priestess – the Christian Neophyte – his still lovely, but much changed Luxima' (Owenson 2002: 249). She murmurs 'the *Gayatra*, pronounced by the Indian women before their voluntary immolation', and jumps into the fire, calling, '"My beloved, I come! – Brahma receive and eternally unite our spirits!"' Superimposing two religious practices that end human life in a particularly grisly way, Catholic heretic burning and Hindu *sati*, Owenson dramatises the extremes of fanaticism and intolerance in both Eastern and Western cultures. Luxima's 'voluntary immolation' (Owenson 2002: 246) may be the product of a delusion; she has been physically ill and mentally disordered in the days leading up to the execution.[16] The word 'immolation' links her act to the sacrifice he and she had earlier intended to make for their respective religions – the sacrifice, for the lovers, of their earthly togetherness. Self-immolation now appears a means to eternal union.

Cross-cultural contact has led to tragedy: the iconic representatives of East and West are on the verge of burning together. But that is not all that goes up in flames. The volatile crowd, 'inflamed' by Luxima's self-sacrifice, sets the whole city on fire:

> [T]he timid spirits of the Hindoos rallied to an event which touched their hearts, and roused them from their lethargy of despair; – the sufferings, the oppression they had so long endured, seemed now epitomized before their eyes, in the person of their celebrated and distinguished Prophetess . . . they rushed forward with a hideous cry, to rescue his priestess – and to avenge the long slighted cause of their religion, and their freedom. (Owenson 2002: 250)

We might compare Luxima's leap into the flames, at least in its effect, if not its motivation, to the self-immolation of Mohamed Bouazizi, the Tunisian street vendor who set himself on fire to protest a dictatorship – and sparked a revolution, the first of the 2011 Arab Spring. Cultural intolerance, Owenson warns, is a dangerous course for colonial rulers.

But nobody burns to death in *The Missionary*. When Hilarion leaps to Luxima's rescue, an Inquisitor is not far behind, with a dagger aimed at the heretic's heart. It misses him, but deals her a deathly wound. Hilarion carries her to a seaside cave, where she dies exhorting the missionary to preach reconciliation between the two faiths. 'But should thy eloquence . . . fail, tell them my story! tell them how I suffered, and how even thou hast failed' to convert Luxima to Christianity. '*I die* as

Brahmin women *die*, a *Hindu* in my feelings and my faith – dying for him I loved, and believing as my fathers have believed' (Owenson 2002: 257). Once again, in case anyone missed it, Owenson's Orientalist novel of ideas hammers home its polemical message. An epilogue notes rumours of a recluse living in a cave in Kashmir: 'a wild and melancholy man! whose religion was unknown, but who prayed at the confluence of rivers, at the rising and setting of the sun' (Owenson 2002: 260). This is clearly Hilarion, but the time and place of his religious practice is the same as Luxima's when she was a Brahmin priestess, suggesting a hybrid or syncretic religion. Has Hilarion gone native? This Romantic saga of cross-cultural love ends with the failure of religious institutions and the violent rejection of colonial rule. Its veiled warning to India's nineteenth-century rulers fell on deaf ears.

Alastor

Owenson's novel captivated the poet Percy Bysshe Shelley, a voracious reader. He wrote to a friend, 'Since I have read this book I have read no other – but I have thought strangely' (quoted in Wright 2002: 42). A number of Shelley's poems reference the East: among others, the well-known sonnet 'Ozymandias' (1817), an ironic portrait of a long-dead despot, and The *Revolt of Islam* (1818), which replays the French Revolution in an Asian setting. His masterpiece *Prometheus Unbound* (1820) is set in the Indian Caucasus and has a heroine named Asia. This poetic drama re-enacts the fall of empire once again as part of a complex, syncretic story of human mental evolution (Butler 1994: 439, 442). Like many nineteenth-century Britons, Shelley had a relative working in the East: his cousin, Lieutenant Thomas Medwin (also a poet), who fought in India and read Shelley his Indian journal when they met in Pisa in 1820 (Leask 1992: 69). Though Shelley produced many lovely lyrics, his major poems are serious, philosophical and political (in his somewhat idiosyncratic understanding of the political). As Shelley scholar Kelvin Everest reminds us, 'Shelley's poetry is *radical* poetry' (Everest 1994: 314). His first notably successful longer poem, *Alastor, or, The Spirit of Solitude* (1816), tells the story of a fantastic journey into the East in which psychological, aesthetic and political themes are intertwined.

Alastor features a Shelley-like protagonist: an exceptionally gifted individual who leaves home to seek 'strange truths in undiscovered lands' (l. 77). Lured onward by a dream vision of a symbolic, alluring 'veiled maid', the Visionary, as Earl Wasserman (1971) calls him, never finds what he seeks, finally dying in a remote location amid mountain crags and autumn leaves. *Alastor* is a quest romance, a genre popular in the first two decades of the nineteenth century. Southey wrote two quest romances set in India, as I have noted. *Thalaba* and *The Curse of Kehama* came equipped with copious, erudite footnotes (mined for obscure lore by subsequent poets, including Byron, as we will see). But *Alastor* eschews this type of apparatus, despite its debt to Shelley's extensive reading in narratives of travel and exploration, as well as literary texts such as those of Owenson and Southey.[17] The poem's preface tells the reader that it 'may be considered as allegorical'. Twentieth-century critics took this as a cue to read *Alastor* as an 'inward, mental voyage toward a psychic origin', a 'meditation on the poetical character'. This is similar to the way Coleridge's *Rime of the Ancient Mariner* was read in the mid-twentieth century, as I discussed in Chapter 1 – as a Christian allegory, taking place in a 'mental landscape' with 'symbolic topography' (Tetreault 1987: 45, 50). Postcolonial critics, as we have seen, moved away from such ahistorical interpretations. By taking the connection between geography and history seriously, they are able to read the *Rime* as a meditation on colonialism and its effect on metropolitan culture.

What happens if we try this with *Alastor*? Its preface also tells us that it is a poem about desire. Like so many young British men in this age of expanding empire, Shelley's Visionary pursues his desire in the East. *Orientalism* pioneered postcolonial criticism's investigation of imperial desire: the ways in which 'the Orient becomes an imaginative investment, the locus of a symbolic quest for identity on the part of the West', expected to 'fulfil the self-realisation of its colonizers in all kinds of ways – geographical, commercial, political and literary' (Rossington 1991: 19). Such an imaginative investment in the East helps lead Walter Scott's Richard Middlemas to India in *The Surgeon's Daughter*, though Middlemas's motives are crasser than those of Shelley's protagonist, as we saw in Chapter 3. The desire that Shelley's Visionary pursues is much loftier and less specific. Its personification in the poem, the 'veiled maid', owes her form to the powerful Orientalist stereotype of the East as feminine, embodied by Owenson's heroine Luxima. She descends in turn, as we saw, from the Hindu goddesses of Jones's hymns. Her 'strange harp', her 'sinuous veil' and 'the outspread arms now bare,/ Her dark locks floating in the breath of night' (ll. 166, 176–8) recall the novel's extravagantly romantic descriptions of the Brahmin priestess. *Alastor*'s vision also takes place in the Vale of Kashmir. The setting and literary genealogy of Shelley's allegorical quest point toward concerns less generalised than 'the poetical character'.

To grasp the significance of the poem's eastern geography, we must first look closely at its form. Wasserman's influential reading established that *Alastor* is narrated not by the Visionary, but by a contrasting character who admires and elegises the dead youth. Wasserman sees the narrator as a more conventional poet (perhaps akin to Wordsworth, from whom Shelley took one of the poem's epigraphs): someone for whom Utopia, if it exists, is located here on earth. The Visionary sets his sights higher, aiming for nothing less than 'infinite perfection at the end of infinite time' – a futile but admirable ambition, Faustian in scale. According to Wasserman, *Alastor* sets these contrasting perspectives in a 'sceptical dialogue' that is ultimately irresolvable (Wasserman 1971: 33). If the Visionary's grandiose desires are imperialist in nature, as I have suggested, the poem's attitude toward this is thus deeply sceptical and ambivalent. The veiled maid is a solipsistic delusion, though an attractive one; the quest fails, ending in the protagonist's death.

A closer look at the Visionary's vision may give us more insight into the specific type of imperialism with which we are concerned. It is not the more familiar imperialism of the later nineteenth century, rooted in a racialist or jingoist worldview. For Romantic idealists like Southey (the younger Southey) and Shelley, the attraction of empire was inseparable from that of the French Revolution. This connection emerges from Shelley's 1820 essay, *A Philosophical View of Reform*. The essay sets forth a characteristically ambitious vision of human history as progressing from tyranny toward liberty. It surveys the nations of the earth, presenting the United States government as 'the first practical illustration of the new philosophy', namely that of the Enlightenment, from Bacon and Berkeley to Hume and Hartley (Shelley 1954: 234). The French Revolution succeeded in getting rid of 'the hierarchy, the aristocracy, and the monarchy, and the whole of that peculiarly oppressive system on which they were based', but the subsequent reaction partly restored the old system (Shelley 1954: 236).

Surveying the globe for more hopeful signs, Shelley looks to India. What he sees there is worth quoting at length:

> Revolutions in the political and religious state of the Indian peninsula seem to be accomplishing, and it cannot be doubted but the zeal of the missionaries of what is called the Christian faith will produce beneficial innovation there, even by the application of dogmas and forms of what is here an outworn incumbrance. The Indians have been enslaved and cramped in the most severe and paralyzing forms which were ever devised by man; some of this new enthusiasm ought to be kindled among them to consume

it and leave them free, and even if the doctrines of Jesus do not penetrate through the darkness of that which those who profess to be his followers call Christianity, there will yet be a number of social forms modeled upon those European feelings from which it has taken its colour substituted to those according to which they are at present cramped, and from which, when the time for complete emancipation shall arrive, their disengagement may be less difficult, and under which their progress to it may be the less imperceptibly slow. Many native Indians have acquired, it is said, a competent knowledge in the arts and philosophy of Europe, and Locke and Hume and Rousseau are familiarly talked of in Brahminical society. But the thing to be sought is that they should as they would if they were free attain to a system of arts and literature of their own. (Shelley 1954: 238)

We can recognise this view of an India 'enslaved' to Oriental despotism, in need of Western models to escape its 'cramped' state, as highly problematic, though Shelley is prescient in citing elite Indians' engagement with European culture (Leask 1992:119). Shelley the atheist surprisingly praises Christian missionaries for helping institute better 'social forms' than the 'severe and paralyzing' ones of Hinduism. But his prose betrays the problem with his analysis through the awkward structure of the last sentence: the 'faltering, unpunctuated conditional' of 'as they would if they were free' (Leask 1992: 119). How meaningful is emancipation from the Brahmins if India remains under British rule?

Alastor, written a few years earlier, also injects Western ideas into an Eastern context. The veiled maid, reminiscent of Jones's Hindu goddesses, is a 'spokeswoman for revolutionary enlightenment' (Leask 1992: 127). She speaks to the sleeping Visionary of 'Knowledge and truth and virtue . . . And lofty hopes of divine liberty' (ll. 158–9). How are we to understand this apparent conflation of the East/West binary in the context of *Alastor's* poetic form? The narrative frame makes clear that the vision of the veiled maid is an illusion, an impossible dream that leads the Visionary to his death. The preface lauds the protagonist's idealism as a 'generous error', 'sacred thirst of doubtful knowledge' and 'illustrious superstition'. These oxymoronic terms of praise suggest ideals at once appealing and unrealisable. Nigel Leask finds in *Alastor* 'a cultural self-awareness which rejects both "orientalist" and assimilationist strategies in constructing India' (Leask 1992: 129). Cultural syncretism, like that pioneered by Jones, is no longer a viable course in 1816.

The vision of the veiled maid comes directly after the most geographically specific section of the poem, describing the Visionary's journey to the Eastern cradle of civilisation:

> His wandering step,
> Obedient to high thoughts, has visited
> The awful ruins of the days of old:
> Athens, and Tyre, and Balbec, and the waste
> Where stood Jerusalem, the fallen towers
> Of Babylon, the eternal pyramids,
> Memphis and Thebes, and whatsoe'er of strange
> Sculptured on alabaster obelisk
> Or jasper tomb, or mutilated sphinx,
> Dark Ethiopia in her desert hills
> Conceals. Among the ruined temples there,
> Stupendous columns and wild images
> Of more than man, where marble demons watch
> The Zodiac's brazen mystery.

(ll. 107–19)

Touring the Middle East and northern Africa, as Saree Makdisi observes, Shelley's protagonist finds time standing bizarrely still:

> nothing has changed in this mythic Orient, nothing has altered the Roman temples of Baalbek, the Phoenician palaces of Tyre, the temples of Athens, the towers of Babylon . . . And yet, of course, time has moved on: these are ruined temples, open wastes, fallen towers, mutilated monuments. (Makdisi 1998: 140)

Here is another strange paradox. Where is everybody? If this is the distant past, why aren't all these palaces and temples populated by the people of those ancient times? And if this is actually the present day, as their ruined state might indicate, then where are all the living inhabitants of the present-day Middle East? The eerie emptiness and silence of this scene suggest some kind of open-air museum. Makdisi calls *Alastor* a 'narrative of non-encounter'. On this basis he argues, 'Shelley's vision of the East is ruthlessly violent, for he symbolically depopulates a space in order to establish the possibility (or even inevitability) of its reclamation as part of some invented 'Western' heritage' (Makdisi 1998: 142).

But this pronouncement does not take into account the narrative structure of Shelley's poem.[18] If we attribute it to the deluded Visionary's fallible perception, the absence of people in the ruins is consistent with his tragic flaw as specified by the poem's subtitle. The 'Spirit of Solitude' is the evil genius (definition of the Greek *alastor*) that leads the Visionary astray. He is an idealist who fails to engage with people and society, and this solipsism, in all of its ramifications, brings on his downfall. We can see by now that *Alastor*'s version of the quest romance is not, as earlier critics assumed, internalised, in the sense of lacking any specific reference outside the psychological or aesthetic. Rather, Shelley's poem explores a particular 'psychopathology of empire' (Leask 1992: 124). Signposting this subject is the imaginary geography of the Visionary's journey. Shelley mines the available repertoire of images of the East – in particular, Owenson's iconic Brahmin priestess Luxima, re-imagined as the illusory 'veiled maid' – for an ambivalent exploration of an extraordinary individual's misguided desire. Worn by his wanderings, the Visionary resembles a victim of colonial disease:

> And now his limbs were lean: his scattered hair
> Sered by the autumn of strange suffering
> Sung dirges in the wind; his listless hand
> Hung like dead bone within its withered skin.
>
> (ll. 248–51)

Drawn to the East by idealistic but wrongheaded desire, he is finally killed by it.[19]

The Giaour

Byron, like Shelley, made the East a major topic of his poetry. Famously cynical about the commercial value of his poetic product, he proposed to 'sell you, mixed with Western sentimentalism,/ Some samples of the finest Orientalism'. 'Stick to the East', he advised the poet Tom Moore, calling it 'the only poetical policy . . . the public are orientalizing, and pave the path for you' (quoted in Leask 2005: 137). (Moore, following his friend's advice, produced *Lalla Rookh* in 1817 and landed a publisher's advance of 3,000 guineas.) Byron was the only Romantic poet who actually travelled to the East, visiting Greece, Turkey and the remote Muslim country of Albania on his extended Grand Tour in 1809–11. His travels provided material for the hugely popular *Childe Harold's Pilgrimage,* whose first two cantos came out in 1812. *The Giaour* (pronounced 'zhower'), published the following year, was the first of a series of Turkish Tales, followed by *The Bride of Abydos* in 1813 and *The Corsair* and *Lara* in 1814. Byron gives his fans a dramatic story of frustrated passion, bloody vengeance and despairing love beyond the grave, set in an exotic, chaotic corner of the Ottoman Empire (Gordon 2002). With its extensive footnotes on Muslim culture and customs, culled from Byron's experiences abroad as well as his reading in Romantic Orientalism, *The Giaour* is more than just exotic fluff. Its narrative form of jumbled fragments with multiple narrators works to complicate the binary opposition between East and West, Islam and Christianity.

At the height of the evangelical campaign to let missionaries into India, ardently supported by Byron's 'chief literary antagonist', Southey, Byron's poem sets both these great monotheisms in a less than flattering light (Butler 1988: 85).

A 'giaour', we learn from Byron's notes, is an infidel, a non-Muslim. The story that emerges from the poem (subtitled 'a fragment of a Turkish tale') is a grim one. The beautiful Leila is a Circassian maiden married to a Muslim nobleman, Hassan. Unfaithful to him with the title character, a young Venetian, Leila is sewn in a sack and drowned by her outraged husband 'in the Mussulman manner', as the poem's Advertisement tells us. The Giaour then joins a band of Albanian mercenaries and takes revenge by killing Hassan in a bloody ambush. Years later he turns up in a Christian monastery, dressed like a monk, but not praying. Just before his death he makes a long, dramatic confession to a priest there. The story, emerging in cryptic stages from the poem's complex structure, sets up familiar dichotomies between East and West, Muslim and Christian, which it then proceeds to undermine, as Alan Richardson argues (2006: 219). This begins with the Advertisement, which specifies the tale's geographical and temporal setting to a seemingly gratuitous degree of exactness: Greece and the Balkans, the very eastern edge of Europe, then ruled by the Ottoman Empire. The time is also specific: the mid-1790s, when 'the Seven Islands [off the west coast of Greece] were possessed by the Republic of Venice, and soon after the Arnauts [Albanians] were beaten back from the Morea [Peloponnesian peninsula], which they had ravaged for some time subsequent to the Russian invasion'. Venice occupied the islands until 1797; Russia invaded the peninsula in 1770, but withdrew in 1794, leaving it to the rampaging Albanians. It was a chaotic period, with various factions contending for power in the shadow of the declining Ottoman Empire. Greece was an Ottoman province, but by no means a secure one. Byron gives us a vision of history as 'a matter not of monolithic, eternally contending cultural blocs but of shifting loyalties and alliances, unstable identities, cultures that interpenetrate as much as they collide'. Specifying the setting in this way prompts readers to 'take a . . . particularised, localised, and historically specific view' of the events of the story (Richardson 2006: 221, 216).

The poem's prologue is narrated by a pro-Hellenic, classically educated voice much like the author's. Critics have read it as setting up a political allegory. The poem opens at the tomb of Themistocles, who helped save Greece from Persian invasion in classical times: 'When shall such a hero live again?' (l. 6). Despite the natural beauty of the Greek landscape, 'lust and rapine wildly reign' (l. 60). An extended simile compares the nation to a beautiful corpse shortly after death, 'Before Decay's effacing fingers/ Have swept the lines where beauty lingers' (ll. 72–3). The narrator recalls Greece's classical glory days and resents its present bondage to the Ottomans. He calls the Greeks 'servile offspring of the free', exhorting them to '[a]rise, and make again your own' their native land (ll. 111, 115). Political meaning is not far to seek in a poem about a dead woman loved by two men, a Christian European and an Ottoman Muslim: East and West contending for the birthplace of freedom. However, as Richardson contends, to succumb to this kind of allegorical reading is to miss the way the rest of the poem works to undermine the oppositions that the prologue sets up (Richardson 2006: 217).

A closer look at the title character complicates our view of him. Making him a Venetian, a citizen of a dying empire (more moribund than the Ottoman Empire, which would survive into the twentieth century), suggests the tenuousness of European power this far to the east (Richardson 2006: 218). Costume is also significant:[20] the dashing adventurer chooses to dress as a Muslim, 'in Arnaut garb,/ Apostate from his own vile faith', according to his enemy Hassan (ll. 615–16). We might be reminded of the Albanian getup, complete with turban, that Byron wears in a famous portrait. But a more relevant comparison would be John Walker Lindh, the 'American Taliban', who joined America's Muslim enemies early in the war with Afghanistan and is now serving a twenty-year prison sentence. There are choices from which one cannot turn back. Allying himself with what we might today call a Muslim militia, 'the Giaour has renounced his Christian faith and his European allegiance' (Richardson 2006: 219). He has become, if not a full-fledged Muslim, a cultural hybrid: neither one thing nor the other, a man in between, operating in a permeable zone of shifting alliances and turbulent local conflict.

The Giaour's hybridity emerges further in relation to his antagonist, Hassan. Bound together in a classic love triangle, the two men share an intense homosocial bond:

But love itself could never pant
For all that Beauty sighs to grant
With half the fervor Hate bestows
Upon the last embrace of foes.

(ll. 647–50)

They share other characteristics as well. Obviously, both are men of action, violent and fearless, a military ethos that the poem tends to glorify. The Giaour also has what Hassan labels 'the evil eye' (glossed in Byron's footnotes as 'a common superstition in the Levant'). But Hassan, too, has an unusual gaze, to which the poem refers more than once. It persists after death: as the Giaour bends over his enemy's corpse, Hassan's 'unclos'd eye' continues 'lowering on his enemy' (ll. 669–70). The antagonists also share, as the Giaour's final confession reveals, an uncompromising attitude to female infidelity. 'Yet did he but what I had done/ Had she been false to more than one' (ll. 1062–3). This overlap or doubling between the male representatives of Islam and Christianity troubles an allegorical reading (Richardson 2006: 220).

What about Leila, loved by both men, whose shocking execution draws the Giaour's revenge? She is little more than a placeholder in the poem. Like the heroines of other Byron poems, such as *Manfred* and *The Siege of Corinth*, 'Leila is viewed entirely from the vantage point of her death – which is therefore simultaneously the starting-point and climax of the story, and fixes her as an icon'. She never speaks; though the whole story revolves around her, it is reconstructed from various male points of view (Franklin 1992: 39). Like Owenson's Luxima, Byron's Leila personifies the enduring Orientalist stereotype of the East as feminine. She embodies the 'unity of the spiritual and the sensual' that gives this icon its enduring allure. Before he kills her, Hassan keeps her in his harem, or 'Serai' (l. 444), an Eastern institution that was the target of Western travellers' prurient speculation for centuries. Byron catalogues Leila's charms in a poetic blazon, starting with her eyes:

> Her eye's dark charm 'twere vain to tell,
> But gaze on that of the Gazelle,
> It will assist thy fancy well,
> As large, as languishingly dark,
> But Soul beamed forth in every spark
> That darted from beneath the lid,
> Bright as the jewel of Giamschid.

(ll. 473–9)

The footnotes gloss this gem as 'the celebrated fabulous ruby of Sultan Giamschid'. They also comment sardonically on the 'vulgar error' of the Western belief that Islam allows women no souls. In fact, 'the Koran allots at least a third of Paradise to well-behaved women', though most 'Mussulmans interpret the text their own way' to exclude them. Like an earlier traveller to Turkey whose letters he had read, Lady Mary Wortley Montagu, Byron was concerned to correct British errors about the East (Sharafuddin 1994: 217).

Unlike Luxima, who becomes a character with an independent voice and a degree of agency, Leila remains a device. She motivates the Giaour's apostasy, 'his abandonment of religion and . . . substitution of an extremely individualized idealized romantic love' (Franklin 1992: 44). This is not, the poem makes clear, a courtly or chivalric love: ''Tis true, I could not whine or sigh,/ I knew but to obtain or die./ I die – but first I have possest' (ll. 1112–14). But the Giaour values the fact that Leila gives him her love freely, making the poem 'paradoxically both a strongly charged plea for female sexual autonomy, and an acknowledgement that as the fabric of society is built on the foundation of female chastity, woman will always be the chief victim of illegitimate love' (Franklin 2000: 47). Like her lover, as Richardson notes, Leila is a hybrid. She is from Circassia, 'a region of the northern Caucasus sited precisely on the imaginary geopolitical line between Europe and Asia', influenced by 'Greeks, Romans, Khazars, and Mongols . . . Georgians, Russians, and Turks . . . a region where Muslim and Christian traditions had long coexisted'. Famed in Orientalist discourse for the beauty of its women, Circassia is also a site of cultural interpenetration (Richardson 2006: 221).

The poem's formal structure is characterised by multiple perspectives, linked to different cultures. We can identify four speakers, including the narrator of the framing section on Greece. The first voice narrating the central action is, significantly, that of a Muslim: a fisherman who watches the central character 'thundering' along the coast 'on blackest steed' (l. 180). As Jerome McGann's classic study points out, the Giaour is 'dramatized largely through the responses he elicits from those who watch him' (McGann 1968: 150). From the fisherman's point of view, the Giaour is an alien: 'I know thee not, I loathe thy race' (l. 191). Byron seems to relish showing his readers how hated Christians are in the East (Butler 1988: 87). But even this hostile observer is riveted by the Venetian's appearance, watching him with a 'gaze of wonder' (l. 201):

> Though young and pale, that sallow front
> Is scath'd by fiery passion's brunt,
> Though bent on earth thine evil eye
> As meteor like thou glidest by,
> Right well I view, and deem thee one
> Whom Othman's sons [Muslims] should slay or shun.
>
> (ll. 194–9)

The Giaour's antagonist, Hassan, is also first shown from the sympathetic perspective of his co-religionist, who describes Hassan's ruined hall after his death in a somewhat kitschy Oriental Gothic, complete with cobwebs, bats and owls. 'Courtesy and Pity died/ With Hassan on the mountain side' (ll. 346–7). According to Mohammed Sharafuddin, Byron 'records Islamic terms and idioms with great accuracy'. He attributes Byron's detail-consciousness in presenting Islamic civilisation to his Western readers not just to his wish to 'distinguish himself from the rack of merely reading orientalists' (as someone who has actually seen the places he describes). More important, Sharafuddin believes, is the poet's concern 'to give weight and dignity to an alternative social and religious reality' (Sharafuddin 1994: 236).

The poem's portrayal of Islam, though not free of Orientalist stereotypes, tempers these with ethnographic detail. It is not an entirely sympathetic view: this is, after all, 'a religion that instructs a man to tie his wife in a sack and throw her into the sea for infidelity' (Butler 1988: 89). Byron's footnote tells his readers that this practice 'was not very uncommon in Turkey'. Another unattractive aspect of Islam as seen in the poem is its fanaticism. A dramatic sequence in the fisherman's speech imagines in Gothic detail the Giaour's fate in the afterlife: he will become a vampire, forced to suck his own family's blood (ll. 748–86). Byron's footnotes attribute the vampire superstition to 'Mr. Southey, in the notes to *Thalaba*', showing himself well read in the footnote-heavy Orientalist poetry of the early 1800s. This sequence, effectively putting a curse on the Giaour, recalls a central moment in Southey's *Curse of Kehama*: the rajah's blighting curse on the hero. Marilyn Butler views the fisherman's curse as the rhetorical centrepiece of *The Giaour*, showcasing the superstitious intolerance of one of the two great monotheisms it portrays.

But the other religion, Christianity, comes off no better than Islam. The priest to whom the Giaour confesses at the end of the poem views him as damned, an 'evil angel' (l. 912). He badgers the sinner to repent with a sermon derisively dismissed by Byron's footnote: 'The monk's sermon is omitted. It seems to have had so little effect upon the patient, that it could have no hopes from the reader.' Both of these two great religions fail Byron's protagonist: neither has a place, in this world or the next, for his beloved Leila. As Butler suggests, 'The poem's villains are the two great monotheistic codes, Christianity and Islam, comparable instruments of control over the lives of men and women' (Butler 1988: 91). Published the year Parliament voted to give Christian missionaries access to millions of colonised Hindus, a goal promoted by his rival Southey, Byron's poem rejects organised religion while presenting a complex, detailed and knowledgeable glimpse into an Eastern culture that he had explored in person as well as in books. Michael

Franklin compares Byron's outlook to that of Sir William Jones, the great Orientalist of the previous century: they share a 'hostility against Eurocentrism', an 'open-minded receptiveness to other cultures' and a concern to 'dispel prejudiced errors of literary Orientalism' (Franklin 2000: 65, 66). For Lord Byron, Saree Makdisi suggests, the East represented 'not only a refuge from modernity . . . but also a space from which to critique modernity and the West itself' (Makdisi 1998: 137).

This brief, selective survey of Romantic Orientalisms has illustrated important developments studied by postcolonial critics. Britain's imperial expansion during the Romantic era, most importantly in India, spurred the production of knowledge about Asia. The Orientalist scholarship of Sir William Jones and the Bengal Asiatic Society helped Britain to administer its empire, but also had an impact on metropolitan British culture – for example, when Jones's study of Persian, Arabic and Sanskrit poetry led him to articulate a Romantic expressivist poetics. Writers' pursuit of Eastern themes helped reshape Romantic literary genres such as the novel and the quest romance. Gender was central to Romantic literary representations of the East as writers from Jones to Shelley revelled in the spiritual and sensuous allure of feminine icons such as Jones's Hindu goddesses, Owenson's Brahmin priestess, Shelley's veiled maid and Byron's tragic Circassian, Leila. Figuring imperial desire as heterosexual desire naturalised imperial domination, but could also be used to raise questions about colonial policy, as in *The Missionary*. Romantic Orientalism took diverse forms, with writers intervening on both sides of important political and cultural debates, such as that on whether missionaries should be allowed to proselytise in British India.

The Romantic era was a transitional period in which the growing empire radically reversed its course on the so-called Eastern Question: how to govern large populations of non-Europeans. This reversal involved a dramatic shift in attitudes toward Asian cultures. Sir William Jones exemplifies a stance that prized knowledge of the East for its own sake, as well as for its instrumental value to colonial administrators. In his 'Essay on the Poetry of the Eastern Nations' he writes:

> [I]f the languages of the Eastern nations were studied in our great seminaries of learning, where every other useful branch of knowledge is taught to perfection, a new and ample field would be opened for speculation; we should have a more extensive insight into the history of the human mind. (Jones quoted in Makdisi 1998: 108)

By the end of the decades discussed in this book, a very different attitude toward Asian culture was in the ascendant. This becomes clear in a document that both summarises a set of opinions and advocates for a specific policy: Thomas Babington Macaulay's famous 'Minute on Indian Education' (1835). Macaulay, like Jones, was both a cultural producer and a colonial administrator. A historian and literary critic of sorts, he was a member of the East India Company's Supreme Council and President of its Committee of Public Instruction, supervising Company policy on the education of the colonised Indian population. The Committee was split into two factions: the Orientalists, and those who wanted to teach Indians the English language and European culture. Macaulay's Minute, addressed to Governor General Bentinck, advocates for the latter position and threatens that he will quit his job if the Orientalist stance prevails.[21]

The Minute is often quoted to sum up the arrogance of Victorian imperialism. Macaulay has talked to his adversaries, he reports:

> I am quite ready to take the Oriental learning at the value of the Orientalists themselves. I have never found one among them who could deny that a single shelf of a good European library was worth the whole native literature of India and Arabia. (Macaulay 1952: 722)

(Jones had been dead for four decades by this time.) Macaulay is steeped in an ideology of progress that views Europe, and Britain in particular, as leading the world forward to a better future. 'It may be safely said, that the literature now extant in [English] is of far greater value than all the literature which three hundred years ago was extant in all the languages of the world together' (Macaulay 1952: 723). His rhetoric ridicules Indian culture. The question, he proclaims, is

> whether, when we can patronize sound Philosophy and true History, we shall countenance, at the public expense, medical doctrines, which would disgrace an English farrier, – Astronomy, which would move laughter in girls at an English boarding school, – History, abounding with kings thirty feet high, and reigns thirty thousand years long, – and Geography, made up of seas of treacle and seas of butter. (Macaulay 1952: 723)

Such a description characterises Indian culture, by implication, as childishly ignorant, unable to tell the difference between factual history and geography and hyperbolic Hindu myths or legends. But Macaulay's memo also makes clear the common ground between him and his opponents. Both sides agreed 'that the dialects commonly spoken among the natives of this part of India, contain neither literary nor scientific information, and are, moreover, so poor and rude that . . . it will not be easy to translate any valuable work into them' (Macaulay 1952: 721). The Orientalists privileged elite languages and texts from the distant past, Sanskrit scripture and legal codes. They viewed present-day Hindu civilisation as a paltry remnant from centuries of decline. As Macaulay points out, the Company had to pay people to learn Sanskrit and Arabic – nobody volunteered. It is important to remember that 'Orientalist' and 'anglicist' approaches to governing India and educating Indians were both imperialist, both intent on devising methods for ruling a population that the colonists deemed 'rude' and inferior.

As I write, the United States (successor empire to Britain) has been at war in the Middle East for over a decade following the events of 11 September 2001. Those events gave new currency to Orientalist stereotypes, in particular those of Muslims. The initial shock of 9/11 triggered widespread, crass denigration of Islamic civilisation, seen as the enemy of freedom and modernity. But the sustained interest in Middle Eastern culture that followed succeeded in making visible to many Americans through the war years the internal diversity of Islam and the Middle East: the difference between Saddam Hussein's secular dictatorship and Taliban-style Islamic theocracy, between Sunnis and Shiites, Pashtun and Hazara.[22] More recently, the Arab Spring of 2011 and the ongoing wave of revolutions in Tunisia, Egypt, Libya and Syria have focused Western attention on the complexities of Eastern civilisation in the turbulent present day. The East India Company's expanding domination of India in the late eighteenth and early nineteenth centuries brought with it, as we have seen, an expanded production of knowledge about the subcontinent and a correspondingly finer-grained appreciation of its peoples and religions in the British metropole. The new strain of (comparatively) realistic Orientalism discussed above wove a detailed Orientalist knowledge into works of Romantic literature. This did not dislodge the persistent tropes of the exotic East already in circulation, nor did it produce anything like what we would today call realistic depictions of Eastern life. But authors such as Owenson and Byron, using the extravagant mediums of the Romantic novel and verse romance, leavened popular entertainment with political polemic and with a type of openness to other cultures less often seen in British writing as the nineteenth century advanced.

Notes

1. Leask 1998 analyses the transition from an exoticism of isolated objects or curios to a carefully contextualised 'absorptive' exoticism.
2. Said's critics include Bhabha, Leask, Suleri, Lowe, MacKenzie and Clifford. An excellent introduction to his work is Loomba 2005: 42–8.
3. Jones's modern editor, Michael Franklin, finds the conclusion of the 'Hymn

to Lacshmi' uncharacteristic of Jones's usual 'dispassionate and tolerant' Enlightenment stance (Franklin 1995a: 162n.).

4. 'While not all literary historians ... attribute the same importance to Jones, Abrams is not alone in seeing him as a representative and even pivotal figure' (Sitter 2008: 386). Sitter traces the fate of Abrams's expressive theory of Romanticism through Deconstruction and New Historicism: the 'sense of Romanticism as a radical but temporary suspension of mimetic order continues to exert a determining influence on the way this literature is studied, taught, canonized, and marketed' (Sitter 2008: 385).

5. Majeed (1992) discusses Mill's book in the context of his utilitarian philosophy (he was a follower of Bentham).

6. Suleri analyses Burke's rhetoric in the Hastings trial (Suleri 1992: 49–74).

7. See Makdisi 1998, Chapter 5, on the Romantic period as a transitional moment between these 'two antithetical paradigms of British colonial rule' (Makdisi 1998: 101).

8. Davidoff and Hall 1987: ch. 3.

9. Renaldi was a British painter of Italian ancestry, almost certainly born in England and trained there before going to India (Archer 1979: 281).

10. Tobin 1999: 116. See Dalrymple 2002 for a fascinating historical study of cross-cultural love in eighteenth-century India.

11. Born and trained in Germany, Zoffany worked in England (and for a time in Italy) from 1760 to 1783. King George III and Queen Charlotte were among his subjects before he fell out of favour. He returned to England in 1789 and died there in 1810. Other British painters in India in the second half of the eighteenth century include Tilly Kettle, William Hodges, Thomas and William Daniell and Arthur William Devis, in addition to Renaldi and Zoffany (Pal and Dehejia 1986: 12).

12. Coleridge's fragment, 'Kubla Khan', which he claimed to have written in 1797 but did not publish until 1816 (at Byron's suggestion), condenses into fifty-four lines several Romantic Orientalist motifs also seen, for example, in *Alastor*: the sacred river, chasm, caverns and alluring 'maid' seen in a dream.

13. Quoted in Franklin 2006a: 181. Franklin notes the contrast between 'the "fairy ground" of the sentimental novel and the commercial realities of book production'.

14. See Saglia 1996 on Radcliffe and Kelly 1976 on the Jacobin novel.

15. Feminist scholarship on *sati* includes Mani 1987 and 1992 and Loomba 1993, as well as Spivak's often-quoted essay (Spivak 1988).

16. The state of mind of the widow when she commits *sati*, and more broadly, the degree of agency she possesses (as opposed to being a passive victim of brainwashing and/or coercion) are important issues for postcolonial feminist scholarship on *sati*; see Mani 1987 and Loomba 1993.

17. 'Like Coleridge in 'Kubla Khan', [Shelley] seeks to suppress the cultural specificity of his sources in order to create vivid "dreamscapes" consistent with his ideological goal of cultural universalism' (Leask 1998: 182).

18. Makdisi does say that he is not concerned with the poem's narrative, but only with 'the terrain on which the narrative takes place' (Makdisi 1998: 151).

19. See Alan Bewell's chapter 'Percy Bysshe Shelley and Revolutionary Climatology' (Bewell 1999) for a postcolonial analysis of the links between power, disease and the environment in Shelley's poetry.

20. 'The word "costume" appears repeatedly in late eighteenth-century and Romantic poetics, a technical term which critics had derived – via eighteenth-century French channels – from the Italian "costume", employed by painters since the Renaissance to describe "guise or habit in artistic representations";

what we might prefer to call *setting* rather than mere clothing' (Leask 1998: 176).

21. Viswanathan notes the irony of the fact that 'English literature appeared as a subject in the curriculum of the colonies long before it was institutionalized in the home country' (Viswanathan 1989: 3). *Masks of Conquest* analyses the ways in which literary education was made to serve the aims of imperial rule.

22. Richardson 2006 offers a thoughtful meditation on teaching Romantic Orientalism after 9/11.

Romantic Readers and Writers, Selves and Others

[T]he place[s] of both the English lady and the unnamable monster are left open by this great flawed text. It is satisfying for a postcolonial reader to consider this a noble resolution for a nineteenth-century English novel.

Gayatri Chakravorty Spivak
'Three Women's Texts and a Critique of Imperialism' (1985: 259)

The 'great flawed text' is, of course, Mary Shelley's *Frankenstein*. This Romantic novel by the daughter of two 1790s radicals – a feminist and an anarchist – birthed an enduring cultural myth of fatal curiosity and monstrous science. The story of Frankenstein's creature, as Shelley imagined it, brings together a number of concerns addressed by postcolonial critics of Romantic literature.[1] Mary Wollstonecraft Godwin Shelley was an exemplary Romantic reader, deeply curious about the corners of the globe traversed by British merchants, soldiers and explorers. With her poet husband, she devoured travel and exploration writing alongside literature, philosophy and history (and recorded it all in her journals). Her densely allusive narrative works through the issues of race and slavery, the education of the colonised, and the cost of imperial expansion – all revolving around postcolonial criticism's central question of Otherness, exclusion, monstrosity. A brief survey of postcolonial studies' impact on the interpretation of *Frankenstein* is thus a fit conclusion for this book.

Twentieth-century academic critics had an uneasy relationship to *Frankenstein*. George Levine and Ulrich Knoepflmacher's preface to their landmark collection, *The Endurance of Frankenstein* (1979), tells of 'a playful conversation at a party', in which 'several of us discovered that we were all closet aficionados of Mary Shelley's novel' (Levine and Knoepflmacher 1979: xi). Not just its closeness to popular culture through stage and film adaptations, or its aesthetic flaws by the criteria of 'high' realism (Austen, Eliot, Conrad), but its status as the work of a teen-aged girl made a taste for *Frankenstein* something for professors to keep in the closet. The preface's faintly patronising tone is familiar to those of us who worked to get women authors taken seriously: 'How much of the book's complexity is actually the result of Mary Shelley's self-conscious art and how much is merely the product of the happy circumstances of subject, moment, milieu?' (Levine and Knoepflmacher 1979: xii).

The essays in the collection nonetheless helped launch the re-thinking of *Frankenstein* in the light of critical theory. Feminist critics led the charge. Ellen Moers's striking reading of the novel as a birth myth (Moers 1979), probing the dark side of motherhood (reprinted in *The Endurance of Frankenstein*), joined Sandra Gilbert and Susan Gubar's famous meditation on Shelley's reworking of Milton in 'Mary Shelley's Monstrous Eve' (Gilbert and Gubar 1979). Barbara Johnson (1982) read *Frankenstein* as 'the story of autobiography's attempt to neutralize the monstrosity of autobiography' (Johnson 1982: 4), especially when the life in question is that of a woman. Johnson's title, 'My Monster/ My Self', suggests the way Shelley's monstrous protagonist condensed feminist preoccupations with difference, exclusion and rage.

Whom, meanwhile, were the feminists excluding? Spivak's famous 1985 essay, quoted above, reads *Jane Eyre* as engineering the Englishwoman's access to individualism, the bourgeois family and the imperialist projects of child-bearing and what she calls 'soul-making' (converting or civilising 'natives') at the expense of a female Other, embodied in the novel by Bertha Mason, the West Indian Creole who is Gilbert and Gubar's famous 'madwoman in the attic' (Gilbert and Gubar 1979). Bertha's climactic torching of Rochester's house, Spivak writes, constitutes 'an allegory of the general epistemic violence of imperialism, the construction of a self-immolating colonial subject for the glorifica-tion of the social mission of the colonizer' (1985: 251). Bertha has to commit spectacular suicide so Rochester and Jane can make babies for the empire. Jean Rhys rewrites Brontë's novel in *Wide Sargasso Sea*, but 'in the interest of the white Creole rather than the native' (Spivak 1985: 253). Busy producing the privileged colonial intellectual as Ariel, Rhys still has no room for Caliban, his deformed, rebellious counterpart in Shakespeare's *Tempest*.[2]

Spivak calls her reading of *Jane Eyre* 'a narrative, in literary history, of the "worlding" of what is now called "the Third World"'. For the postcolonial critic, Mary Shelley's nineteenth-century Caliban makes possible 'an analysis – even a deconstruction – of a "worlding" such as *Jane Eyre*'s' (Spivak 1985: 243, 244). By 'worlding' I take Spivak to mean the creation, through literary representation, of certain parts of the globe as inferior, relative or contingent, subsequent and subordinate to the 'First World', i.e. Europe. Frankenstein's monster, as Shelley imagines him, successfully resists such 'worlding'. The 'subject created by the fiat of natural philosophy is the tangential unresolved moment in *Frankenstein*'. He cannot possibly be tamed, civilised, or humanised. Victor Frankenstein tries to bring him 'within the circuit of the Law' when he tells a Geneva magistrate his improbable story, accuses the monster of murder, and asks that he be arrested and punished. The magistrate says he'll try: 'But I fear . . . that this will prove impracticable' (Shelley 2012: 144). The magistrate's 'sheer social reasonableness', Spivak writes, 'reminds us that the absolutely Other cannot be selfed, that the monster has "properties" which will not be contained by "proper" measures' (Spivak 1985: 258). Beyond any specific category of difference or otherness – gender, race, class – Shelley's creation comes to symbolise a principle of absolute outsiderhood that occupies the very heart of postcolonial criticism.[3]

Peter Brooks (though not a postcolonial critic) helpfully formulates this principle in his chapter entitled 'What Is a Monster?': 'A monster is that which cannot be placed in any of the taxonomic schemes devised by the human mind to understand and to order nature. It exceeds the very basis of classification, language itself: it is an excess of signification, a strange byproduct or leftover in the process of making meaning' (Brooks 2012: 387). Resistant to classification, to 'worlding', a monster will not be pinned down. His very existence rips open the envelope of the novel's epistolary form. 'Victor never writes his family, Walton's missive never ends, and something monstrous escapes', writes Mary Favret in her classic analysis of Romantic epistolarity (Favret 1993: 177). The letters of *Frankenstein* feature as their 'recipient-function' the 'English lady', Walton's sister Margaret Saville, whose place, along with the monster's, is 'left open by this great flawed text', as Spivak points out. We do not know if Mrs Saville ever gets the letters. She certainly 'does not respond to close the text as a frame' (Spivak 1985: 259).

This formal openness is enhanced by Shelley's choice to tell her story through 'multiple, competing voices'. Walton, Victor and the creature are all fallible narrators: any reading of the novel must address 'questions of narrative authority' (Favret 1993: 178, 179). Whose voice, if any, should be believed? Who can speak or write authoritatively about these bizarre, implausible events? Again and again, the creature is denied a voice, as Kari Winter pointed out in 1992. 'All his violent actions result from his desire to be heard, his desperation to make Frankenstein listen to him'.

This is one of the connections that Winter makes between Shelley's novel and the slave narrative, a genre that claims a voice for those whom a racist society refuses to hear. 'In *Frankenstein*, Shelley attempts to give voice to those people in society who are traditionally removed from the centres of linguistic power, people who are defined as alien, inferior, or monstrous solely because of physical features (such as sex or race) or material conditions (such as poverty)' (Winter 1992: 50, 51).

Slavery, debated in Britain throughout Mary Shelley's lifetime, was very much part of the cultural matrix in which her novel arose. The historian H. L. Malchow (1996) presents the novel, its stage adaptations, and the monster's subsequent use as a metaphor in political rhetoric and caricature as part of the process of developing a popular vocabulary for representing racial and cultural difference. Shelley certainly read about slavery: in Bryan Edwards's 1793 *History . . . of the . . . West Indies*, for example, which details Tacky's Revolt, a large-scale 1760 slave uprising in Jamaica. She also read Mungo Park's popular *Travels in the Interior Districts of Africa* (1799), discussed in Chapter 1. Park narrates his interactions with African slaves and documents the cruelty of the African and transatlantic slave trades. The creature's physiognomy, Malchow notes, echoes descriptions of Africans – large and powerful, dark and sinister – though he concedes that not all aspects of his appearance point in that direction (for example, his yellow skin). '[R]eaching into childhood fantasy and imagination, [Shelley] dredged up a bogeyman that had been prepared by a cultural tradition of the threatening Other – whether troll or giant, gypsy or Negro – from the dark inner recesses of xenophobic fear and loathing' (Malchow 1996: 18).

But Shelley's creature transcends his monstrous appearance, as the reader learns when he tells Victor Frankenstein the story of his life. The tension or contradiction between the visual and the verbal – the power of language to 'deconstruct the defining and classifying power of the gaze' – is key to the power of *Frankenstein* (Brooks 2012: 389). The creature is curious, thoughtful, emotionally needy, and has a sense of right and wrong. He is 'dreadfully wronged by a society that cannot see the inner man for the outer form' (Malchow 1996: 19). Malchow finds in Shelley's creation:

> a compound of both sides of the slavery debate. He *is* wild and danger-ous, unpredictable and childlike, but at the same time has perhaps (as the Creature himself says) been made such by the circumstances of an unjust exclusion. And yet the depth of his rage and destructiveness seems to stem from more than environment and frustration; it suggests an inherent

bestiality . . . How much the Monster's excitable character is the result of his unique physiology, and how much of his environment, is an ambiguity exactly paralleling the central conundrum of the antislavery debate. (Malchow 1996: 19–20)

Are the slave's seeming character flaws, listed ad nauseam by pro-slavery propagandists, artefacts of the institution of slavery, or are they inherent in the African character? The only way to know for sure is to emancipate him – a dangerous experiment, as the same writers were quick to point out. By the time Shelley wrote, the slave-owning class could point to the bloody trajectory of the Haitian Revolution as an object lesson in the dangers of '"a race of devils" in conditions of autonomy' (Malchow 1996: 26).

This is the excuse Victor Frankenstein gives for tearing up the female creature he has started to make: 'one of the first results of those sympathies for which the daemon thirsted would be children, and a race of devils would be propagated upon the earth, who might make the very existence of the species of man a condition precarious and full of terror' (Shelley 2012: 119). Victor's nightmare vision contrasts with the future that the creature predicts when he asks Victor to make him a companion. The two of them will 'go to the vast wilds of South America', he says, and live on 'acorns and berries', not even killing animals for food (Shelley 2012: 102–3). Denying the Creature 'control and fulfillment in sexuality', Allan Lloyd Smith points out, also echoes slavery, which broke up families and denied marriage and parenting to slaves (Smith 2005: 216).

Another thing denied to slaves was education. The most interesting recent addition to postcolonial criticism of *Frankenstein* is Eduardo Cadava's 'The Monstrosity of Human Rights' (2006).[4] Frederick Douglass's well-known account of his education in his 1845 autobiography 'draws directly from a passage in Mary Shelley's *Frankenstein* where the monster tells Victor how he acquired language'. Douglass's 'self-portrait turns out to be a portrait of the monster, of himself as a monster'. Created in relation to the British debate over slavery, Shelley's novel highlights the importance of language and the creature's eloquent use of it to assert his entitlement to the basic right to be considered a human being (Cadava 2006: 1560, 1562). The creature's vicarious education brings him to realise his own monstrosity: 'And what was I? . . . Was I then a monster, a blot upon the earth, from which all men fled, and whom all men disowned?' (Shelley 2012: 83). As Douglass puts it in *My Bondage and My Freedom*, 'Genealogical trees do not flourish among slaves' (quoted in Cadava 2006: 1562). Douglass's account of reading speeches and dialogues in the *Columbian Orator* 'echoes the monster's response to finding the treasured books that became the sources of his language and education' (Cadava 2006: 1562): 'The more I read, the more I was led to abhor and detest my enslavers. I could regard them in no other light than a band of successful robbers . . . I would at times feel that learning to read had been a curse rather than a blessing', Douglass declares (quoted in Cadava 2006: 1562). The bitter ironies of colonial education – a longstanding theme of postcolonial studies – are summed up by Caliban's famous complaint: 'You gave me language, and my profit on't/ Is, I know how to curse' (*The Tempest* I, ii, 363–4).

But slavery has not been the only preoccupation of postcolonial critics of *Frankenstein*. Joseph W. Lew (1991) finds a critique of Orientalism in Shelley's novel, tracing the ways in which it 'both imitates and inverts the plot of *Alastor*', her husband's quest romance, discussed in Chapter 4. 'Frankenstein's creature is the ultimate dream-maiden, the 'epipsy-chidion' who forces us (and perhaps even Percy Shelley) to confront the constructed nature of our desire' (Lew 1991: 258, 272). Lew links Shelley's physical description of the creature, with his 'yellow skin' and 'hair . . . of a lustrous black, and flowing' (Shelley 2012: 35), to the Bengalis, who 'by 1818 . . . had suffered several generations of [British] misrule' (Lew 2012: 273). D. S. Neff (1997) takes this in a somewhat different direction, connecting the creature to India's mixed-race or Euro-Asian population. Malchow's book studies representations of the 'half-breed' in Victorian popular culture as 'an outcast, a misfit, and a biological unnatural' (Malchow 1996: 199). Tracing fears of 'rampaging half-caste forces in India' through Southey's *Curse of Kehama*, another work Mary Shelley knew well, Neff reads the character of Arvalan in that poem as 'a Gothicized version of a dispossessed Anglo-Indian child', demanding vengeance for his mistreatment – the vengeance that Frankenstein's creature violently takes (Neff 1997: 390, 391).

Neff also connects *Frankenstein* to another novel discussed in Chapter 4, which Mary Shelley certainly read, since it was a favourite of her husband's: Sydney Owenson's *The Missionary*. Could Victor Frankenstein be partly modelled on Hilarion, the missionary with a passion for converting Hindus to Christianity? Confronted by his creature, Victor is traumatised, Neff suggests, by what Homi Bhabha calls the menace of mimicry. His 'reforming, civilizing mission is threatened by the displacing gaze of its disciplinary double' (quoted in Neff 1997: 397). 'The creature, like the half-castes in London, identifies strongly with and tries to assimilate the beliefs and appearances of those he understands to be his betters, converted and colonized by [the De Lacey] family's values'

(Neff 1997: 398). But his hope of successful mimicry is dashed by what Bhabha (invoking another postcolonial critic, Frantz Fanon) calls a 'primal scene' of blackness – like the one in Fanon's *Black Skin, White Masks* where a child looks at the black man and cries, 'Mama, see the Negro! I'm frightened'. Fanon's devastated reaction echoes the wrenching moment in *Frankenstein* when the creature looks into a mirroring pool. He cannot believe, he says, 'that I was in reality the monster that I am' (Shelley 2012: 78–9). His denial resumes until Felix De Lacey's violent rejection in a second 'primal scene', which leads him to 'declare . . . everlasting war against the species' (Shelley 2012: 95).

Anne Mellor's more recent essay (part of her important body of work on Mary Shelley, starting in the 1980s) also connects *Frankenstein* to the idea of racial mixing or hybridity (Mellor 2003). Mellor points to the place where readers first glimpse him: the far north of Russia, on the Arctic ice, where Walton's ship is stuck. Walton describes the creature by contrast with Victor Frankenstein, who 'was not, as the other traveller seemed to be, a savage inhabitant of some undiscovered island, but a European' (Shelley 2012: 14). 'A yellow-skinned man crossing the steppes of Russia and Tartary, with long black hair and dun-coloured eyes – most of Shelley's nineteenth-century readers would immediately have recognized the Creature as a member of the Mongolian race, one of the five races of man first classified in 1795 by Johann Friedrich Blumenbach, the scholar who . . . founded the modern science of physical anthropology' (Mellor 2003: 174). Mary Shelley had a personal connection to Blumenbach's racial theories through William Lawrence, professor of anatomy at St Bartholomew's Hospital in London, a disciple of the German scientist and Percy and Mary Shelley's personal physician. Lawrence built on Blumenbach's work by assigning '*moral characteristics* to each racial type' (Mellor 2003: 179). Mongolians are inferior to whites, he decrees, due to their 'stationary' or stagnant culture. And they are violent: look at Attila and Genghis Khan (quoted in Mellor 2003: 179).

By 1818 'the image of the Mongols or Asians as a yellow-skinned, black-haired, and beardless race was well established . . . in European culture'. *Frankenstein*, Mellor argues, made the yellow man a giant. By the end of the nineteenth century the giant Yellow Man 'had become a synecdoche for the population of China as a whole . . . These hordes of yellow men soon became known as the "yellow peril"' (Mellor 2003: 181). Second World War propaganda posters, with images of Japanese soldiers as menacing giants attacking white women, constitute another strand of twentieth-century visual culture partly traceable to Shelley's myth. But the novel, Mellor claims, rather than a racist condemnation of Frankenstein's creature, actually encodes 'a possible *solution* to racial stereotyping and racial hatred'. This would include racial hybridity, or 'amalgamation' (Mellor 2003: 192). Her argument draws on contemporaneous women writers who endorsed interracial love, as well as on Shelley's later novel, *The Last Man* (1826).

Twenty-first-century criticism of *Frankenstein* has been more interested in the history of science than in postcolonial studies (possibly because earlier postcolonial critics covered so much ground). One branch of Romantic science that has drawn comment is geographical exploration. While Shelley was writing *Frankenstein*, Jessica Richard notes, Sir John Barrow, Secretary to the Admiralty, published a series of articles in the *Quarterly Review* to drum up government and popular support for Arctic exploration (Richard 2003: 297). Barrow got what he wanted: weeks after the novel came out, an expedition headed north. It did not succeed in locating the North Pole or finding a passage to the Pacific (Garrison 2008: 4). Shelley added the polar frame narrative to *Frankenstein* between September 1816 and April 1817, perhaps capitalising on the popular appeal of polar exploration. 'Victor's tale of over-reaching scientific undertakings', Richard argues, 'is deliberately situated against the Arctic expeditions that were about to set sail' (Richard 2003: 296).

But Richard does not, Karen Piper points out, mention the indigenous peoples of the Arctic, the Inuits or 'Esquimaux' and Sami or 'Laplanders'. Nor does Mary Shelley, though she had certainly read about them in the *Quarterly Review* and in collections of travel writing like Pinkerton's (1808–14). Her description of the creature's appearance, with his yellow skin, flowing black hair, 'shriveled complexion and straight black lips' (Shelley 2012: 35), is 'hauntingly similar' to descriptions of the inhabitants of Greenland in Pinkerton's collection. Travellers described the Sami as strikingly ugly – like Frankenstein's 'hideous' creature (Piper 2007: 64–5).[5] Strong and fast, with a superhuman ability to endure cold, hunger and fatigue, the creature is well adapted for survival in the Arctic. Chasing his creation, Victor becomes dependent on him, guided by marks the creature makes on trees or rocks, eating food he supplies (Piper 2007: 65). We see this kind of dependence in colonial narratives of contact with indigenes (think of the New England Pilgrims and Squanto). The creature is nomadic, homeless: 'wherever he is, he does not belong there. The very fact that he has been sighted by a European reveals, in [*Frankenstein*], that he needs to be further away, or dead . . . Victor can never really kill him . . . but only push him out to the far reaches of the world in an attempt to erase or undo that moment of first contact that had proven so deadly for everyone.' Apropos of Victor's violent destruction of the female creature, Piper asks, 'Could it be . . . that the dilemma in *Frankenstein* is less about whether to create creatures than whether or not to destroy them?' (Piper 2007: 67, 71, 69).

In the 'final and wonderful catastrophe' that ends Shelley's narrative, Walton finds the creature mourning his dead creator. The explorer gets a taste of his eloquence as he expresses profound remorse, but protests his treatment: 'Am I to be thought the only criminal, when all human kind sinned against me?' Assuring Walton that he and humanity have nothing more to fear, the creature vows suicide:

> Do not think that I shall be slow to perform this sacrifice . . . I shall collect my funeral pile, and consume to ashes this miserable frame, that its remains may afford no light to any curious and unhallowed wretch, who would create such another as I have been. (Shelley 2012: 160, 161)

The image of the pyre is a double allusion, incongruously conflating Occident and Orient. The mythical strongman Hercules, 'a giant created in an unnatural way and left to fend for himself in a cruel world', kills himself on a funeral pyre, according to Ovid's *Metamorphoses*, which Mary Shelley read (in the original Latin) throughout 1815 (Thompson 2004: 36). But the pyre also calls to mind the self-immolating Indian widow of *sati*, the barbaric-seeming custom debated by India's colonial rulers as Shelley wrote:

> This curious double exposure superimposes a classical masculine icon of empire on the figure of empire's humblest subaltern, fusing them in mutual self-destruction. Allusively, Frankenstein insists on the unstable hybridity of selves in a world of complex global interdependence . . . Between cultures and within them, selves depend on their opposites and include them: I embrace multitudes. (Bohls 1995: 244–5)

British intellectuals were not the only ones to voice their opinions on the contentious issue of *sati*. I will close by introducing the Indian poet and activist Henry Louis Vivian Derozio (1809–31), author of the commemorative poem 'On the Abolition of Suttee' (1829). The poem opens by citing the new colonial edict: 'The practice of Suttee, or of burning or burying alive the Widows of Hindoos, is hereby declared illegal, and punishable by the Criminal Courts' (Derozio 2008: 286):

> Red from his chambers came the morning Sun
> And frowned, dark Ganges! on thy fatal shore,
> Journeying on high; but when the day was done
> He set in smiles, to rise in blood no more.
> Hark! heard ye not? the Widow's wail is o'er:

No more the flames from impious pyres ascend,
See Mercy now primeval peace restore,
While paeans glad the arch ethereal rend,
For India hails at last, her father, and her friend.

(Derozio 2008: 287)

The poem appeared in the *India Gazette* on 10 December 1829 under Derozio's name. The father and friend to whom the poem refers is Lord William Bentinck, Governor General of Bengal: '*Bentinck*, be thine the everlasting meed!' Derozio does not acknowledge the prominent Bengali reformer Rammohun Roy's campaign against *sati*. The second half of the eight-stanza poem decries the bad treatment of women in Indian society: 'Nurtured in darkness, born to many woes' (Derozio 2008: 284, 288). The tone is that of a liberal reformer and loyal colonial subject.

Clearly an 'official' poem, perhaps even commissioned, 'On the Abolition of Suttee' differs from much of the other poetry that Derozio published in Calcutta newspapers and in two volumes dated 1827 and 1828. The poems he published under the pen name 'Leporello', for example, were 'light, humorous, and personal' (Derozio 2008: 284). His long verse romance, *The Fakeer of Jungheera* (1828), includes *sati* as part of its plot: the heroine, Nuleeni, is rescued from her dead husband's pyre by her lover, a Muslim fakir (holy man), who also happens to be the leader of a band of robbers. *The Fakeer* features the extensive footnotes so popular in the Romantic verse romances that the poet grew up reading. He was a fan of Byron, Moore, L. E. L. (Letitia Elizabeth Landon), and in particular Percy Shelley (Chaudhuri 2008: xxxviii).

Derozio's footnotes disclose a more complex, conflicted attitude toward *sati*. Opposed to women's misery in all forms, the poet seems to have had doubts as late as 1828 about banning the custom outright. One note approvingly quotes an article from the *India Magazine*: 'It will be impossible . . . to make an attempt at overthrowing this system, before education is generalized, without wounding the tenderest feelings of human nature.' Improving the condition of Hindu women in general, and widows in particular, needs to precede statutory action: 'It is however our firm, and sincere wish that the day may soon come when rays of intellectual greatness will awaken the benighted natives of India from their long trance of bigotry and error', the unnamed author of the article concludes (Derozio 2008: 229). Once the colonial government had enacted the ban on *sati*, Derozio publicly celebrated it, but the *Fakeer* footnote suggests that beforehand – like other Indian intellectuals at the time – he struggled to reconcile reformist ideals with respect for religious customs rooted in 'the tenderest feelings of human nature'.

Derozio lived his short life at a time of remarkable openness and cultural ferment in colonial Calcutta. Calcutta in the 1820s was a cosmopolitan city, 'polyglot and multi-ethnic', characterised by a 'social flux' quite different from the later period of British India when racial hierarchies had rigidified (Chaudhuri 2008: lxix, lxx). The poet was biracial, his father of Portuguese extraction (the first European nation to colonise India) and his mother possibly British.[6] He called himself 'East Indian', a designation for 'Europeanized people of mixed race as well as native Christians in India who were an adjunct or comprador class to early colonialists' (Paranjape 2011: 567). The East Indian community considered itself distinct from both Hindus and Muslims, groups that each had their own code of civil laws. They petitioned the colonial government to be tried under British law, drafting petitions to Parliament in a series of public meetings at which Derozio was vocal (Derozio 2008: 342–56).

Educated by the Scottish schoolmaster David Drummond, Derozio imbibed Scottish Enlightenment philosophy and liberal values. Drummond's school educated Indian, Eurasian and European children in the same classes, unthinkable in later Victorian India (Chaudhuri 2008: l). His modern editor emphasises the 'radicalism of lifestyle and philosophy that Derozio introduced to Calcutta'. We glimpse the lifestyle in Leporello's 'On Drunkenness' (1824), a tongue-in-cheek newspaper essay sporting an epigraph from Byron: 'Man, being reasonable, must get drunk' (Derozio 2008: 70). Derozio worked as a teacher at Hindu College from 1826 until 1831, the year he died, tragically young, of cholera. He resigned after the College's managing committee voted to fire him for, among other offences, teaching the works of the atheist philosopher Hume. His students, who came to be known as the Derozians, were 'the most brilliant, outrageous and defiant young men of many a generation of Indians' (Chaudhuri 2008: lix). The teacher wrote a touching sonnet 'To the Students at the Hindu College':

> O! how the winds
> Of circumstance, and freshening April showers
> Of early knowledge, and unnumbered kinds
> Of new perceptions shed their influence;
> And how you worship Truth's omnipotence!

> (Derozio 2008: 315)

The poem appeared in 1830 in the first Indian literary annual, the *Bengal Annual*, described as 'the most elegant volume that ever issued from the Indian press' (Derozio 2008: 297).[7]

The Fakeer of Jungheera is an implausible, digressive melange of a poem. Set in seventeenth-century Mughal India, it unfolds a melodramatic saga of doomed love in a lush subtropical landscape. Derozio incorporates the British aesthetics of the picturesque, choosing the 'romantic' rocky island of Jungheera in the Ganges as his setting. But he also 'draws on Persian ideas of the *shair*, or poet, a living tradition in India . . . which was . . . entering English for the first time through translations by Orientalists' such as William Jones (Paranjape 2011: 556). (Derozio published several versions of Persian odes by Hafiz, though it is not clear whether he knew the language.) Rescued by her lover from the funeral pyre, Nuleeni enjoys a brief honeymoon on the island before he goes off to fight the army of Prince Shuja (a historical figure), led by Nuleeni's father, seeking vengeance for his family's dishonour.[8] She finds him dying on the battlefield and holds him as he breathes his last. The next morning a peasant comes upon

> a form
> So bold, in life it might have ruled a storm –
> And fondly ivying round it were the arms
> Of a fair woman, whose all-powerful charms
> Even death had failed to conquer –

(Derozio 2008: 227)

Makarand Paranjape reads Nuleeni's death as a second, successful *sati*, committed 'in the more deadly if less fiery fashion sanctioned by the conventions of western romanticism'. *The Fakeer of Jungheera* is not an anti-*sati* polemic, but an exotic diversion for a primarily British and Euro-Asian readership. A postcolonial reading of the poem, Paranjape suggests, 'would see in it the impossibility of the full blossoming of a productive love and life-affirming narrative under colonialism'. Read allegorically, 'India as Nuleeni really has few choices . . . Her father, husband and lover – all three men who control her life – turn against her happiness' (Paranjape 2011: 558, 559–60). Paranjape disagrees with those who read Derozio as a proto-nationalist poet, arguing that 'the "national" as a valid social or cultural space was not yet available' at the time he wrote. His 'modernity lay not so much in his politics as in his aesthetic practices . . . his vernacularizing of western sources and influences, grafting them on local material to create a new, hybridised idiom of expression'. Derozio was an 'East Indian cosmopolitan', occupying a fluid, multi-ethnic public sphere that would drastically shrink after British hegemony was secured (Paranjape 2011: 550, 565–6).

The elusive image of the body on the pyre connects these two Romantic writers and readers: Mary Shelley in London, reading up on the global geography of empire, and Derozio in Calcutta, revelling in the poetry of Byron and Shelley and nurturing a taste for the picturesque. Such transnational linkages and deliberate self-hybridisation have become commonplace in the current era of globalisation. Formal empire has given way to neo-colonialism, and British to US hegemony, but the imperial culture that brought forth these Romantic texts cannot be relegated to an inert past. Whether we consider the extension of Orientalism in the post-9/11 demonisation of Islam, or the plight of African and Caribbean nations still confronting harsh inequities in the long-term wake of Atlantic slavery, we must recognise the continuing usefulness of postcolonial studies. Romantic literature records real or imagined encounters between privileged selves and exoticised or abjected Others during a time of rapid modernisation and widespread war. Postcolonial critics' skill at connecting cultural forms to geopolitics exposes Romantic texts as peculiarly timely for twenty-first-century readers.

Notes

1. Some critics choose to refer to Frankenstein's creation as a 'creature', others as a 'monster'. Each term carries a persuasive rationale: the more neutral designation, 'creature', suspends judgement, while 'monster' acknowledges the problem of perception that drives the novel's plot. Here I will alternate as my context and other critics' diction suggests.
2. She is referring to Roberto Fernández Retamar's influential 1971 essay recasting the Latin American intellectual as Caliban rather than Ariel, with whom José Enrique Rodó had identified him in 1900 (Spivak 1985: 245).
3. Moretti (1988), in an essay first published in 1978, highlights the monster's racial identity, although his focus is European proletarian agency imaginatively transmuted.
4. See Winter (2009) for another recent meditation on *Frankenstein* and liberal conceptions of human rights.
5. See Bohls 1995: 230–45 for an analysis of the creature's relation to aesthetic discourse.
6. Paranjape believes Chaudhuri is mistaken in thinking Sophia Johnson was Derozio's mother; she was his uncle's wife, while his mother's identity remains unknown (Paranjape 2011: 568).
7. Milinda Banerjee discusses possible homoerotic elements in Derozio's bond with his students and the 'intertwining of the cult of . . . friendship with a cult of scandalous knowledge' (Banerjee 2009: 64).
8. 'Nowhere does Derozio seem to be aware of . . . the inter-religious dimensions of his story. *Sati* was a rite for Hindu widows. Not only is Nuleeni's abductor-rescuer . . . a Muslim, so are Prince Shuja and his "Muslim chivalry". A Hindu father's appeal to a Muslim ruler to avenge his daughter's failure to commit *sati* is, to say the least, remarkable' (Paranjape 2011: 558).

Bibliography

Abrams, M. H. (1971), *Natural Supernaturalism: Tradition and Revolution in Romantic Literature*, New York: W. W. Norton and Co.

Abu Taleb, Mirza [1810] (2005), *Westward Bound: Travels of Abu Taleb*, ed. M. Hasan, Oxford: Oxford University Press.

Altick, Richard (1978), *The Shows of London,* Cambridge, MA: Belknap Press of Harvard University Press.

Andrews, Malcolm (1989), *The Search for the Picturesque: Landscape Aesthetics and Tourism in Britain, 1760–1800,* Stanford: Stanford University Press.

Aravamudan, Srinivas (1999a), 'Introduction', in S. Aravamudan (ed.), *Fiction,* in P. Kitson and D. Lee (eds), *Slavery, Abolition and Emancipation: Writings in the British Romantic Period,* London: Pickering and Chatto, vol. 6, pp. vii–xxiii.

Aravamudan, Srinivas (1999b), *Tropicopolitans: Colonialism and Agency, 1688–1804,* Durham, NC: Duke University Press.

Aravamudan, Srinivas (2005), 'Introduction', in William Earle, *Obi, or, The History of Three-Fingered Jack*, ed. S. Aravamudan, Peterborough, Ontario: Broadview Press, pp. 7–51.

Archer, Mildred (1979), *India and British Portraiture, 1770–1825,* London and New York: Sotheby Parke Bernet; Karachi and Delhi: Oxford University Press.

Archer, Mildred and Ronald Lightbown (1982), *India Observed: India as Viewed by British Artists, 1760–1860,* London: Victoria and Albert Museum.

Asiatic Researches, or, Transactions of the Society, Instituted in Bengal, for Inquiring into the History and Antiquities, the Arts, Sciences, and Literature of Asia (1799), vol. 1, London.

Association for Promoting the Discovery of the Interior Parts of Africa [1810] (1967), *Proceedings,* 2 vols, facsimile edn, intro. Robin Hallett, London: Dawsons of Pall Mall.

Austen, Jane [1814] (1998), *Mansfield Park,* ed. Claudia L. Johnson, New York: W. W. Norton and Co.

Austen, Jane [1818] (2002), *Northanger Abbey*, ed. Claire Grogan, Peterborough, Ontario: Broadview Press.

Bakhtin, Mikhail (1981), *The Dialogic Imagination: Four Essays*, ed. M. Holquist, trans. C. Emerson and M. Holquist, Austin: University of Texas Press.

Banerjee, Milinda (2009), 'The Trial of Derozio, or the Scandal of Reason', *Social Scientist* 37: 60–88.

Bartram, William [1791] (1958), *Travels Through North and South Carolina, Georgia, East and West Florida, the Cherokee Country, the Extensive Territories of the Muscogulges, or Creek Confederacy, and the Country of the Chactaws*, ed. F. Harper, New Haven: Yale University Press.

Batten, Charles, Junior (1978), *Pleasurable Instruction: Form and Convention in Eighteenth-Century Travel Literature*, Berkeley: University of California Press.

Baum, Joan (1994), *Mind-Forg'd Manacles: Slavery and the English Romantic Poets*, North Haven, CT: Archon Books.

Baumgartner, Barbara (2001), 'The Body as Evidence: Resistance, Collaboration, and Appropriation in *The History of Mary Prince*', *Callaloo* 24.2: 253–75.

Bayly, C. A. (1988), *Indian Society and the Making of the British Empire*, Gordon Johnson (ed.), *The New Cambridge History of India,* part II, vol. 1, Cambridge: Cambridge University Press.

Bayly, C. A. (1989), *Imperial Meridian: The British Empire and the World, 1780–1830*, London: Longman.

Bayly, C. A (1998), 'The First Age of Global Imperialism, *c.* 1760–1830', *Journal of Imperial and Commonwealth History* 26: 28–47.

Beckford, William (1790), *A Descriptive Account of the Island of Jamaica*, 2 vols, London: T. and J. Egerton.

Bentley, G. E. (2001), *The Stranger From Paradise: A Biography of William Blake*, New Haven: Yale University Press.

Bernal, Martin (1991), *Black Athena: The Afroasiatic Roots of Classical Civilisation*. London: Vintage Books.

Bewell, Alan (1999), *Romanticism and Colonial Disease*, Baltimore: Johns Hopkins University Press.

Bhabha, Homi (1994), *The Location of Culture*, London: Routledge.

Bilby, Kenneth M. (2005), *True-Born Maroons*, Gainesville: University Press of Florida.

Blackburn, Robin (1988), *The Overthrow of Colonial Slavery, 1776–1848*, London: Verso.

Blair, David (2006), 'Scott, Cartography, and the Appropriation of Scottish Place', in P. Brown and M. Irwin (eds), *Literature and Place, 1800–2000*, Oxford: Peter Lang, pp. 87–107.

Blake, William (1970), 'The Little Black Boy' (1789), in *Songs of Innocence and of Experience*, ed. G. Keynes, London: Oxford University Press.

Blake, William (2008), *Blake's Poetry and Designs*, ed. Mary Lynn Johnson and John E. Grant, New York: W. W. Norton and Co.

Bohls, Elizabeth A. (1994), 'The Aesthetics of Colonialism: Janet Schaw in the West Indies, 1774–1775', *Eighteenth-Century Studies* 27: 363–90.

Bohls, Elizabeth A. (1995), *Women Travel Writers and the Language of Aesthetics, 1716–1818*, Cambridge: Cambridge University Press.

Boulukos, George (2008), *The Grateful Slave: The Emergence of Race in Eighteenth-Century British and American Culture*, Cambridge: Cambridge University Press.

Brathwaite, Kamau (Edward) (1971), *The Development of Creole Society in Jamaica*, Oxford: Clarendon Press.

Brooks, Peter (2012), 'What Is A Monster? (According to Frankenstein)', in Mary Shelley, *Frankenstein*, ed. J. P. Hunter, New York: W. W. Norton and Co, pp. 368–90.

Bunn, David (1994), '"Our Wattled Cot": Mercantile and Domestic Space in Thomas Pringle's African Landscapes', in W. J. T. Mitchell (ed.), *Landscape and Power*, Chicago: University of Chicago Press, pp. 127–73.

Burnard, Trevor (2004), *Mastery, Tyranny, and Desire: Thomas Thistlewood and his Slaves in the Anglo-Jamaican World*, Chapel Hill, NC: University of North Carolina Press.

Burns, Robert (2001), *The Canongate Burns: The Complete Poems and Songs of Robert Burns*, ed. A. Noble and P. S. Hogg, Edinburgh: Canongate.

Bush, Barbara (1990), *Slave Women in Caribbean Society, 1650–1838*, Kingston: Heinemann; Bloomington and Indianapolis: Indiana University Press; London: James Currey.

Butler, Marilyn (1975), *Jane Austen and the War of Ideas*, Oxford: Clarendon Press.

Butler, Marilyn (1981), *Romantics, Rebels, and Reactionaries: British Literature and its Background, 1760–1830*, Oxford: Oxford University Press.

Butler, Marilyn (1988), 'The Orientalism of Byron's *Giaour*', in B. Beatty and V. Newey (eds), *Byron and the Limits of Fiction*, Totowa, NJ: Barnes and Noble, pp. 78–96.

Butler, Marilyn (1990), 'Plotting the Revolution: The Popular Narratives of Romantic Poetry and Criticism', in K. R. Johnston, G. Chattin, K. Hanson et al. (eds), *Romantic Revolutions*, Bloomington: Indiana University Press, pp. 133–57.

Butler, Marilyn (1994), 'Orientalism', in D. B. Pirie (ed.), *Penguin History of Literature: The Romantic Period*, New York: Penguin, pp. 394–447.

Butler, Marilyn (1999), 'Antiquarianism (Popular)', in I. McCalman (ed.), *An Oxford Companion to the Romantic Age: British Culture, 1776–1832*, Oxford: Oxford University Press, pp. 328–38.

Buzard, James (1995), 'Translation and Tourism: Scott's *Waverley* and the Rendering of Culture', *Yale Journal of Criticism* 8: 331–59.

Cadava, Eduardo (2006), 'The Monstrosity of Human Rights', *PMLA* 121: 1558–65.

Carretta, Vincent (2005), *Equiano the African: Biography of a Self-Made Man*, Athens, GA: University of Georgia Press.

Chaudhuri, Rosinka (2008), 'Introduction', in *Derozio, Poet of India: The Definitive Edition*, ed. R. Chaudhuri, New Delhi: Oxford University Press, pp. 21–81.

Clarkson, Thomas (1786), *An Essay on the Slavery and Commerce of the Human Species, Particularly the African*, London: T. Cadell.

Clarkson, Thomas (1808), *History of the Rise, Progress, and Accomplishment of the Abolition of the African Slave-Trade, by the British Parliament*, 2 vols, London: Longman, Hurst, Rees, and Orme.

Clifford, James (1988), 'On Orientalism', in *The Predicament of Culture: Twentieth-Century Literature, Ethnography, and Art*, Cambridge, MA: Harvard University Press, pp. 255–76.

Coleridge, Samuel Taylor (1969), 'Lecture on the Slave-Trade', in *Lectures 1795 on Politics and Religion*, ed. L. Patton and P. Mann, *Collected Works of Samuel Taylor Coleridge*, Princeton: Princeton University Press, vol. 1.

Coleridge, Samuel Taylor [1798] (1999), *The Rime of the Ancient Mariner*, ed. P. H. Fry, Boston: Bedford/St Martin's.

Colley, Linda (1992), *Britons: Forging the Nation, 1707–1837*, New Haven: Yale University Press.

Cowper, William [1788] (1999), 'The Negro's Complaint', in A. Richardson (ed.), *Verse*, in P. Kitson and D. Lee (eds), *Slavery, Abolition and Emancipation: Writings in the British Romantic Period*, London: Pickering and Chatto, vol. 4, pp. 75–7.

Cox, Jeffrey N. (2002), 'Theatrical Forms, Ideological Conflict, and the Staging of *Obi*', in Charles Rzepka (ed.), *Obi: A Romantic Circles Praxis Volume* <http://romantic.arhu.umd.edu/praxis/obi/> (accessed 27 June 2012).

Craig, Cairns (2004), 'Coleridge, Hume, and the Chains of the Romantic Imagination', in L. Davis, I. Duncan and J. Sorensen (eds), *Scotland and the Borders of Romanticism*, Cambridge: Cambridge University Press, pp. 20–37.

Crais, Clifton and Pamela Scully (2009), *Sara Baartman and the Hottentot Venus: A Ghost Story and a Biography*, Princeton: Princeton University Press.

Craton, Michael (1978), *Searching for the Invisible Man: Slaves and Plantation Life in Jamaica*, Cambridge, MA: Harvard University Press.

Craton, Michael (1982), *Testing the Chains: Resistance to Slavery in the British West Indies*, Ithaca, NY: Cornell University Press.

Crawford, Robert (2000), *Devolving English Literature*, 2nd edn, Edinburgh: Edinburgh University Press.

Crawford, Thomas (1960), *Burns: A Study of the Poems and Songs*, Edinburgh: Oliver and Boyd.

Crosby, Alfred (2004), *Ecological Imperialism: The Biological Expansion of Europe, 900–1900*, Cambridge: Cambridge University Press.

Dalrymple, William (2002), *White Mughals: Love and Betrayal in Eighteenth-Century India*, New York: Viking.

Davidoff, Leonore and Catherine Hall (1987), *Family Fortunes: Men and Women of the English Middle Class, 1780–1850*, Chicago: University of Chicago Press.

Davis, Charles T. and Henry Louis Gates (eds) (1985), *The Slave's Narrative*, Oxford and New York: Oxford University Press.

Davis, Leith (1998), *Acts of Union: Scotland and the Literary Negotiation of the British Nation, 1707–1830*, Stanford: Stanford University Press.

Davis, Leith, Ian Duncan and Janet Sorensen (eds) (2004), *Scotland and the Borders of Romanticism*, Cambridge: Cambridge University Press.

Davis, Leith and Maureen McLane (2007), 'Orality and Public Poetry', in I. Brown (ed.), *Edinburgh History of Scottish Literature*, vol. 2, pp. 125–32.

Day, Aidan (1996), *Romanticism*, New York: Routledge.

Derozio, Henry Louis Vivian (2008), *Derozio, Poet of India: The Definitive Edition*, ed. R. Chaudhuri, New Delhi: Oxford University Press.

Devine, T. M. (1999), *The Scottish Nation: A History, 1700–2000*, New York: Viking.

Devine, T. M. (2003), *Scotland's Empire and the Shaping of the Americas, 1600–1815*, Washington, DC: Smithsonian Books.

Drew, John (1987), *India and the Romantic Imagination*, Delhi: Oxford University Press.

Duckworth, Alistair M. (1971), *The Improvement of the Estate: A Study of Jane Austen's Novels*, Baltimore: Johns Hopkins University Press.

Duffy, Michael (1998), 'World-Wide War and British Expansion, 1793–1815', in W. R. Louis (ed. in chief), *The Oxford History of the British Empire*, vol. II, P. J. Marshall (ed.), *The Eighteenth Century*, Oxford: Oxford University Press, pp. 184–207.

Duncan, Ian (1992), *Modern Romance and the Transformations of the Novel: The Gothic, Scott, Dickens*, Cambridge: Cambridge University Press.

Duncan, Ian with Leith Davis and Janet Sorensen (2004), 'Introduction', in Leith Davis, Ian Duncan and Janet Sorensen (eds), *Scotland and the Borders of Romanticism*, Cambridge: Cambridge University Press, pp. 1–19.

Duncan, Ian (2006), 'Walter Scott, *Waverley*', in F. Moretti (ed.), *The Novel*, vol. 2, *Forms and Themes*, Princeton: Princeton University Press, pp. 173–80.

Duncan, Ian (2007), *Scott's Shadow: The Novel in Romantic Edinburgh*, Princeton: Princeton University Press.

Duncan, Ian (2010), 'Introduction', in James Hogg, *The Private Memoirs and Confessions of a Justified Sinner*, ed. I. Duncan, Oxford: Oxford University Press.

Earle, William (2005), *Obi, or, The History of Three-Fingered Jack,* ed. S. Aravamudan, Peterborough, Ontario: Broadview Press.

Edney, Matthew (1997), *Mapping an Empire: The Geographical Construction of British India, 1765–1843,* Chicago: University of Chicago Press.

Edwards, Bryan (1794), *The History, Civil and Commercial, of the British Colonies in the West Indies: In Two Volumes,* London.

Empson, William (1964), 'The Ancient Mariner', *Critical Quarterly* 6: 298–319.

Equiano, Olaudah [1789] (2003), *The Interesting Narrative and Other Writings,* ed. V. Carretta, New York: Penguin.

Erdman, David V. (1969), *Blake, Poet Against Empire: A Poet's Interpretation of the History of His Own Times,* revised edn, Princeton: Princeton University Press.

Everest, Kelvin (1994), 'Shelley', in D. B. Pirie (ed.), *'The Penguin History of Literature: The Romantic Period,* New York: Penguin, pp. 311–41.

Fabian, Johannes (1983), *Time and the Other: How Anthropology Makes its Object,* New York: Columbia University Press.

Favret, Mary A. (1993), *Romantic Correspondence: Women, Politics, and the Fiction of Letters.* Cambridge: Cambridge University Press.

Felsenstein, Frank (1999), *English Trader, Indian Maid: Representing Gender, Race, and Slavery in the New World: an Inkle and Yarico Reader,* Baltimore: Johns Hopkins University Press.

Ferguson. Moira (1992), *Subject to Others: British Women Writers and Colonial Slavery, 1670–1834,* New York: Routledge.

Ferguson, Moira (1997), 'Introduction', in *The History of Mary Prince, a West Indian Slave, Related by Herself,* ed. M. Ferguson, revised edn, Ann Arbor: University of Michigan Press, pp. 1–51.

Ferris, Ina (2008), 'Scholarly Revivals: Gothic Fiction, Secret History, and Hogg's *Private Memoirs and Confessions of a Justified Sinner',* in J. Heydt-Stevenson and C. Sussman (eds), *Recognizing the Romantic Novel,* Liverpool: Liverpool University Press, pp. 267–84.

Festa, Lynn (2006), *Sentimental Figures of Empire in Eighteenth-Century Britain and France,* Baltimore: Johns Hopkins University Press.

Fisher, Michael H. (1996), *The First Indian Author in English: Dean Mahomed (1759–1851) in India, Ireland, and England,* Delhi: Oxford University Press.

Fraiman, Susan (1995), 'Jane Austen and Edward Said: Gender, Culture, and Imperialism', *Critical Inquiry* 21.4: 805–21.

Franklin, Caroline (1992), *Byron's Heroines,* Oxford: Clarendon Press.

Franklin, Michael (1995a), 'Introduction' and notes, in William Jones, *Selected Poetical and Prose Works,* ed. Michael J. Franklin, Cardiff: University of Wales Press.

Franklin, Michael (1995b), *Sir William Jones,* Cardiff: University of Wales Press.

Franklin, Michael (1998), 'Accessing India: Orientalism, anti-"Indianism" and the Rhetoric of Jones and Burke', in T. Fulford and P. Kitson (eds), *Romanticism and Colonialism: Writing and Empire, 1780–1830*, Cambridge: Cambridge University Press, pp. 48–66.

Franklin, Michael (2000a), 'The Building of Empire and the Building of Babel: Sir William Jones, Lord Byron, and their Productions of the Orient', in M. Procházka (ed.), *Byron: East and West*, Prague: Univerzita Karlova v Praze, pp. 63–78.

Franklin, Michael (2006b), 'Representing India in Drawing-Room and Classroom, or, Miss Owenson and "Those Gay Gentlemen, Brahma, Vishnu, and Co."', Diane Long Hoeveler and Jeffrey Cass (eds), *Interrogating Orientalism: Contextual Approaches and Pedagogical Practices*, Columbus: Ohio State University Press, pp. 159–81.

Franklin, Michael (2006), '"Passion's Empire": Sydney Owenson's "Indian Venture," Phoenicianism, Orientalism, and Binarism', *Studies in Romanticism* 45: 181–97.

Fryer, Peter (1984), *Staying Power: The History of Black People in Britain*, London: Pluto Press.

Fulford, Tim (2006), *Romantic Indians: Native Americans, British Literature, and Transatlantic Culture, 1756–1830*, Oxford: Oxford University Press.

Fulford, Tim (2008), 'Poetry, Peripheries and Empire', in J. Chandler and M. McLane (eds), *The Cambridge Companion to British Romantic Poetry*, Cambridge: Cambridge University Press, pp. 178–94.

Fulford, Tim and Peter Kitson (eds) (1998), *Romanticism and Colonialism: Writing and Empire, 1780–1830*, Cambridge: Cambridge University Press.

Fulford, Tim and Debbie Lee (2002), 'Mental Travellers: Joseph Banks, Mungo Park, and the Romantic Imagination', *Nineteenth-Century Contexts* 24: 117–37.

Garrison, Laurie (2008), 'Imperial Vision in the Arctic: Fleeting Looks and Pleasurable Distractions in Barker's Panorama and Shelley's *Frankenstein*', *Romanticism and Victorianism on the Net* 52: 1–23.

Garside, Peter (2001), 'Introduction', in James Hogg, *The Private Memoirs and Confessions of a Justified Sinner*, ed. P. Garside, Edinburgh: Edinburgh University Press.

Garside, Peter, James Raven and Rainer Schöwerling (2000), *The English Novel, 1770–1829: A Bibliographical Survey of Fiction Published in the British Isles*, 2 vols, Oxford: Oxford University Press.

Gilbert, Sandra M. and Susan Gubar (1979), *The Madwoman in the Attic: The Woman Writer and the Nineteenth-Century Literary Imagination*, New Haven: Yale University Press.

Gilroy, Paul (1993), *The Black Atlantic: Modernity and Double Consciousness*, Cambridge, MA: Harvard University Press.

Glover, Richard (1958), 'Introduction', in Samuel Hearne, *A Journey from Prince of Wales's Fort in Hudson's Bay to the Northern Ocean 1769, 1770,*

1771, 1772, ed. Richard Glover, Toronto: Macmillan Company of Canada, pp. vii–xliii.

Goldie, Terry (1989), *Fear and Temptation: The Image of the Indigene in Canadian, Australian, and New Zealand Literatures*, Kingston: McGill-Queen's University Press.

Gordon, George, Lord Byron [1813] (2002), *The Giaour*, in A. Richardson (ed.), *Three Oriental Tales*, Boston: Houghton Mifflin.

Greenfield, Bruce (1992), *Narrating Discovery: The Romantic Explorer in American Literature, 1790–1855*, New York: Columbia University Press.

Grove, Richard (1996), *Green Imperialism: Colonial Expansion, Tropical Island Edens and the Origins of Environmentalism, 1600–1860*, Cambridge: Cambridge University Press.

Hall, Douglas (1999), *In Miserable Slavery: Thomas Thistlewood in Jamaica, 1750–86*, Barbados: University of the West Indies Press.

Hartman, Saidiya V. (1997), *Scenes of Subjection: Terror, Slavery, and Self-Making in Nineteenth Century America*, Oxford: Oxford University Press.

Hearne, Samuel [1795] (1958), *A Journey from Prince of Wales's Fort in Hudson's Bay to the Northern Ocean 1769, 1770, 1771, 1772*, ed. Richard Glover, Toronto: Macmillan Company of Canada.

Hechter, Michael (1975), *Internal Colonialism: The Celtic Fringe in British National Development, 1536–1966*, Berkeley: University of California Press.

Henry, Lauren (1998), '"Sunshine and Shady Groves": What Blake's Little Black Boy Learned from African Writers', in T. Fulford and P. Kitson (eds), *Romanticism and Colonialism: Writing and Empire, 1780–1830*, Cambridge: Cambridge University Press, pp. 67–86.

Heydt-Stevenson, Jillian and Charlotte Sussman (2008), '"Launched upon the Sea of Moral and Political Inquiry": The Ethical Experiments of the Romantic Novel', in J. Heydt-Stevenson and C. Sussman (eds), *Recognizing the Romantic Novel*, Liverpool: Liverpool University Press, pp. 13–48.

Hodges, William [1793] (2001), *Travels in India, during the Years 1780, 1781, 1782, and 1783* (excerpts), in I. Ghose (ed.), *Travels, Explorations and Empires, India*, general ed. T. Fulford, London: Pickering and Chatto, vol. 6, pp. 131–56.

Hogg, James [1824] (2010), *The Private Memoirs and Confessions of a Justified Sinner*, ed. I. Duncan, Oxford: Oxford University Press.

JanMohamed, Abdul (1985), 'The Economy of Manichean Allegory: The Function of Racial Difference in Colonialist Literature', *Critical Inquiry* 12.1: 59–87.

Johnson, Barbara (1982), 'My Monster/My Self'', *Diacritics* 12: 2–10.

Johnson, Claudia (1988), *Jane Austen: Women, Politics, and the Novel*, Chicago: University of Chicago Press.

Johnson, Samuel and James Boswell [1785] (1984), *A Journey to the Western*

Islands of Scotland and *The Journal of a Tour to the Hebrides*, ed. Peter Levi, New York: Penguin.

Jones, William (1995), *Selected Poetical and Prose Works*, ed. Michael J. Franklin, Cardiff: University of Wales Press.

Jordan, Elaine (2000), 'Jane Austen Goes to the Seaside: *Sanditon*, English Identity, and the "West Indian" Schoolgirl', in Y.-M. Park and R. S. Rajan (eds), *The Postcolonial Jane Austen*, London: Routledge, pp. 29–55.

Kahir, Tabish (2001), 'Remembering to Forget Abu Taleb', *Wasafiri* 16.34: 34–8.

Kaul, Suvir (2009), *Eighteenth-Century British Literature and Postcolonial Studies*, Edinburgh: Edinburgh University Press.

Kelly, Gary (1976), *The English Jacobin Novel, 1780–1805*, Oxford: Clarendon Press.

Keymer, Thomas and Jon Mee (2004), 'Preface', in T. Keymer and J. Mee (eds), *The Cambridge Companion to English Literature, 1740–1830*, Cambridge: Cambridge University Press, pp. xi–xv.

Kiely, Robert (1972), *The Romantic Novel in England*, Cambridge, MA: Harvard University Press.

Kitson, Peter (1999), 'Introduction', in P. Kitson (ed.), *Theories of Race*, in P. Kitson and D. Lee (eds), *Slavery, Abolition and Emancipation: Writings in the British Romantic Period*, London: Pickering and Chatto, vol. 8, pp. vii–xxvi.

Korte, Barbara (2000), *English Travel Writing from Pilgrimages to Postcolonial Explorations*, trans. Catherine Matthias, Basingstoke: Macmillan.

Kowaleski-Wallace, Elizabeth (1997), *Consuming Subjects: Women, Shopping, and Business in the Eighteenth Century*, New York: Columbia University Press.

Lamb, Jonathan (2000), '"The Rime of the Ancient Mariner": A Ballad of the Scurvy', in R. Wrigley and G. Revill (eds), *Pathologies of Travel*, Amsterdam: Rodopi, pp. 157–77.

Lambert, David (2004), 'Deadening, Voyeuristic, and Reiterative? Problems of Representation in Caribbean Research', in S. Courtman (ed.), *Beyond the Blood, the Beach and the Banana: New Perspectives in Caribbean Studies*, Kingston: Ian Randle Publishers, pp. 3–14.

Lambert, David (2005), *White Creole Culture, Politics, and Identity During the Age of Abolition*, Cambridge: Cambridge University Press.

Lamont, Claire (2003), 'Scott and Eighteenth-Century Imperialism: India and the Scottish Highlands', in T. d'Haen, P. Liebregts and W. Tigges (eds), *Configuring Romanticism*, Amsterdam: Rodopi, pp. 35–50.

Larrabee, Mary Jeanne (2006), '"I Know What a Slave Knows": Mary Prince's Epistemology of Resistance', *Women's Studies* 35: 453–73.

Leask, Nigel (1992), *British Romantic Writing and the East: Anxieties of Empire*, Cambridge: Cambridge University Press.

Leask, Nigel (1998), '"Wandering Through Eblis": Absorption and

Containment in Romantic Exoticism', in T. Fulford and P. Kitson (eds), *Romanticism and Colonialism: Writing and Empire, 1780–1830*, Cambridge: Cambridge University Press, pp. 165–88.

Leask, Nigel (2002), *Curiosity and the Aesthetics of Travel Writing, 1770–1840*, Oxford: Oxford University Press.

Leask, Nigel (2005), 'Easts', in Nicholas Roe (ed.), *Romanticism: An Oxford Guide*, Oxford: Oxford University Press, pp. 136–48.

Leask, Nigel (2010), *Robert Burns and Pastoral: Poetry and Improvement in Late Eighteenth-Century Scotland*, Oxford: Oxford University Press.

Lee, Debbie (1998), 'Yellow Fever and the Slave Trade: Coleridge's *The Rime of the Ancient Mariner*', *ELH* 65: 675–700.

Lee, Debbie (2001), 'Introduction: Visitors in Africa: Current Debates and Principles of Editorial Selection', in D. Lee (ed.), *Travels, Explorations, and Empires: Africa*, London: Pickering and Chatto, vol. 5, pp. xix–xxxvi.

Lee, Debbie (2002a), *Slavery and the Romantic Imagination*, Philadelphia: University of Pennsylvania Press.

Lee, Debbie (2002b), 'Grave Dirt, Dried Toads, and the Blood of a Cat: How Aldridge Worked His Charms', in C. Rzepka (ed.), *Obi: A Romantic Circles Praxis Volume* <http://romantic.arhu.umd.edu/praxis/obi/> (accessed 27 June 2012).

Levine, George and U. C. Knoepflmacher (1979), *The Endurance of* Frankenstein: *Essays on Mary Shelley's Novel*, Berkeley: University of California Press.

Lew, Joseph W (1991), 'The Deceptive Other: Mary Shelley's Critique of Orientalism in *Frankenstein*', *Studies in Romanticism* 30: 255–83.

Linebaugh, Peter and Marcus Rediker (2000), *The Many-Headed Hydra: Sailors, Slaves, Commoners, and the Hidden History of the Revolutionary Atlantic*, Boston: Beacon Press.

Loomba, Ania (1993), 'Dead Women Tell No Tales: Issues of Female Subjectivity, Subaltern Agency and Tradition in Colonial and Post-colonial Writings on Widow Immolation in India', *History Workshop Journal* 33: 209–27.

Loomba, Ania (2005), *Colonialism/Postcolonialism*, 2nd edn, London: Routledge.

Loomba, Ania and Jonathan Burton (eds) (2007), *Race in Early Modern England: A Documentary Companion*, New York: Palgrave Macmillan.

Low, Donald (ed.) (1974), *Robert Burns: The Critical Heritage*, London: Routledge and Kegan Paul.

Lowe, Lisa (1991), *Critical Terrains: French and British Orientalisms*, Ithaca, NY: Cornell University Press.

Lowes, John Livingston (1927), *The Road to Xanadu: A Study in the Ways of the Imagination*, Princeton: Princeton University Press.

Lupton, Kenneth (1979), *Mungo Park the African Traveller*, Oxford: Oxford University Press.

Lynch, Deidre (1996), 'At Home With Jane Austen', in D. Lynch and W. B. Warner (eds), *Cultural Institutions of the Novel*, Durham, NC: Duke University Press, pp. 159–92.

Macaulay, Thomas Babington (1952), *Prose and Poetry*, ed. G. M. Young, London: Rupert Hart-Davis.

McCalman, Iain (1986), 'Anti-Slavery and Ultra-Radicalism in Early Nineteenth-Century England: The Case of Robert Wedderburn', *Slavery and Abolition* 7: 99–117.

McCalman, Iain (1988), *Radical Underworld: Prophets, Revolutionaries and Pornographers in London, 1795–1840*, Cambridge: Cambridge University Press.

McCalman, Iain (1991), 'Introduction', in Robert Wedderburn, *The Horrors of Slavery and Other Writings*, ed. I. McCalman, New York: Markus Wiener Publishing.

McCrone, David, Angela Morris and Richard Kiely (1995), *Scotland, the Brand: The Making of Scottish Heritage*, Edinburgh: Edinburgh University Press.

Macdonald, D. L. (1994), 'Pre-Romantic and Romantic Abolitionism: Cowper and Blake', *European Romantic Review* 4: 163–182.

Mack, Douglas S. (2006), *Scottish Fiction and the British Empire*, Edinburgh: Edinburgh University Press.

McGann, Jerome (1968), *Fiery Dust: Byron's Poetic Development*, Chicago: University of Chicago Press.

McGann, Jerome (1983), *The Romantic Ideology*, Chicago: University of Chicago Press.

McGann, Jerome (1990), 'The Meaning of the Ancient Mariner', in G. A. Rosso and D. P. Watkins (eds), *Spirits of Fire: English Romantic Writers and Contemporary Historical Methods*, London: Associated University Presses, pp. 208–39.

McGinn, Clark (2011), 'Vehement Celebrations: The Global Celebration of the Burns Supper Since 1801', in Murray Pittock (ed.), *Robert Burns in Global Culture*, Lewisburg, PA: Bucknell University Press, pp. 189–203.

McGoogan, Ken (2004), *Ancient Mariner: The Arctic Adventures of Samuel Hearne, the Sailor Who Inspired Coleridge's Masterpiece*, New York: Carrol and Graf.

McGuirk, Carol (1985), *Robert Burns and the Sentimental Era*, Athens, GA: University of Georgia Press.

McGuirk, Carol (1991), 'Burns, Bakhtin, and the Opposition of Poetic and Novelistic Discourses: A Response to David Morris', *The Eighteenth Century: Theory and Interpretation* 32: 58–72.

McGuirk, Carol (2007), 'Writing Scotland: Robert Burns', in Ian Brown (ed.), *Edinburgh History of Scottish Literature*, Edinburgh: Edinburgh University Press, vol. 2, pp. 168–77.

Mackay, James A. (1992), *RB: A Biography of Robert Burns*, Edinburgh: Mainstream.

MacKenzie, John M. (1995), *Orientalism: History, Theory, and the Arts*, Manchester: Manchester University Press.

Macpherson, James (1996), *The Poems of Ossian and Related Works*, ed. H. Gaskill, Edinburgh: Edinburgh University Press.

Macqueen, James (1831), 'The Colonial Empire of Great Britain', *Blackwood's Edinburgh Magazine* 30: 744–64.

Majeed, Javed (1992), *Ungoverned Imaginings: James Mill's* The History of British India *and Orientalism*, Oxford: Clarendon Press.

Makdisi, Saree (1998), *Romantic Imperialism: Universal Empire and the Culture of Modernity*, Cambridge: Cambridge University Press.

Makdisi, Saree (2003), *William Blake and the Impossible History of the 1790s*, Chicago: University of Chicago Press.

Makdisi, Saree (2008), 'Austen, Empire and Moral Virtue', in J. Heydt-Stevenson and C. Sussman (eds), *Recognizing the Romantic Novel*, Liverpool: Liverpool University Press, pp. 192–207.

Malchow, H. L. (1996), *Gothic Images of Race in Nineteenth-Century Britain*, Stanford: Stanford University Press.

Mani, Lata (1987), 'Contentious Traditions: The Debate on Sati in Colonial India', *Cultural Critique* 7: 119–56.

Marsters, Kate Ferguson (2000), 'Introduction', in Mungo Park, *Travels in the Interior Districts of Africa*, ed. K. F. Marsters, Durham, NC: Duke University Press, pp. 1–28.

Mathurin, Lucille (1975), *The Rebel Woman in the British West Indies During Slavery*, Kingston: Institute of Jamaica.

Mee, Jon (2000), 'Austen's Treacherous Ivory: Female Patriotism, Domestic Ideology, and Empire', in Y.-M. Park and R. S. Rajan (eds), *The Postcolonial Jane Austen*, London: Routledge, pp. 74–92.

Mellor, Anne K. (1995), 'Sex, Violence, and Slavery: Blake and Wollstonecraft', *Huntington Library Quarterly* 58.3/4: 345–70.

Mellor, Anne K. (2003), '*Frankenstein*, Racial Science, and the "Yellow Peril"', in Noah Heringman (ed.), *Romantic Science: The Literary Forms of Natural History*, Albany, NY: State University of New York Press, pp. 173–96.

Mill, James [1817] (1975), *The History of British India* (abridged), ed. William Thomas, Chicago: University of Chicago Press.

Mintz, Sidney (1985), *Sweetness and Power: The Place of Sugar in Modern History*, New York: Penguin.

Moers, Ellen (1979), 'Female Gothic', in George Levine and Ulrich Knoepflmacher (eds), *The Endurance of Frankenstein*, Berkeley: University of California Press, pp. 77–87.

Moretti, Franco [1978] (1988), 'Dialectic of Fear', in *Signs Taken for Wonders*, trans. Susan Fischer, David Forgacs and David Miller, London: Verso, pp. 83–108.

Morris, David B. (1987), 'Burns and Heteroglossia', *The Eighteenth Century: Theory and Interpretation* 28: 3–27.

Morton, Timothy (1998), 'Blood Sugar', in T. Fulford and P. J. Kitson (eds), *Romanticism and Colonialism: Writing and Empire, 1780–1830*, Cambridge: Cambridge University Press, pp. 87–106.

Moss, Sarah (2002), '"The Bounds of His Great Empire": *The Ancient Mariner* and Coleridge at Christ's Hospital', *Romanticism* 8.1: 49–61.

Murphy, Peter (1993), *Poetry as an Occupation and an Art in Britain, 1760–1830*, Cambridge: Cambridge University Press.

Neff, D. S. (1997), 'Hostages to Empire: The Anglo-Indian Problem in *Frankenstein, The Curse of Kehama*, and *The Missionary*', *European Romantic Review* 8: 386–408.

Noble A. and P. S. Hogg (2001), 'Introduction', in *The Canongate Burns: The Complete Poems and Songs of Robert Burns*, ed. A. Noble and P. S. Hogg, Edinburgh: Canongate, pp. ix–xcii.

Nussbaum, Felicity A. (2003), *The Limits of the Human: Fictions of Anomaly, Race, and Gender in the Long Eighteenth Century*, Cambridge: Cambridge University Press.

Oldfield, J. R. (1995), *Popular Politics and British Anti-Slavery: The Mobilization of Public Opinion Against the Slave Trade, 1787–1807*, Manchester: Manchester University Press.

Owenson, Sydney, Lady Morgan [1811] (2002), *The Missionary*, ed. J. M. Wright, Peterborough, Ontario: Broadview Press.

Pal, Pratapaditya and Vidya Dehejia (1986), *From Merchants to Emperors: British Artists in India, 1757–1930*, Ithaca, NY: Cornell University Press.

Paquet, Sandra Pouchet (1992), 'The Heartbeat of a West Indian Slave: *The History of Mary Prince*', *African American Review* 26.1: 131–46.

Paranjape, Makarand R. (2011), '"East Indian" Cosmopolitanism: *The Fakeer of Jungheera* and the Birth of Indian Modernity', *Interventions* 13: 550–69.

Park, Mungo [1799] (2000), *Travels in the Interior Districts of Africa*, ed. K. F. Marsters, Durham, NC: Duke University Press.

Parry, Benita (2004), *Postcolonial Studies: A Materialist Critique*, London: Routledge.

Parry, J. H., Philip Sherlock and Anthony Maingot (1987), *A Short History of the West Indies*, 4th edn, London: Macmillan.

Paton, Diana (2007), 'The Afterlives of Three-Fingered Jack', in B. Carey and P. J. Kitson (eds), *Slavery and the Cultures of Abolition*, Cambridge: D. S. Brewer, pp. 42–63.

Pereira, Ernest and Michael Chapman (1989), 'Introduction', in E. Pereira and M. Chapman (eds), *African Poems of Thomas Pringle*, Pietermaritzburg: University of Natal Press, pp. xi–xxvi.

Pettinger, Alasdair (ed.) (1998), *Always Elsewhere: Travels of the Black Atlantic*, London: Cassell.

Pinkerton, John (ed.) (1808–14), *A General Collection of the Best and Most*

Interesting Voyages and Travels in All Parts of the World, 17 vols, London: Longman, Hurst, Rees, Orme, Brown, Cadell and Davies.

Piper, Karen (2007), 'Inuit Diasporas: *Frankenstein* and the Inuit in England', *Romanticism* 13: 63–75.

Pittock, Murray (1991), *The Invention of Scotland: The Stuart Myth and the Scottish Identity, 1638 to the Present*, London: Routledge.

Pittock, Murray (2008), *Scottish and Irish Romanticism*, Oxford: Oxford University Press.

Pratt, Mary Louise (1992), *Imperial Eyes: Travel Writing and Transculturation*, New York: Routledge.

Price, Richard and Sally Price (1988), 'Introduction', in John Gabriel Stedman, *Narrative of a Five Years Expedition Against the Revolted Negroes of Surinam*, ed. R. Price and S. Price, Baltimore: Johns Hopkins University Press, pp. xiii–xcvii.

Prince, Mary [1831] (1997), *The History of Mary Prince, a West Indian Slave, Related by Herself*, , ed. M. Ferguson, revised edn, Ann Arbor: University of Michigan Press.

Pringle, Thomas [1835] (1966), *Narrative of a Residence in South Africa*, Cape Town: C. Struik.

Pringle, Thomas (1989), *African Poems of Thomas Pringle*, ed. E. Pereira and M. Chapman, Pietermaritzburg: University of Natal Press.

Pringle, Thomas (2011), *The South African Letters of Thomas Pringle*, ed. R. Vigne, Cape Town: Van Riebeeck Society.

Quilley, Geoff (2003), 'Pastoral Plantations: The Slave Trade and the Representation of British Colonial Landscape in the Late Eighteenth Century', in G. Quilley and K. D. Kriz (eds), *An Economy of Colour: Visual Culture and the Atlantic World, 1660–1830*, Manchester: Manchester University Press, pp. 106–28.

Rajan, Balachandra (1999), *Under Western Eyes: India From Milton to Macaulay*, Durham, NC: Duke University Press.

Rauwerda, A. M. (2001), 'Naming, Agency, and "A Tissue of Falsehoods" in *The History of Mary Prince*', *Victorian Literature and Culture* 29.2: 397–411.

Ray, Rajat Kanta (1998), 'Indian Society and the Establishment of British Supremacy, 1765–1818', in W. R. Louis (ed. in chief), *The Oxford History of the British Empire*, vol. II, P. J. Marshall (ed.), *The Eighteenth Century*, Oxford: Oxford University Press, pp. 508–29.

Richard, Jessica (2003), '"A Paradise of My Own Creation": *Frankenstein* and the Improbable Romance of Polar Exploration', *Nineteenth-Century Contexts* 25: 295–314.

Richardson, Alan (1990), 'Colonialism, Race, and Lyric Irony in Blake's "The Little Black Boy"', *Papers in Language and Literature* 26: 233–48.

Richardson, Alan (1997), 'Romantic Voodoo: Obeah and British Culture, 1797–1807', in M. Fernandez-Olmos and L. Paravisini-Gebert (eds), *Sacred*

Possessions: Vodou, Santería, Obeah, and the Caribbean, New Brunswick, NJ: Rutgers University Press, pp. 171–94.

Richardson, Alan (ed) (1999a), *Verse*, in P. Kitson and D. Lee (eds), *Slavery, Abolition and Emancipation: Writings in the British Romantic Period*, London: Pickering and Chatto, vol. 4.

Richardson, Alan (1999b), 'Introduction', in *Verse*, in P. Kitson and D. Lee (eds), *Slavery, Abolition and Emancipation: Writings in the British Romantic Period*, London: Pickering and Chatto, vol. 4, pp. ix–xix.

Richardson, Alan [1813] (2002), 'Introduction', in A. Richardson (ed.), *Three Oriental Tales*, Boston: Houghton Mifflin.

Richardson, Alan (2006), 'Byron's *The Giaour*: Teaching Orientalism in the Wake of September 11', in D. L. Hoeveler and J. Cass (eds), *Interrogating Orientalism: Contextual Approaches and Pedagogical Practices*, Columbus: Ohio State University Press, pp. 213–23.

Robertson, James (2003), *Joseph Knight*, London: Fourth Estate.

Roe, Nicholas (2005), 'Introduction', in *Romanticism: An Oxford Guide*, Oxford: Oxford University Press, pp. 1–12.

Rossington, Michael (1991), 'Shelley and the Orient', *Keats-Shelley Review* 6: 18–36.

Saglia, Diego (1996), 'Looking at the Other: Cultural Difference and the Traveller's Gaze in *The Italian*', *Studies in the Novel* 28: 12–37.

Saglia, Diego (2002), 'William Beckford's "Sparks of Orientalism" and the Material-Discursive Orient of British Romanticism', *Textual Practice* 16: 75–92.

Said, Edward (1978), *Orientalism*, New York: Vintage.

Said, Edward (1993), *Culture and Imperialism*, New York: Knopf.

Salih, Sarah (2007), 'Putting Down Rebellion: Witnessing the Body of the Condemned in Abolition-Era Narratives', in B. Carey and P. J. Kitson (eds), *Slavery and the Cultures of Abolition*, Cambridge: D. S. Brewer, pp. 64–86.

Schwab, Raymond (1984), *The Oriental Renaissance: Europe's Rediscovery of India and the East, 1680–1880*, trans. G. Patterson-Black and V. Reinking, New York: Columbia University Press.

Scott, Walter [1827–8] (2000), *Chronicles of the Canongate*, ed. C. Lamont, Edinburgh: Edinburgh University Press.

Scott, Walter [1814] (2007), *Waverley*, ed. P. Garside, Edinburgh: Edinburgh University Press.

Sharafuddin, Mohammed (1994), *Islam and Romantic Orientalism: Romantic Encounters With the Orient*, London: I. B. Tauris.

Sharpe, Jenny (2002), *Ghosts of Slavery: A Literary Archaeology of Black Women's Lives*, Minneapolis: University of Minnesota Press.

Shelley, Mary [1818] (2012), *Frankenstein*, ed. J. P. Hunter, New York: W. W. Norton and Co.

Shelley, Percy Bysshe (1954), 'A Philosophical View of Reform' (1820), in *Shelley's Prose, or, The Trumpet of a Prophecy*, ed. D. L. Clark, Albuquerque: University of New Mexico Press, pp. 229–61.

Shelley, Percy Bysshe [1816] (1998), *Alastor, or, The Spirit of Solitude*, in D. Wu (ed.), *Romanticism: An Anthology*, 2nd edn, Oxford: Blackwell, pp. 824–41.

Shum, Matthew (2009), 'The Prehistory of *The History of Mary Prince*: Thomas Pringle's 'The Bechuana Boy', *Nineteenth-Century Literature* 64: 291–322.

Siskin, Clifford (1998), *The Work of Writing: Literature and Social Change in Britain, 1700–1830*, Baltimore: Johns Hopkins University Press.

Sitter, Zak (2008), 'William Jones, "Eastern" Poetry, and the Problem of Imitation', *Texas Studies in Literature and Language* 50: 385–405.

Smith, Allan Lloyd (2005), '"This Thing of Darkness": Racial Discourse in Mary Shelley's *Frankenstein*', *Gothic Studies* 6: 208–22.

Smith, Bernard (1985), *European Vision and the South Pacific*, 2nd edn, New Haven: Yale University Press.

Smith, Jeremy J. (2009), 'Copia Verborum: The Linguistic Choices of Robert Burns', *Review of English Studies*, n.s., 58.233: 73–88.

Smith, Olivia (1984), *The Politics of Language, 1791–1819*, Oxford: Clarendon Press.

Solow, Barbara L. and Stanley L. Engerman (eds) (1987), *British Capitalism and Caribbean Slavery: The Legacy of Eric Williams*, Cambridge: Cambridge University Press.

Sorensen, Janet (2000), *The Grammar of Empire in Eighteenth-Century British Writing*, Cambridge: Cambridge University Press.

Sorensen, Janet (2002), 'Internal Colonialism and the British Novel', *Eighteenth-Century Fiction* 15: 53–8.

Southey, Robert [1797] (2011), 'Poems on the Slave Trade', in *Poems*, Bristol, Eighteenth-Century Collections Online (ECCO) (accessed 9 November 2011).

Speitz, Michele (2011), 'Blood Sugar and Salt Licks: Corroding Bodies and Preserving Nations in *The History of Mary Prince, A West Indian Slave, Related by Herself*', in P. Youngquist and F. Botkin (eds), *Circulations: Romanticism and the Black Atlantic: A Romantic Circles Praxis Volume* <http://www.rc.umd.edu/praxis/circulations/HTML/praxis.2011.speitz.html> (accessed 12 July 2012).

Spivak, Gayatri Chakravorty (1985), 'Three Women's Texts and a Critique of Imperialism', *Critical Inquiry* 12: 243–61.

Spivak, Gayatri Chakravorty (1988), 'Can the Subaltern Speak?', in Cary Nelson and Lawrence Grossberg (eds), *Marxism and the Interpretation of Culture*, Basingstoke: Macmillan Education, pp. 271–313.

Spivak, Gayatri Chakravorty (1999), *A Critique of Postcolonial Reason: Toward a History of the Vanishing Present*, Cambridge, MA: Harvard University Press.

St Clair, William (2004), *The Reading Nation in the Romantic Period*, Cambridge: Cambridge University Press.

Stafford, Barbara Maria (1984), *Voyage Into Substance: Art, Nature, and the Illustrated Travel Account, 1760–1840*, Cambridge, MA: MIT Press.

Stafford, Fiona (1996), 'Introduction', in James Macpherson, *The Poems of Ossian and Related Works*, ed. H. Gaskill, Edinburgh: Edinburgh University Press.

Stafford, Fiona (2005), 'Ossian, Primitivism, Celticism', in S. Gillespie and D. Hopkins (eds), *The Oxford History of Literary Translation in English*, Oxford: Oxford University Press, pp. 416–26.

Stedman, John Gabriel [1796] (1988), *Narrative of a Five Years Expedition Against the Revolted Negroes of Surinam*, ed. R. Price and S. Price, Baltimore: Johns Hopkins University Press.

Stewart, Maaja A. (1993), *Domestic Realities and Imperial Fictions: Jane Austen's Novels in Eighteenth-Century Contexts*, Athens, GA: University of Georgia Press.

Suarez, Michael and Michael Turner (eds) (2011), *The Cambridge History of the Book in Britain, vol. V, 1695–1830*, Cambridge: Cambridge University Press.

Suleri, Sara (1992), *The Rhetoric of English India*, Chicago: University of Chicago Press.

Sussman, Charlotte (2000), *Consuming Anxieties: Consumer Protest, Gender, and British Slavery, 1713–1833*, Stanford: Stanford University Press.

Sypher, Wylie (1942), *Guinea's Captive Kings: Anti-Slavery Literature of the XVIII Century*. Chapel Hill, NC: University of North Carolina Press.

Szwydky, Lissette Lopez (2011), 'Rewriting the History of Black Resistance: The Haitian Revolution, Jamaican Maroons, and the "History" of Three-Fingered Jack in English Popular Culture, 1799–1830', in P. Youngquist and F. Botkin (eds), *Circulations: Romanticism and the Black Atlantic: A Romantic Circles Praxis Volume* <http://www.rc.umd.edu/praxis/circulations/HTML/praxis.2011.szwydky.html> (accessed 27 June 2012).

Teltscher, Kate (1995), *India Inscribed: European and British Writing on India, 1600–1800*, Delhi: Oxford University Press.

Teltscher, Kate (2000), 'The Shampooing Surgeon and the Persian Prince: Two Indians in Early Nineteenth-Century Britain', *Interventions* 2: 409–23.

Tetreault, Ronald (1987), *The Poetry of Life: Shelley and Literary Form*, Toronto: University of Toronto Press.

Thomas, Hugh (1997), *The Slave Trade*, New York: Simon and Schuster.

Thompson, Terry (2004), ' "A Majestic Figure of August Dignity": Herculean Echoes in *Frankenstein*', *ANQ* 17: 36–41.

Tobin, Beth Fowkes (1999), *Picturing Imperial Power: Colonial Subjects in Eighteenth-Century British Painting*, Durham, NC: Duke University Press.

Todorova, Kremena (2001), ' "I Will Say the Truth to the English People":

The History of Mary Prince and the Meaning of English History', *Texas Studies in Literature and Language* 43.3 (Fall): 285–302.

Trevor-Roper, Hugh (2008), *The Invention of Scotland: Myth and History*, New Haven: Yale University Press.

Trumpener, Katie (1997), *Bardic Nationalism: The Romantic Novel and the British Empire*, Princeton: Princeton University Press.

Tuite, Clara (2000), 'Domestic Retrenchment and Imperial Expansion: The Property Plots of *Mansfield Park*', in Y.-M. Park and R. S. Rajan (eds), *The Postcolonial Jane Austen*, London: Routledge, pp. 93–115.

Viswanathan, Gauri (1989), *Masks of Conquest: Literary Study and British Rule in India*, New York: Columbia University Press.

Wallace, Tara Ghoshal (2002), 'The Elephant's Foot and the British Mouth: Walter Scott on Imperial Rhetoric', *European Romantic Review* 13: 311–24.

Walvin, James (1994), *Black Ivory: A History of British Slavery*, Washington, DC: Howard University Press.

Walvin, James (2000), *Britain's Slave Empire*, Stroud: Tempus.

Wasserman, Earl (1971), *Shelley: A Critical Reading*, Baltimore: Johns Hopkins University Press.

Wästberg, Per (2010), *The Journey of Anders Sparrman: A Biographical Novel*, trans. T. Geddes, London: Granta Books.

Watt, James (2004), 'Scott, the Scottish Enlightenment, and Romantic Orientalism', in I. Duncan, L. Davis and J. Sorensen (eds), *Scotland and the Borders of Romanticism*, Cambridge: Cambridge University Press, pp. 94–112.

Webster, Mary (2011), *Johann Zoffany, 1733–1810*, New Haven: Yale University Press.

Wedderburn, Robert (1991), *The Horrors of Slavery and Other Writings*, ed. I. McCalman, New York: Markus Wiener Publishing.

Wheatley, Phillis (1989), *The Poems of Phillis Wheatley*, ed. Julian D. Mason Jnr, Chapel Hill, NC: University of North Carolina Press.

Wheeler, Roxann (2000), *The Complexion of Race: Categories of Difference in Eighteenth-Century British Culture*, Philadelphia: University of Pennsylvania Press.

Williams, Eric [1944] (1994), *Capitalism and Slavery*, Chapel Hill, NC: University of North Carolina Press.

Williams, Helen Maria (2001), *Letters Written in France in the Summer of 1790*, ed. N. Fraistat and S. S. Lanser, Peterborough, Ontario: Broadview Press.

Williams, Raymond (1973), *The Country and the City*, New York: Oxford University Press.

Willis, Deborah (2010), *Black Venus 2010: They Called Her 'Hottentot'*, Philadelphia: Temple University Press.

Wilson, Kathleen (2004), 'Introduction: Histories, Empires, Modernities', in

K. Wilson (ed.), *A New Imperial History: Culture, Identity, and Modernity in Britain and the Empire, 1660–1840*, Cambridge: Cambridge University Press, pp. 1–26.

Winter, Kari J. (1992), *Subjects of Slavery, Agents of Change: Women and Power in Gothic Novels and Slave Narratives, 1790–1865*, Athens, GA: University of Georgia Press.

Winter, Sarah (2009), 'The Novel and Prejudice', *Comparative Literature Studies* 46: 76–102.

Withers, Charles W. J. (2010), 'Geography, Enlightenment, and the Book: Authorship and Audience in Mungo Park's African Texts', in Miles Ogborn and Charles W. J. Withers (eds), *Geographies of the Book*, Farnham: Ashgate, pp. 191–220.

Wollstonecraft, Mary [1794] (1989), *An Historical and Moral View of the French Revolution: The Works of Mary Wollstonecraft*, ed. Janet Todd and Marilyn Butler, 7 vols, New York: New York University Press, vol. 6.

Wood, Marcus (2000), *Blind Memory: Visual Representations of Slavery in England and America, 1780–1865*, New York: Routledge.

Wood, Marcus (2002), *Slavery, Empathy, and Pornography*, Oxford: Oxford University Press.

Wordsworth, Dorothy (1941), *Recollections of a Tour Made in Scotland, A.D. 1803, Journals of Dorothy Wordsworth*, ed. E. de Selincourt, 2 vols, New York: Macmillan.

Wordsworth, William (1971), *The Prelude: A Parallel Text*, ed. J. C. Maxwell, New Haven: Yale University Press.

Wordsworth, William [1802] (2002), 'Preface', in William Wordsworth and Samuel Taylor Coleridge, *Lyrical Ballads and Related Writings*, ed. W. Richey and D. Robinson, Boston: Houghton Mifflin, pp. 390–416.

Wordsworth, William and Samuel Taylor Coleridge [1798] (2002), *Lyrical Ballads and Related Writings*, ed. William Richey and Daniel Robinson, Boston: Houghton Mifflin.

Wright, Julia M. (2002), 'Introduction', in Sydney Owenson, *The Missionary*, ed. J. M. Wright, Peterborough, Ontario: Broadview Press.

Youngquist, Paul (2005), 'The Afro Futurism of DJ Vassa', *European Romantic Review* 16: 181–92.

Youngquist, Paul and Frances Botkin (2011), 'Introduction: Black Romanticism: Romantic Circulations', in P. Youngquist and F. Botkin (eds), *Circulations: Romanticism and the Black Atlantic: A Romantic Circles Praxis Volume* <http://www.rc.umd.edu/praxis/circulations/index.html> (accessed 27 June 2012).

Index